Communications
in Computer and Information Science   **666**

Commenced Publication in 2007
Founding and Former Series Editors:
Alfredo Cuzzocrea, Dominik Ślęzak, and Xiaokang Yang

More information about this series at http://www.springer.com/series/7899

Weixia Xu · Liquan Xiao
Jinwen Li · Chengyi Zhang
Zhenzhen Zhu (Eds.)

Computer Engineering and Technology

20th CCF Conference, NCCET 2016
Xi'an, China, August 10–12, 2016
Revised Selected Papers

Springer

Editors
Weixia Xu
National University of Defense Technology
Changsha
China

Liquan Xiao
National University of Defense Technology
Changsha
China

Jinwen Li
National University of Defense Technology
Changsha
China

Chengyi Zhang
National University of Defense Technology
Changsha
China

Zhenzhen Zhu
National University of Defense Technology
Changsha
China

ISSN 1865-0929   ISSN 1865-0937 (electronic)
Communications in Computer and Information Science
ISBN 978-981-10-3158-8   ISBN 978-981-10-3159-5 (eBook)
DOI 10.1007/978-981-10-3159-5

Library of Congress Control Number: 2016958510

Printed on acid-free paper

This Springer imprint is published by Springer Nature
The registered company is Springer Nature Singapore Pte Ltd.
The registered company address is: 152 Beach Road, #22-06/08 Gateway East, Singapore 189721, Singapore

Preface

We are pleased to present the proceedings of the 20th Annual Conference on Computer Engineering and Technology (NCCET 2016). Over its short 20-year history, NCCET has established itself as one of the major national conferences dedicated to the important and emerging challenges in the field of computer engineering and technology. Following the previous successful events, NCCET 2016 provided a forum to bring together researchers and practitioners from academia and industry to discuss cutting-edge research on computer engineering and technology.

We are delighted that the conference continues to attract high-quality submissions from a diverse and national group of researchers. This year, we received 120 submissions, among which 21 papers were accepted. Each paper received three or four peer reviews from our Technical Program Committee (TPC) comprising 42 members from academia and industry.

The pages of this volume represent only the end result of an enormous endeavor involving hundreds of people. Almost all this work is voluntary, with some individuals contributing hundreds of hours of their time to the effort. Together, the 42 members of the TPC, the 16 members of the External Review Committee (ERC), and the 13 other individual reviewers consulted for their expertise wrote nearly 400 reviews.

Every paper received at least two reviews and many had three or more. With the exception of submissions by the TPC, each paper had at least two reviews from the TPC and at least one review from an outside expert. For the fourth year running most of the outside reviews were done by the ERC, which was selected in advance, and additional outside reviews beyond the ERC were requested whenever appropriate or necessary. Reviewing was "first read double-blind," meaning that author identities were withheld from reviewers until they submitted a review. Revealing author names after initial reviews were written allowed reviewers to find related and previous material by the same authors, which helped greatly in many cases to understand the context of the work, and also ensured that the author feedback and discussions at the PC meeting could be frank and direct. We allowed PC members to submit papers to the conference. Submissions co-authored by a TPC member were reviewed exclusively by the ERC and other outside reviewers, and these same reviewers decided whether to accept the PC papers; no PC member reviewed a TPC paper, and no TPC papers were discussed at the TPC meeting.

After the reviewing was complete, the PC met at the National University of Defense Technology, Changsha, during June 30–31 to select the program. Separately, the ERC decided on the PC papers in e-mail and phone discussions. Finally, 21 of the 120 submissions (18%) were accepted for the conference.

First of all, we would like to thank all researchers who submitted manuscripts. Without these submissions, it would be impossible to provide such an interesting technical program. We thank all PC members for helping to organize the conference program. We thank all TPC members for their tremendous time and efforts during the paper review and selection process. The efforts of these individuals were crucial in constructing our successful technical program. Last but not least, we would like to thank the organizations and sponsors that supported NCCET 2016. Finally, we thank all the participants of the conference and hope that they had a truly memorable NCCET 2016 in Xi'an, China.

August 2016   Xu Weixia
                                                                         Han Wei
                                                                  Zhang Minxuan
                                                                     Xiao Liquan

Organization

General Co-chairs

Xu Weixia   National University of Defense Technology, China
Han Wei   Xi'an Aviation Institute of Computing Technology, China
Zhang Minxuan   National University of Defense Technology, China

Program Chair

Xiao Liquan   National University of Defense Technology, China

Publicity Co-chairs

Zhang Chengyi   National University of Defense Technology, China
Li Jinwen   National University of Defense Technology, China

Local Arrangements Co-chairs

Tian Ze   Xi'an Aviation Institute of Computing Technology, China
Li Jinwen   National University of Defense Technology, China

Registration and Finance Co-chairs

Li Yuanshan   National University of Defense Technology, China
Zhang Junying   National University of Defense Technology, China

Program Committee

Han Wei   Xi'an Aviation Institute of Computing Technology, China
Jin Lifeng   Jiangnan Institute of Computing Technology, China
Xiong Tinggang   709 Institute of China Shipbuilding Industry, China
Zhao Xiaofang   Institute of Computing Technology,
     Chinese Academy of Sciences, China
Yang Yintang   Xi Dian University, China

Technical Program Committee

Xiao Liquan   National University of Defense Technology, China
Zhao Xiaofang   Institute of Computing Technology,
     Chinese Academy of Sciences, China
Han Wei   Aviation Industry Corporation of China

Xiong Tinggang	China Shipbuilding Industry Corporation, China
Yang Yintang	Xidian University, China
Jin Lifeng	Institute of Computing Technology, Jiangnan, China
Dou Qiang	National University of Defense Technology, China
Du Huimin	Xi'an University of Posts and Telecommunications, China
Fan Dongrui	Institute of Computing Technology, Chinese Academy of Sciences, China
Fan Xiaoya	Northwestern Polytechnical University, China
Fu Yuzhuo	Shanghai Jiao Tong University, China
Guo Donghui	Xiamen University, China
Guo Wei	Tianjin University, China
Huang Jin	Xidian University, China
Jiang Jiang	Shanghai Jiao Tong University, China
Li Ping	University of Electronic Science and Technology of China, China
Li Yun	Yangzhou University, China
Lin Kaizhi	Inspur, China
Lin Zhenghao	Tongji University, China
Sun Yongjie	National University of Defense Technology, China
Tian Ze	Aviation Industry Corporation of China, China
Wang Yaonan	Hunan University, China
Wang Yiwen	University of Electronic Science and Technology of China, China
Wang Yongwen	National University of Defense Technology, China
Xue Chengqi	Southeast University, China
Yang Xiaojun	Institute of Computing Technology, Chinese Academy of Sciences, China
Yu Zongguang	CETC, China
Zeng Yun	Hunan University, China
Zhang Lixin	Institute of Computing Technology, Chinese Academy of Sciences, China
Zhang Minxuan	National University of Defense Technology, China
Zhang Shengbin	Northwestern Polytechnical University, China
Zhang Shujie	Huawei, China
Zhao Yuelong	South China University of Technology, China
Zhou Ya	Guilin University of Electronic Technology, China
Jiang Xu	Hong Kong University of Science and Technology, SAR China
Zhonghai Lu	Royal Institute of Technology, KTH, Sweden
Zheng Wang	Lancaster University, UK
Pengcheng Li	The University of Rochester, USA
Guangda Zhang	The University of Manchester, UK
Xueqing Li	Pennsylvania State University, USA
Yi-Chung Chen	The University of Manchester, UK
Ping Chi	University of California, Santa Barbara, USA

Contents

Processor Architecture

Application Specific Processors

Computer Application and Software Optimization

Technology on the Horizon

Processor Architecture

Single/Double Precision Floating-Point Division and Square Root Unit Based on SRT-8 Algorithm

Yuanxi Peng, Tingting He, Yuanwu Lei[✉], and Baozhou Zhu

College of Computer, National University of Defense Technology,
Changsha 410073, China
yuanwulei@nudt.edu.cn

Abstract. To meet the precision requirement of different applications and reduce latency of operation for low precision, a unified structure for IEEE-754 double-precision/SIMD single-precision floating-point division and square root operation based on SRT-8 algorithm was introduced. Special instructions were designed and independent mantissa computing unit and normalization unit are implemented. Moreover, parallel adders and QDS structure was adopted to hide the latency of look-up table, generating fast addend was used to decrease critical path, and "On-the-fly" conversion was employed for saving area-cost. Experimental results show that our proposed design can achieve low latency and low hardware overhead.

Keywords: Single/double precision · SRT-8 · Division · Square root · DSP

1 Introduction

Modern applications have a wide range use of floating-point division and square root operations [1], however their precision requirement is different. For example, scientific computation requires as high as possible operational precision, while some applications, such as grayscale image processing, require lower precision computing. So, this paper researches a structure easy to implement IEEE-754 single/double precision floating-point division and square root, to satisfy the precision requirement of different applications.

Many algorithms [2] are presented to implement division and square root, which could be divided into two categories. The first category is based on multiplications, such as Newton algorithm and Goldschmidt algorithm [3], has the character of fast convergence, but their hardware structures are complicated. The other category, such as SRT [4–7], is based on addition and subtraction, and its structure is simple and easy to round with linear convergence. It's more suitable to design of flexible precision than these based on multiplication.

This work is supported by the Aerospace Science Foundation of China (No. 2013ZC88003), and the Natural Science Foundation of China (No. 61402499).

W. Xu et al. (Eds.): NCCET 2016, CCIS 666, pp. 3–14, 2016.
DOI: 10.1007/978-981-10-3159-5_1

In order to improve operation efficiency of SRT algorithm, many researchers have done many related works. In order to reduce hardware resource, [8, 9] integrated division and square root into a unit according to their similarity of implementation by reusing, but the latency of square root is obviously longer than division so that iteration frequency is low [10, 11] adopted redundant digits to express operands to eliminate the latency of addition carry, and used minimum redundant digit set to simplify generating remainder. Because the larger the redundant digit set is, the more operations are needed for generating remainder.

Obviously, there are still many challenges to SRT algorithm in the tradeoff between performance and consumption. To get a higher efficient design, this work proposed several methods. The advantages of the proposed design are as following:

(1) Independent mantissa computing and normalization structure and splitting iterative instructions were adopted to implement double-precision or SIMD (single instruction multiple data) single-precision floating-point operation. Splitting iterative instructions were designed for operating lower precisions cost less latency.
(2) Using simpler logic to implement quotient conversion on-the-fly to minimize additional required hardware.
(3) In division and square root iteration, their addend is parallel directly generating instead of computing step by step to reduce latency and improve frequency.

2 Background

SRT is a digit-recurrence algorithm to calculate division and square root. Comparing with the traditional method to compute division and square root, SRT algorithm ensures more quotient digits by the function of quotient digit selection each digit-recurrence. Traditional digit-recurrence radix is 2, 1 bit quotient digit is produced each iteration. This work researched SRT algorithm with radix 8(SRT-8), and 3-bit quotient digits are produced at each iteration.

The operation processing is similar for division and square root in SRT-8 algorithm. Equation (1) is consolidated to iteration for division and square root.

$$W[j+1] = 8 \times W[j] + F[j]. \tag{1}$$

In Eq. (1), $W[j]$ denotes the remainder after jth iteration, and $F[j]$ is the addend for iteration. As for division, $F[j]$ equals to $-d \times q_{j+1}$ where d is divisor, and q_{j+1} is the quotient digit and selected according to $W[j]$ and divisor. The division iterative can be written as Eq. (2):

$$W[j+1] = 8 \times W[j] - d \times q_{j+1}. \tag{2}$$

For square root, $F[j]$ equals to $-2Q[j]q_{j+1} - q_{j+1}^2 8^{-(j+1)}$, where $Q[j]$ is the quotient after jth iteration, and q_{j+1} is the quotient digits and selected according to W $[j]$ and $Q[j] = \sum_{i=1}^{k} q_i 8^{-i}$. The square root iterative can be written as Eq. (3).

$$W[j+1] = 8 \times W[j] - 2Q[j]q_{j+1} - q_{j+1}^2 8^{-(j+1)}. \tag{3}$$

The division or square root result can be reach to target precision by sequential addition and shifting.

3 Structure Supporting Single/Double Precision Operation

In this section, the structure of double/SIMD single precision floating-point unit for division and square root based on SRT-8 algorithm is proposed. Special instructions and novel scheduling process were designed to implement division and square root operation.

3.1 Structure of Independent Mantissa Computation and Normalization

Because of the similarities in the digit-recurrence algorithm, division and square root can be integrated into the same unit. The structures of independent mantissa computing unit and normalization unit are designed for separating division or square root mantissa operation and normalization, as shown in Fig. 1. The independent structure is easy to execute flexible precision floating-point operation joined with corresponding splitting iterative instructions scheduling. Its operation process is sending the operands to mantissa computing unit for computing mantissa quotient or square root firstly, then, sending source operands and mantissa operation result to normalization unit for final processing. Double/SIMD single precision operation is implemented by changing times of instructions scheduling.

Each iteration of division or square root can be completed within one cycle for mantissa computing unit. Its iteration begins with SRT-8 core operation, then, storing the quotient and residue result, and according to the result preparing data and latching data for the next iteration. The data prepared has two different cases due to whether it is the first iteration. For the first one, the iteration data is obtained from source operands, otherwise, the iteration data is obtained from the last iteration results.

To enhance instruction level parallel, the proposed unit supports SIMD operation by two single-precision data path as show in Fig. 2. Two quotient digit selection (QDS) modules are set in mantissa computing unit. When operand's format is double-precision floating-point, QDS(H) will work, otherwise, the operand's format is double single-precision, QDS(H) and QDS(L) will work at same time corresponding to high-order single-precision operand and low-order single-precision operand. Double-precision format data and double single-precision format data adopted same 57 bits data path. Normalization unit adopted double path structure supporting double-precision and single-precision format floating-point operations.

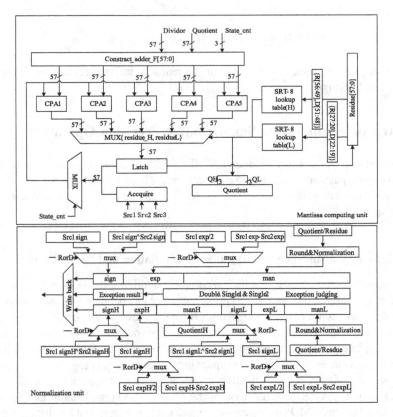

Fig. 1. Structures of independent mantissa computing unit and normalization unit

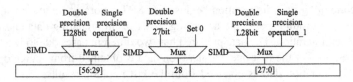

Fig. 2. SIMD data path for single-precision operation

3.2 Splitting Iteration Instructions

According to IEEE-754 floating-point standard, the mantissas of single-precision and double-precision floating-point are 24 bits and 53 bits, respectively. The proposed mantissa computing unit based on SRT-8 algorithm generates 3 bits quotient digits for each iteration. Then, 8 iterations and 18 iterations are needed for single-precision operation and double-precision operation, respectively. However, some operations need lower precision, they can be processed with less iterations.

Splitting iteration instructions are easy to achieve flexible precision floating-point division and square root operations through different times of execution. In this section,

7 cycles for double precision and 4 cycle for single precision division and square root splitting iteration instructions were proposed. They can support different precision floating-point operations by multiple and combined scheduling instructions.

We designed SRT-8 instructions which were instructions (FSRTDD and FSRTDS) for supporting division SRT iteration and instructions (FSRTRD and FSRTRS) for supporting square root SRT-8 iteration. At the same time, normalization instructions (FNORMD and FNORMS) are designed to final normalization processing, which executes one cycle.

The double-precision SRT-8 instructions FSRTDD and FSRTRD designed support six iterations for division and square root, and 18 bits quotient digits are produced each scheduling instruction, while the SIMD single-precision SRT-8 instructions FSRTDS and FSRTRS designed support three iterations for division and square root, and 9 bits quotient digits are produced each scheduling instruction. How many times are needed to schedule depend on target operation precision. Once the enough precision result is obtained, the source operands and the mantissa result will be sent to normalization unit and operated by the normalization instruction corresponding to target precision data format. When floating-point division or square root is executed, the SRT-8 instruction need be scheduled three times for single precision or double precision. If operation is lower precision, flexible precision result matching single or double FP format can be achieved by changing instruction executing times.

Because of each instruction scheduling supports six or three iterations, the intermediate result need be stored in appointed register files for the next scheduling, which includes partial quotient, residue and some scheduling information. In the first scheduling, its source operands are dividend and divisor, while its source operands are residue, divisor and the third operand for other scheduling. The third operand comes from destination operand stored in the last scheduling, which is composed of partial quotient digits and scheduling times.

The following displayed is the scheduling process for two kinds of precision division. Because of the scheduling process of instruction FSRTRD and FSRTRS for square root are similar to the division instruction, its description is omitted (Tables 1 and 2).

Table 1. Instruction scheduling of single-precision division

Cycle	Instruction
1	FSRTDS R1, R2, R3, R5:R4;
2–4	SNOP;
5	FSRTDS R5, R2, R4, R7:R6;
6–8	SNOP;
9	FSRTDS R7, R2, R6, R9:R8;
10–12	SNOP;
13	FNORMS R1, R2, R9, R10;

Table 2. Instruction scheduling of double-precision division

Cycle	Instruction
1	FSRTDD R1, R2, R3, R5:R4;
2–7	SNOP;
8	FSRTDD R5, R2, R4, R7:R6;
9–14	SNOP;
15	FSRTDD R7, R2, R6, R9:R8;
16–21	SNOP;
22	FNORMD R1, R2, R9, R10;

The instruction FSRTRD and FSRTRS need three source operands. In the first scheduling for division, source operand 1 is dividend, source operand 2 is divisor, and source operand 3 is zero. In the follow scheduling, source operand 1 is remainder, source operand 2 is still divisor, and source operand 3 is composed of quotient digits and recording of iteration scheduling. At the same time, source operand 1 and source operand 3 are destination operands from last scheduling. The instructions FNORMD and FNORMS are used for normalization. The instruction SNOP inserted is used to wait for iteration processing.

4   Implementation of Unified Unit for Division and Square Root

In this section, the implementation of mantissa computing unit is introduced based on SRT-8 algorithm.

4.1   Quotient Digit Selection

Quotient Digit Selection (QDS) is significant part of SRT algorithm. The leading digits of residual and divisor are as inputs for the QDS function, and the quotient digits are produced corresponding to current iteration.

For constructing the QDS function, some issues need to be solved, including by the following:

1. The range area of quotient digit selection that is quotient set;
2. How many bits of remainder and divisor the input of the function;
3. How to map quotient from remainder joined on divisor;

A symmetrical redundancy quotient set is used for high speed operation. That is:

$$q = k \in \{\bar{a}, \bar{a}+1 \cdots, -1, 0, 1, \cdots, a-1, a\}.$$

The set determines the redundancy factor ρ, and the factor ρ is defined by $\rho = \frac{a}{8-1}$. And $1 > \rho > \frac{1}{2}$ so, parameter 'a' belongs to (5, 6, 7) for SRT-8.

$$\begin{cases} P_{\min} = L_k = (-\rho + k)d \\ P_{\max} = U_k = (\rho + k)d \end{cases} \tag{4}$$

In Eq. (4), L_k and U_k are the low bound and the up bound of remainder when quotient is k, and $U_{k-1} > L_k$. $\{-5, 5\}$ is selected as the range area of quotient. According to Eq. (4) and the confirmed quotient set, the range of remainder corresponding to each quotient can be obtained, as shown in Table 3. Among the overlap area, the larger quotient digit is selected. Figure 4 is P-D diagram for digit selection. The largest value of remainder is $\frac{40}{7}d$, so the bits of input $W[j]$ are larger 3 than input d at least for meeting the range of remainder.

Table 3. W[j] bounds/7

Quotient q	0	1	2	3	4	5
$L_k(d)$	$-5d$	2d	9d	16d	23d	30d
$U_k(d)$	5d	12d	19d	26d	33d	40d

The divisor $d \in [1, 2)$ is divided into smaller interval $[d_i, d_{i+1})$ whose length is $2^{-\delta}$, and $d_1 = 1/2$, $d_{i+1} = d_i + 2^{-\delta}$. Then, the leading δ bits of divisor are used to represent the approximation of divisor. When the internal is in $[d_i, d_{i+1})$ and q_{j+1} equals to k, the residual belongs to $m_k(i) \leq 8Q_j < m_{k+1}(i)$, m_k needs meet the two constrains as following:

$$\begin{cases} m_k(i) \geq \max\{L_k(d_i), L_k(d_{i+1})\} \\ m_k(i) \leq \min\{U_{k-1}(d_i), U_{k-1}(d_{i+1})\} \end{cases}$$

The minimum length of the selection constant is arranged C bits, then $m_k(i) = A_k(i)2^{-C}$, $A_k(i)$ is integer.

$$\begin{cases} L_k(d_i + 2^{-\delta}) \leq A_k(i)2^{-C} \leq U_{k-1}(d_i), Q[j] \geq 0 \\ L_k(d_i) \leq A_k(i)2^{-C} \leq U_{k-1}(d_i + 2^{-\delta}), Q[j] < 0 \end{cases}$$

The worst-case k = 5, d = 1 it derives

$$\delta \geq \log_2 \frac{a - \rho}{(2\rho - 1)d_{\min}} = \lceil \log_2 10 \rceil = 4.$$

The minimum value of δ is 4 amount to input d need 4 bits. According the above analysis, the input W[j] is larger 3 than d, so the minimum value of C is 7.

Square root and division can use the same quotient selection, which is proofed in [4] in detail.

4.2 Parallel SRT-8 Iteration Unit

As shown in Fig. 3, the iteration unit includes five adders corresponding to five absolutes of possible quotient in quotient digit set, and a quotient digit selection (QDS) modules for generating quotient digits each iteration. Addition and QDS can be parallel execution, then, the next residue is selected from five addition results depend on the quotient digits selected.

4.3 Parallel Generating Addend F

While QDS function is working, all possible cases for addend F is generated concurrently, in order to hide the latency of quotient selection, and the all F are sent to five parallel adders.

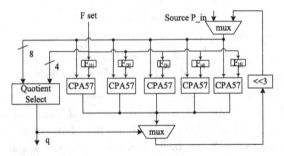

Fig. 3. SRT-8 iteration unit

In division, the input of adder F is simple. The $F = qd$ includes five cases: d, 2d, 3d, 4d and 5d. All of them, d is divisor. 2d and 4d can be obtained by d shifted. 3d is the sum of d and 2d. 5d is the sum d and 4d. The F sets generated are sent to five adders to operate $W[j+1] = W[j] \times 8 \pm F[j]$ for producing next remainder.

In square root, Q and QM representing positive quotient and negative quotient, the expression of F[j] is converted to the following:

$$F[j] = \begin{cases} -2Q[j]q_{j+1} - q_{j+1}^2 8^{-(j+1)}, q_{j+1} \geq 0 \\ 2QM[j]|q_{j+1}| + (2 \times 8 - |q_{j+1}|)|q_{j+1}|8^{-(j+1)}, q_{j+1} < 0 \end{cases}$$

The generating process of F is complex from function computing step by step, but also the process needs longer latency. In order to reduce the latency for generating F, the design adopted direct look-up table to produce F corresponding to each quotient digits. The string 'a..aa' and 'b..bb' replace the value of $Q[j]$ and $QM[j]$ respectively. Then, the updates of F are as shown in Table 4.

Table 4. Generating F[j] directly

q_{j+1}	Expression	F[j] item
1	$-2Q[j] - 8^{-(j+1)}$	a..aa0001
-1	$2QM[j] + 15 * 8^{-(j+1)}$	b..bb1111
2	$-4Q[j] - 4 * 8^{-(j+1)}$	a..a00100
-2	$4QM[j] + 12 * 8^{-(j+1)}$	b..b11000
3	$-2Q[j] - 4Q[j] - 9 * 8^{-(j+1)}$	a..aa000110 + a..aa0000
-3	$2QM[j] + 4QM[j] + 39 * 8^{-(j+1)}$	b..bb0101001 + b..bb0000
...	...	...

As shown in Fig. 4, 10 possible F sets are generated corresponding to 10 different quotient digits simultaneously based on values assigned in advance. The right F are chosen by the logic of multi-Choice, Count_iteration (the signal for recording iterations), $Q[j]$, $QM[j]$ as input index.

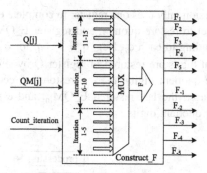

Fig. 4. Parallel generating addend F

4.4 Quotient Conversion "On-the-Fly"

In SRT-8 algorithm, the quotient is typically collected in a representation where the digits can take on both positive and negative values. Thus, at some point, all of the values must be combined and converted into a standard representation. This requires a full-width addition for the conversion, which can be a slow operation. Techniques exist for performing this conversion "on-the-fly", therefore the extra cycle may not be needed [13]. But if this scheme is complex, it will add more required hardware. Then, this conversion "on-the-fly" may bring the problem that the penalty for requiring the additional cycle is obviously much larger than the benefit from it. Focused on the issue, we proposed a conversion "on-the-fly" with little additional required hardware for controlling logic. The follow equations are the definition of positive quotient and negative quotient respectively.

$$Q[j] = \sum_{i=1}^{k} q_i r^{-i} \text{ and } QM[j] = Q[j] - r^{-j}$$

As shown in Fig. 5, the implementation in [12] of the algorithm uses two registers to store Q[j] and QM[j].

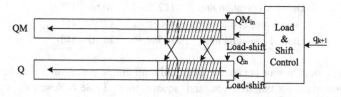

Fig. 5. Traditional quotient conversion on-the-fly

These registers can be shifted three digits left with insertion in the least significant position depend on q_{j+1}. They also require parallel loading to replace Q[j] with QM [j + 1] and vice versa.

The proposed conversion only uses one register to complete on the fly. As shown in Fig. 6, register Q was set to restore quotient and register E_QM_{in} to restore negative quotient digits corresponding to each q_j. $Neg\_q = 7 - q_j$ for $q < 0$; $Neg\_q = q_{j-1}$ for $q > 0$. The next quotient digits are restored in register Q by shifting right. If positive quotient is selected, the quotient digital q_{j+1} is restored directly, otherwise, the last restored q_j will be replaced the last restored E_QM_{in}, and q's complement will be restored as the updating quotient digits.

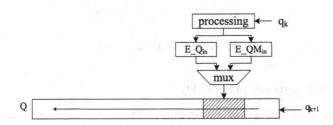

Fig. 6. Quotient conversion on-the-y with simple logic

5 Experiments

We have implemented the proposed single/double precision floating-point division and square root unit and instructions on X-DSP. All modules were encoded in Verilog and synthesized with 45 nm technology library in typical conditions (1 V, 25 °C), and clock cycle was set as 450 ps. At the same time, the other possible designs were implemented as comparisons which were iteration unit for division and square root respectively.

As shown in Table 5, experiment results show that unified unit for division and square root need only be increased by small area cost upon individual SRT-8 division or square root units.

Table 5. Results from synthesis

Operation unit	Area (μm^2)	Power	Critical
Division operation unit	12222.63	10.66	427
Square root operation unit	16039.41	12.48	441
Unified operation unit	18589.36	14.10	446

The implemented unit is capable of calculating single precision a double precision floating-point data format division and square root. Table 6 describes cycles and latency according to different target precision operations need.

Error analyze, the precision of divider was verified by recursion division. The proposed design and C program respectively operated recursion division using same data. Then, compare their results. C program was run on Intel processor. The experimental results show the design can obtain the precision of floating-point division same with Intel processor.

Table 6. Performance of different target precisions

Data format precision	Cycles	Latency (ns)
Single precision 9-bit	5	2.25
Single precision 18-bit	9	4.05
Single precision 24-bit	15	6.75
Double precision 18-bit	8	3.60
Double precision 32-bit	15	6.75
Double precision 53-bit	22	9.90

This paper proposed improved implementation of on-the-fly conversion. The design without on-the-fly conversion, the design with on-the-fly conversion proposed by [12] and the design with on-the-fly conversion proposed by above section were implemented respectively and synthesized in same experimental environment. The experimental data was shown in Table 7 taking double precision operation as example.

Table 7. Comparison of different structures

Structure	Area	Power	Cycles	Latency (ns)
Design without on-the-fly	17925.22	12.64	24	13.50
[13] 's design	19707.41	15.39	22	12.60
Our design	18589.36	14.10	22	12.60

Obviously, the design with on-the-fly conversion cost more area than the design without on-the-fly conversion, but latency is decreased by the structure for computing. In addition, our design area-cost is decreased by 6% comparing to the [13]'s design.

In previous works [13–15], generation of F in square root was implemented by complex computing process. Comparing with directly parallel generating F proposed, previous design will enlarge the latency of critical path, when division and square root were implemented in unify hardware structure, because generation of F in square root need larger latency than division by computing. For analyzing the contribution of design latency, we implemented design unit with past method of generating F for comparing. The experimental data is shown that its area is 15839.21 μm^2 and is decreased by 15% comparing proposed design, however, its critical path is 570 ps and is longer than the proposed design.

6 Conclusions

This work presents the design and implementation of single/double precision floating-point division and square root unit based on SRT-8 algorithm. Structure of independent mantissa computing and normalization joined with splitting iteration instructions are adopted for implementing flexible precision floating-point operation. With the above mentioned improved and optimized strategies, the design obtained higher performance than others. Especially for low precision operation, make them cost less latency.

References

1. Oberman, S.F., Flynn, M.J.: Design issues in division and other floating-point operations. J. IEEE Trans. Comput. **46**(2), 154–161 (1997)
2. Inwook, K., Earl, E.S.: A Goldschmidt division method with faster than quadratic convergence. IEEE Trans. Very Large Scale Integr. Syst. **19**(4), 759–763 (2011)
3. Stuart, F.O., Michael, J.F.: Division algorithms and implementations. IEEE Trans. Comput. **46**(8), 833–854 (1997)
4. Peter, K.: Digit selection for SRT division and square root. IEEE Trans. Comput. **54**(3), 727–739 (2005)
5. Dong, W., Milobs, D.E.: A Radix-16 combined complex division/square root unit with operand prescaling. IEEE Trans. Comput. **61**(9), 1243–1255 (2012)
6. Ingo, R., Tobias, G.N.: Digit-set-interleaved Radix-8 division/square root Kernel for double-precision floating point. In: 2010 International Symposium on System on Chip (SoC), Tampere, Finland, pp. 150–153 (2010)
7. Ercegovac, M.D., Lang, T.: Division and Square Root: Digit Recurrence Algorithms and Implementations. Kluwer Academic Publishers, Norwell (1994)
8. Frandrianto, J.: Algorithm for high-speed shared Radix-8 division and Radix-8 square root. In: Proceedings of 9th Symposium on Computer Arithmetic, pp. 68–75 (1989)
9. Nannarelli, A.: Radix-16 combined division and square root unit. In: 2011 20th IEEE Symposium on Computer Arithmetic, pp. 169–176 (2011)
10. Amaricai, A., Boncalo, O.: SRT Radix-2 dividers with (5, 4) redundant representation of partial remainder. IEEE Trans. 1016–1020 (2013)
11. Issad, M., Anane, M., Bessalah, H.: Influence de la Base sur les Performance de la Division SRT. Journes Francophones sur Adquation algorithm architecture 91–94 (2005)
12. Ercegovac, M.D., Lang, T., Milo, D.: On-the-fly rounding. IEEE Trans. Comput. **41**(12), 1497–1503 (1992)
13. Nannarelli, A.: Radix-16 combined division and square root unit. In: 2011 20th IEEE Symposium on Computer Arithmetic, Germany, pp. 169–176 (2011)
14. Ingo, R., Noll, T.G.: A Digit-set-interleaved Radix-8 division/square root Kernel for double-precision floating point. In: 2010 International Symposium on System on Chip (SoC), Tampere, Finland, pp. 150–153 (2010)
15. Wetter, H., Schwarz, E.M., Haess, J.: The IBM eServer z990 floating-point unit. IBM J. Res. Dev. **48**(3), 311–322 (2004)

Language-Extension-Based Vectorizing Compiling Scheme on SDR-DSP

Xiaoqiang Ni[✉], Liu Yang, and Chiyuan Ma

School of Computer, National University of Defense Technology,
Deya Street 109, Changsha 410073, People's Republic of China
xiaoqiangni@nudt.edu.cn

Abstract. In this paper we propose a Language-Extension-based Vectorizing Compiling Scheme (LEVCS) for a newly developed DSP. The DSP is mainly designed for Software-Defined Radio (SDR) and is called SDR-DSP. The SDR-DSP architecture mixes the styles of VLIW (Very Long Instruction Word) and SIMD (Single Instruction Multiple Data). To explore the potential of SDR-DSP and achieve high performance, vectorization is one of the must equipped critical methods. Because auto-vectorization techniques cannot satisfy the requirements of the typical application, LEVCS is used to direct the vectorization. The C-extending programming language used in LEVCS is called SDR-DSP-C. LEVCS uses flexible data reorganization to make vectorization on SDR-DSP more efficient. We use LEVCS to vectorize five benchmark kernels: Fast Fourier Transform (FFT), Finite Impulse Responsefilter (FIR) and Infinite Impulse Response filter (IIR), Dot product implementation (Dotprod), Sum of vectors (vecsum). Experiment results show that LEVCS is functional correct and can achieve 2.883–8.074 speedups comparing to TI-DSPs.

Keywords: SIMD · VLIW · SDR-DSP · Vectorizing compiling scheme

1 Introduction

With the development of wireless communication techniques, the performance requirement of DSP becomes higher and higher. Software-defined radio (SDR) is a new communication technique, which implements radio functions in software. SDR becomes popular because it meets the trend for better flexibility and scalability [1]. To meet the requirements of high-throughput and low-power, SDR processor requires more complicated architecture than traditional digital signal processor [2]. SIMD processing becomes one of the main architecture of DSP to meet real-time performance requirements of SDR solutions [4]. We design and develop a new DSP architecture for high performance applications, which is named SDR-DSP. It has a new instruction set and it is based on VLIW [6] and SIMD [7]. It includes two processing units, which are called SU (scalar unit) and VU (vector unit). SDR-DSP also has FPU (floating point units) and it can support single floating-point and double floating-point efficiently.

Today most DSP applications is implemented using a combination of both C code and assembly code. For the critical code which is important to performance, DSP

© Springer Nature Singapore Pte Ltd. 2016
W. Xu et al. (Eds.): NCCET 2016, CCIS 666, pp. 15–23, 2016.
DOI: 10.1007/978-981-10-3159-5_2

programmers use highly optimized assembly code [11]. The DSP compilers always supply libraries written in assembly code to support SIMD application.

The CEVA-X C family of DSP cores features acombination of VLIW and Vector engines that enhance typical DSP capabilities with advanced vector processing. The CEVA-XC4000 is the third generation of the CEVA-XC family [9]. Its VLIW architecture shares many similarities with TI (TexasInstrument)' C64x DSP family [8] but only supports fixed-point computation. The lack of FPU implies that the CEVA-dsp cannot efficiently support floating-point applications [10]. CEVA-DSP compiler uses the mode of combining C code with assembly code. It mainly uses assembly intrinsic for SIMD operations [11].

The C6678 DSP is a high-performance fixed/floating-point DSP based on TI's Keystone multi-core DSP architecture C66x. The C66x Digital Signal Processor (DSP) extends the performance of the C64x+ and C674x DSPs through enhancements and new features. Many of the new features target increased performance for vector processing [12]. TI's C66x compiler also uses the mode of combining C code with assembly code. It supports SIMD by using the mode of interfacing C and C++ with assembly language [13].

Writing assembly code is difficult and time consuming. The assembly programmer has to handle time consuming machine-level issues such as registers allocation and instruction scheduling. The work on vectorization must be done manually by assembly programmers. It will be more convenient if these issues can be taken care of by the compiler [11]. If compiler supports high-level vectorized language, programmers can utilize architecture characteristics by using high-level language.

SDR has a large amount of frequently changing radio communication algorithm [3], the high-level language developing environment for SDR-DSP is urgent. The architecture of SDR-DSP requires more complicated compiling techniques to develop data parallelism and instruction parallelism. SDR-DSP has special VU to support SIMD. Making good use of the SIMD architecture characteristics of SDR-DSP is critical to the performance. So the support to vectorization of SDR-DSP compiler is very important.

Today the techniques of autovectorization of compilers are not mature. Saeed Maleki et al. evaluate the vectorization capabilities of today's most popular compilers [14]: GCC (version 4.7.0), ICC (12.0) and XLC (11.1). They use different benchmarks which include a set of synthetic benchmarks, two applications from PACT and the Media Bench applications. The results of the evaluation show today's compilers can at most vectorize 45–71% of the loops in the synthetic benchmark and only 18–30% in the collection of application. Today's popular compilers are not effective in autovectorization and it is difficult in compiling field. It needs long time and large amount of research to find scientific optimized ways to solve this problem. SDR-DSP is designed for wireless communication and the requirement to develop high performance applications is urgent. It is essential for us to find a new scheme of vectorizing compiling for SDR-DSP.

This paper gives a Language-Extension-based Vectorizing Compiling Scheme for SDR-DSP. For convenience, we call it LEVCS. We design a C-extending programming language called SDR-DSP C and develop a vectorizing compiler to support SDR-DSP C. LEVCS can support SDR-DSP C and flexible data reorganization. In this paper, Sect. 2 describes the architecture of SDR-DSP. Section 3 introduces LEVCS, including language extending for vectorization and Data reorganization for vectorization. Section 4 gives the results of the experiment and performance analysis.

2   Architecture of SDR-DSP

As shown in Fig. 1, SDR-DSP consists of two processing units: SU (scalarunit) and VU (vectorunit). SDR-DSP can issue ten instructions per clock cycle. It supports instruction-level parallelism based on VLIW and data-level parallelism based on SIMD.

- SDR-DSP includes unified instruction-fetch unit and instruction-dispatch unit. The dispatch unit issues instructions for SU and VU simultaneously.
- SU performs scalar tasks and controls the flow of the execution of VU. VU performs computation-intensive parallel tasks.
- SDR-DSP has a vector memory (VM) to store vector data. Vector Data Accessing Unit is used to load and store vector data. It supports efficient data supply and transport for wide vector computation.
- VU includes a set of isomorphic VEs and the number of VEs is configurable. Each VE has local register file, accumulators and parallel functional units (MAC, ALU and BP). The parallel functional units support fixed-point and floating-point operations.

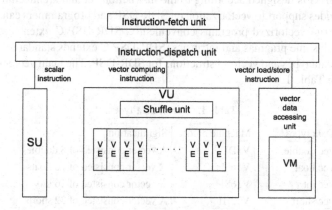

Fig. 1.   Architecture of SDR-DSP

A lot of applications need to reorganize data within VEs in VU. To support shuffle operation, SDR-DSP has data-shuffling unit to exchange data among different VEs. There is a special shuffle-modes memory which is separate from vector memory (VM). It contains various shuffle modes. Shuffle operation permutes data among local registers in various VEs by byte, half word or word. The shuffle operation among VEs can make data exchange more efficient.

3   Introduction to LEVCS

Because of the SIMD characteristics of SDR-DSP architecture and the data-intensive characteristics of SDR applications, the efficient vectorizing compiler of SDR-DSP is very important.

Language Extending for Vectorization. For some C programs, SDR-DSP compiler uses autovectorization to analyze the parallel parts in the programs. Then the parallel parts which satisfy the conditions to be vectorized will be recognized and transformed to the vectorized code running on VU.

Because of the limitation of autovectorization we have described in Sect. 1, lots of complex C programs cannot be vectorized automatically. Some programs include complex loops which are very difficult to be analyzed and vectorized. Some programs benefit from complex SDR-DSP instructions, such as saturation arithmetic, reduction, shuffle and soon. These instructions cannot be mapped easily from high level language [5] and autovectorization for them is more difficult. To compensate the lack of the auto-vectorization of compiler, we put forward LEVCS for SDR-DSP. In LEVCS, we design and implement a C-extending programming language for SDR-DSP which is called SDR-DSP C.

SDR-DSP C is designed according to the instruction set and architecture of SDR-DSP. It provides support to vectorization on SDR-DSP and programmers can use SDR-DSP C to write vectorized programs conveniently. SDR-DSP C extends standard C language with some pragmas and intrinsics. SDR-DSP C extends standard C language with vector data types and vector instructions for SDR-DSP. The main vector data types are shown in Table 1.

Table 1. Vector data-types.

Data types	Machine mode	Signification
vec double	V8DI	A vector consisted of 8 doubles
vec float	V16SF	A vector consisted of 16 floats
vec int	V16SI	A vector consisted of 16 ints
vec short	V32HI	A vector consisted of 32 shorts
vec char	V64QI	A vector consisted of 64 chars

SDR-DSP has some complex vector instructions, such as multi-mode shuffle, multi-width reduction, complex multiplication and soon. Using these instructions effectively can greatly improve applications' performance. So we design new syntax corresponding to all of these instructions in SDR-DSP C. For example, to implement shuffle instructions, we add v_vshufw, v_vshuff, v_vshufh and v_vshufb in SDR-DSP C, to implement reduction instructions, we add v_reduc2, v_reduc4, v_ reduc8 and v_reduc16 in SDR-DSP C. SDR-DSP C adds several pragmas to direct compiling optimization, such as: #pragma vect, #pragma novect, #pragma unroll(n).

In LEVCS, we develop a high-level language developing environment for SDR-DSP. It includes a vectorizing compiler which support SDR-DSP C. It also includes assembler, linker, debugger and simulator. Programmers can use SDR-DSP C to develop vetrorized programs for SDR-DSP and use SDR-DSP compiler to parse and translate these programs into intermediate language and then output the optimized assemble code. Then the code can be assembled and linked. It supplies a friendly and convenient environment for programmers to develop applications for SDR-DSP.

Data Reorganization for Vectorization. The data-level parallelism in the applications of wireless communication, video and image processing always include regular data-level parallelism and irregular data-level parallelism. An application with regular data access can be considered to have regular data-level parallelism. If it has irregular data access and complex control flow, such as data-dependent control flow, the data-level parallelism is considered to be irregular. For regular data-level parallelism, vectorization on SIMD architecture always can get good effect. But for irregular data-level parallelism, the result of vectorization is always not satisfied. In such cases, the performance cannot get improved, and sometimes may be reduced. When the SIMD width is more wide, this problem becomes more serious. So based on maintaining the high effeciency of regular data-level parallelism, the supporting to irregular data-level parallelism is very important. Flexible and efficient data reorganization is essential.

Traditional SIMD architecture uses guarded instructions to support data-dependent controlflow [16]. This method uses masks to disable some SIMD lanes. But for complex branches, this method will waste computing resources and becomes inefficient. Woop [17] uses the scheme of branch fusion. SIMD lanes on different branch paths are executed sequentially and are synchronized in the branch joint. The efficient utilization of SIMDlanes are still not good.

Maven VT microarchitecture [18] uses a unique lane buffering equipment. When meeting branch, the simd lanes on various branch paths will be buffered and will be executed sequentially. In the buffering equipment, SIMD lanes with the same executing paths can be merged to improve the utilization of SIMD lanes. In this method, extra hardware is needed and the hardware cost increases.

Vector Thread Architecture [19] configures an instruction cache for each SIMD lanes. Each simd lanes can fetch instruction independently (threadfetch). This method can support data-dependent control flow effectively but the expansibility are not good. Each SIMD lanes need an instruction buffer, the hardware cost will be into lerable when SIMD width becomes more and more wide.

Dynamic Wrap [20, 21] can support branches efficiently in GPUs. It reorganizes the threads executing various branch paths in multiple wraps in to newwraps, each wrap includes threads executing the same branch path. This methods needs to allocate registers for each wrap to implement the reorganization of abundant wraps and it brings heavy register costs.

Instruction shuffle scheme is a new mechanism that can handle control-flow efficiently [22]. It stores instructions on various branch paths into a unified instruction buffer array. Instruction shuffle unit issues corresponding instructions to the SIMD lanes for various branch paths. This mechanism can implement parallel execution of various branch paths, But extra instructions are needed to support instruction shuffle and the hardware cost also increased. The reorder of the output data is still a problem.

Conditional Stream [23] supports irregular data-level parallelism on IMAGINE processor. It classified the data streams and put the data of the same operations together. The original kernel with control flow is departed into multiple kernels without control flow. This method destroys the original order of data. Many applications in communication, video and image processing are data-order dependent so there covery of data order are more complex.

Most applications of wireless communication, video and image processing are written in high-level language and the source codes in these applications are always complex and flexible. Efficient High-level language compiling is essential. It is very difficult and time consuming to do data reorganization manually. It will be more convenient if these issues can be solved by the compiler. If compiler supports data reorganization, programmers can focus on the algorithms by using high-level language.

Data reorganization is critical to vectorization, so it is essential for us to implement flexible and efficient data reorganization in the compiler for wide SIMD Architecture.

Implementing flexible and efficient data reorganization in the compiler of wide SIMD architecture is essential. LEVCS can do data reorganization for wide SIMD architecture. It implements flexible data reorganization for wide SIMD. It mainly has three modules to implement data reorganization for various requirements: Data reorganization based on Multi-Modulo, Data reorganization for wide vector filling and Data reorganization for Branch.

Many algorithms in wireless communication require complex data exchange, such as FFT [15], FIR, IIR, Hartley transform, Discrete Cosine Transform, Viterbi Decoding and soon. In such algorithms, there are many irregular access to vectors which is a problem to performance. There alparts and imaginary parts of complex numbers are always stored continuously. But in some algorithms, the real parts and imaginary parts always participate in different vector computing, or are different operators of one vector computing. In order to utilize the SIMD architecture efficiently, data reorganization is required.

To implement efficient vector data exchange, LEVCS supports data reorganization based on multi-modulo. According to the requirement of the algorithms, when data is loaded from VM to VR (vector reigister) or is stored from VR into VM, data need to be shuffled based on various modulos. The multiple modulos are designed to direct data reorganization. For each kind of modulo, there is a corresponding item in SMT.

The data are loaded from VM into VRs which will participate in vector operations. In some applications, the data loaded are not long enough to fulfill the vector. In some applications, the data loaded into 16 VEs as a vector includes data for various vector operation or various sources vectors of one vector operation. In these cases, if the data are not reorganized, these data cannot be operated in parallel, some VEs will be idle when the vector operation is executed. The wide simd architecture cannot be fully utilized. LEVCS implements Data reorganization for wide vector filling using inner reorganization, horizontal reorganization and vertical reorganization.

LEVCS identifies loops that can be simdized. Firstly, inner reorganization is used. Inner reorganization is used for one vector operation in inner loops. If the effective vector length is less than simdwidth, some VEs will be idle without data. In such case, short vectors will be combined into wide vector to let more VEs to work in parallel. If vector length still cannot fulfill the requirements of simd width, the loops will be unrolled. After loop unrolling, more data will be reorganized to do vector filling. The compiler should find enough parallel computation and the stride of various short vectors needs to be appropriate. If the data stride is too big, the cost of loading these data will be too higher to be accepted.

If inner reorganization still cannot fulfill the requirements, horizontal reorganization is used. Horizontal reorganization is for multiple irrelevant vector operations in inner loops. Suppose a vector includes several groups of elements. Various groups contain various sources for various vector operations and each group is not wide enough for the vector width. If such vectors are not reorganized, while one group of elements participate in one vector operation, the VEs corresponding to the other groups of elements will be idle. In such case, LEVCS does horizontal reorganization. The horizontal reorganization combines various groups of multiple vectors together to form new vectors.

If data reorganization of inner loops cannot fulfill the requirements, LEVCS will take outer loops into consideration and do vertical reorganization. Vertical reorganization is for multiple irrelevant vector operations in various layers of loops. Multiple irrelevant vector operations are reorganized together to form wide vectors. LEVCS will continue to unroll outer loops to get enough data for vectors when needed.

For the wide SIMD architecture, the problems brought by branches become more serious. In order not to increase the cost of hardware, Data Reorganization for Branch solves this problem in compiling. LEVCS can do flexible data reorganization according to various cases of branches. All VEs in VU can work in parallel and need not to process various branch paths redundantly. The execution efficiency of loops with branches can be improved.

4 Results and Discussion

In the experiment, we use LEVCS to vectorize FFT,FIR, IIR, dotprod and vecsum programs. The programs are compiled with the vetorizing compiler of SDR-DSP. After being assembled and linked, we get the executable program and run it on the cycle accurate simulator. We use $T_{SDR-DSP}$ to represent the cycle counts of the kernel in the program.

We also execute floating-point FFT program on TMS320C66X simulator in CCS5.1. We can get same result with the result on SDR-DSP. We use optimization level -O3 to compile the C program [24] and get the cycle counts T_{C66X}. Comparing the two experiment results, we can get the speedup from Eq. (1)

$$speedup = T_{C66X}/T_{SDR-DSP} \tag{1}$$

From that, we can see the vectorized program using LEVCS can get correct result and achieve higher performance than C program running on TI-DSP. The result of the experiment (Table 2) shows: developing vectorized program with SDR-DSP C and using the vectorizing compiler of SDR-DSP can make good use of the SIMD characteristics of SDR-DSP. We can achieve with TI-DSP. The experiment proves that LEVCS designed in this paper has validity and efficiency.

Table 2. Experiment result

	$T_{SDR-DSP}$	T_{C66X}	Speedup
FFT_float (1024)	14608	117940	8.074
FIR_float (1024 * 16)	29493	85019	2.883
IIR_float (1024)	6159	29722	4.826
vector_dotprod_float (1024)	675	4131	6.828
vector_sum_float (1024)	526	4131	7.854

5 Conclusion

In order to explore the performance of digital signal processor SDR-DSP, this paper designs and implements LEVCS, a Language-Extension-based Vectorizing Compiling Scheme for SDR-DSP. This design provides a vectorized programming method with a new C-extending programming language named SDR-DSP C. The corresponding vectorizing compiler is developed for SDR-DSP, including the support for SDR-DSP C and flexible data reorganization. The result of experiment shows that we can implement vectorizationon SDR-DSP correctly and can get good speedups by using LEVCS. In practice, LEVCS can be used to vectorize the computing kernels of the applications on SDR-DSP.

References

1. Harada, H., Kuroda, M., Morikawa, H., Wakana, H., Adachi, F.: The overview of the new generation mobile communication system and the role of software defined RADIO Technology. IEICE Trans. Commun. **E86-B**(12), 3374–3384 (2003)
2. Jo, G.-D., Sheen, M.-J., Lee, S.-H., Cho, K.-R.: ADSP-Based reconfigurable SDR platform for 3G systems. IEICE Trans. Commun. **E88-B**(2), 678–686 (2005)
3. Wally, H.W.: Tuttlebee: Software Defined Radio: Enabling Technologies. Wiley, Chichester (2002)
4. He, X., Jin, X., Wang, M., Zhou, D., Goto, S.: A 98 GMACs/W 32-core vector processor in 65 nm CMOS. IEICE Trans. Fundam. Electron. Commun. Comput. Sci. **E94-A**(12), 2609–2618 (2011)
5. Tanaka, H., Takeuchi, Y., Sakanushi, K., Mai, M., Tagawa, H., Ota, Y., Matsumoto, N.: Generation of pack instruction sequence for media processors using multi-valued decision diagram. IEICE Trans. Fundam. Electron. Commun. Comput. Sci. **E90-A**(12), 2800–2809 (2007)
6. Fisher, J.: Very long instruction word architectures and the ELI-512. In: Proceedings of the Tenth Annual International Symposium on Computer Architecture, pp. 140–150 (1983)
7. Lorenz M,, Wehmeyer L, Drager T.: Energy aware compilation for DSPs with SIMD instructions. In: Proceedings of the Joint Conference on Languages, Compilers and Tools for Embedded Systems, LCTES/SCOPES 2002, pp. 94–101. ACM Press (2002)
8. Gardner, J.S.: CEVA exposes DSP six pack XC4000 family uses coprocessors to buff up the baseband. The Linley Group, Microprocessor Report, March 2012
9. CEVA-XC4000. CEVA, Inc. (2012). http://www.ceva-dsp.com/CEVA-XC4000.html

10. Balaish, E.: Architecture oriented C optimizations, White Paper, CEVA, Inc., January 2010
11. Balaish, E.: Combining C code with assembly code in DSP applications. White Paper, CEVA, Inc., August 2009
12. Texas Instruments: TMS320C6678 Multicore Fixed and Floating-Point Digital Signal Processor Data Manual. SPRS691C, February 2012
13. Texas Instruments: TMS320C6000 optimizing compiler v7.3 user's guide. SPRU187T, July 2011
14. Maleki, S., Gao, Y., Jess Garzarçn, M., Wong, T., Padua, D.A.: An evaluation of vectorizing compilers. In: PACT, pp. 372–382 (2011)
15. Jung, Y., Yoon, H., Kim, J.: New efficient FFT algorithm and pipeline implementation results for OFDM/DMT applications. IEEE Trans. Consum. Electron. **49**(1), 14–20 (2003)
16. Bouknight, W.J., Denenberg, S.A., McIntyre, D.E., Randall, J.M., Sameh, A.H., Slotnick, D.L.: The Illiac IV system. In: Proceedings of the IEEE, vol. 60, no. 4, pp. 369–388, April 1972
17. Swoop, P., Schmittler, J.: RPU: a programmable ray processing unit for realtime ray tracing. ACM Trans. Graph. **24**(3), 434–444 (2005)
18. Lee, Y., Avizienis, R., Bishara, A., et al.: Exploring the tradeoffs between programmability and efficiency in data-parallel accelerators. In: Proceedings of the IEEE International Symposium on Computer Architecture, San Jose, USA, pp. 129–140, June 2011
19. Krashinsky, R. Hampton, M., Gerding, S., Batten, C.: The vector-thread architecture, In: Proceedings of the IEEE International Symposium on Computer Architecture, Saint-Malo, France, pp. 37–48, June 2004
20. Fung, W.W.L., Sham, I., Yuan, G., et al.: Dynamic Warp Formation And Scheduling For efficient GPU control flow. In: Proceedings of the 40th Annual IEEE/ACM International Symposium on Microarchitecture, Washington, DC, USA, pp. 407–420 (2007)
21. Fung, W.W.L., Sham, I., Yuan, G., et al.: Dynamic warp formation: efficient MIMD control flow on SIMD graphics hardware. ACM Trans. Archit. Code Optim. **6**(2), 1544–3566 (2009)
22. Wang, Y., Chen, S., Zhang, K., Wan, J., Xiaowen Chen, H., Chen, H.W.: Instruction shuffle: achieving MIMD-like performance on SIMD architectures. IEEE Comput. Archit. Lett. **11**(2), 37–40 (2012)
23. Kapasi, U., Dally, W.J., Rixner, S., et al.: Efficient conditional operations for data-parallel architectures. In: Proceedings of the 33rd Annual ACM/IEEE International Symposium on Microarchitecture, pp. 159–170. ACM, New York (2000)
24. Texas Instruments: TMS320C6000 Optimizing Compiler v7.4 User's Guide, SPRU187 (2012)

A Methodology for Performance Verification of Microprocessors

Yongwen Wang[✉], Libo Huang, and Zhong Zheng

School of Computer, National University of Defense Technology,
Changsha 410073, China
yongwen@nudt.edu.cn

Abstract. The tested performance of a microprocessor chip is more important than the predicted performance of it's model. However, performance deviations are often introduced during the design stages. In order to identify and fix the performance defects, a hierarchical performance verification methodology is proposed. Parameter sensitive performance models and coverage driven stimulus are built at the unit-level. Implementation oriented performance calibration and RTL simulation based benchmarks are made at the core-level. Prototyping and counter-based performance analysis systems are built in the system level. An example is given to demonstrate the application and effectiveness of the proposed methodology.

Keywords: Performance verification · Performance model · Microprocessor · Methodology

1 Introduction

The industry has already been able to predict the clock frequency and the functionality of microprocessors in the design stages. However, it is still a great challenge to predict the performance on real programs. Which causes a gap between the performance predicted and the performance tested on the final silicon. In order to narrow this gap and make the real performance consistent with the prediction, performance verification technology is required.

The idea of performance verification is borrowed from the idea of function verification. Function verification has already been obligate in chip design flow and many methodologies have been studied, while performance verification is much less universal and there are hardly any reference methodology.

Performance models are used to predict the overall performance of a microprocessor in the early design phase. This is done by modeling the latency of instructions, the dependencies between instructions, and the allocation of limited resources in the implementation. However, the performance data reflect the behaviors of the models instead of the real silicon. Calibration technologies have

This work is supported in part by National Natural Science Foundation of China under grants 61170045.

W. Xu et al. (Eds.): NCCET 2016, CCIS 666, pp. 24–31, 2016.
DOI: 10.1007/978-981-10-3159-5_3

been studied to make the performance models more accurate. But it won't make the real silicon more accurate when discrepancies are introduced for a new design.

In this paper, a performance verification methodology is proposed to identify and fix the performance discrepancies during the design stages. The rest of the paper is organized as follows: in Sect. 2 related works are analyzed. The proposed methodology is described in Sect. 3. An example is demonstrated to show the application of the methodology in Sect. 4. Finally, this paper is concluded in Sect. 5.

2   Related Works

Performance verification focuses on the performance related discrepancies introduced during the design stage. Thus performance evaluation is very important for performance verification. Many technologies have been studied on these topics in recent decades. Related works can be classified into two categories: performance modeling and benchmarking.

2.1   Performance Modeling

There are two types of performance models, analysis based and simulation based. Analysis based model is created by means of probability theory, queuing theory, Markov model, Petri nets or other mathematical tools. They are commonly used for system-level performance analysis. The degree of accuracy required for microprocessor architecture analysis is beyond the ability of general mathematical models, only a few researchers have attempted to establish a analysis based microprocessor model [1–3]. We have also studied the use of Petri nets for design space exploration [4].

Simulation based model is well known as simulator, which is the main stream method of micro-architecture research. A variety of simulators have been developed successfully [5–8] and surveyed widely [9,10].

In order to make simulators more accurate, a target processor should be chosen. In another word, the simulator should be compared with the target processor which is accurate. Black calibrated the simulator with PowerPC 604 [11], Desikan compared the simulator with Alpha 21264 [12]. There are not many studies on model calibration, partly because performance model is good enough for most academic studies and there are no requirements for a real target processor.

Performance evaluated on models only reflect the behaviors of a simulator. If the simulation model behaves differently to the target processor, the performance improvements may not be achieved on real processors. This is the challenge faced by many microprocessor developers.

2.2   Benchmarking

Benchmarks should represent the behaviors of real-world applications. But it is difficult to decide which application to use for performance evaluation.

Common benchmarks are standard programs for performance evaluation. Some comprehensive benchmarks are derived from real-world applications, which are usually large in scale and long in run time, such as the SPEC CPU, SPLASH, PARSEC and so on. Synthetic benchmarks are based on statistical analysis of frequently used programs, such as Dhrystone, CoreMark and Whetstone. Kernels are extracted from the scientific computing loop code, such as for Linpack and Livermoore. These programs have been widely used and reviewed [13,14].

In addition to the common benchmark suites, researchers will need to develop their own specific testing programs, such as the alpha, beta, gamma and a series of test programs for PowerPC [11] and Microbench testing suites for Godson [3].

However, both benchmarks and specific testing programs can be executed only after the system environment can execute programs. When processor being designed is not complete or correct enough to execute programs, the testing programs can not be used. But when the programs are be evaluated on the designed processor, it might be more difficult to modify the design when performance bottlenecks are found. So it is challenging to evaluate the performance when benchmarks can not be executed.

In summary, most related works are studied by means of simulator and is not responsible for the final processor chip. The lack of effective performance testing and analyzing methodology makes it difficult to narrow the gap between the real performance and expected performance.

3   Methodology

In this paper, we present the idea of performance verification to identify and fix the performance discrepancies introduced during design stages. The methodology is hierarchical in accordance with the microprocessor design flow, including unit-level, core-level and system-level, as shown in Fig. 1.

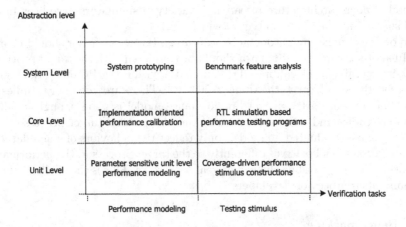

Fig. 1. Hierarchical performance verification methodology

3.1 Unit-Level: Parameter Sensitive Modeling and Coverage Driven Test Cases Construction

Performance modeling is important for the constituent units of the processor. According to the bottom-up design flow, higher-level performance evaluation can not begin until the lower-level units are functionally correct. Unit-level design are usually small in scale, which makes it more efficient to debug than higher-level. If performance bottlenecks escape from the unit-level to the system level, debug costs will be increased dramatically.

The performance of a microprocessor can be broken-down and represented by different performance parameters. Units of microprocessor should focus on the abstracted performance parameters. The performance might not be as detailed as the RTL model, however, the parameters concerned must be abstracted.

Functional units are not complex enough to execute instructions, and benchmarks can not be used for unit-level performance verification. It is difficult to build efficient stimulus to quickly sensitized the performance bottlenecks. In order to assess the quality of test stimulus, the concept of property coverage is introduced. Performance characteristics to be sensitized are defined as cover points. By coverage metrics, we can quantify the effectiveness of performance verification.

3.2 Core-Level: Implementation-Oriented Calibration and RTL Simulation Based Benchmarks

This paper does not mean how to develop a new performance model, but means how to calibrate a simulator to the target processor.

The metrics must be defined for performance calibration. The execution time of the program will give a final performance result, but only the final results are not enough, because internal performance states are not reflected in the final results. If these states appear inconsistent, performance analysis might show the misleading hints.

Approaches to discover and resolve inconsistencies in performance models are called performance debug. Artificial comparison is obviously inefficient, automatical tools should be developed to compare the model with the target processor. Functional verification features might be referenced to accelerate the process of calibration.

When all the RTL units are integrated into a CPU core, a core-level design that can execution instructions is ready, which is the earliest available performance model of the target processor. This core-level RTL implementation has the following features:

- Instruction sequences or programs can be run.
- There are still many function defects.
- There are no peripherals, timers, interrupt controllers, or other system-level components and operating system can not be booted.
- The simulation speed is very slow.
- It's performance behaviors are the same with the target processor.

According to the features above, small-scaled directed testing programs should be developed. The main goal is to sensitize the performance bottlenecks at the instruction execution level.

3.3 System-Level: System Prototyping and Benchmark Analysis

When coming to the system-level design stage, the accelerator or FPGA platform should be ready, which are very close to the target processor. Operating system and real programs can be run on this platform.

3.4 Interactions of Different Abstraction Levels

Each level of the performance verification methodology are not isolated. The co-simulation, reusing and guideline interactive relations are shown in Figs. 2 and 3. Unit-level test stimulus are extracted from the program traces of core-level. And core-level testing programs are derived from system-level benchmarks. Core-level programs can be reused in system-level testing.

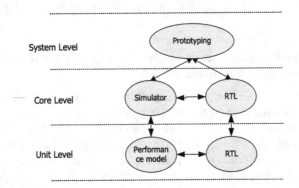

Fig. 2. Performance modeling interaction of different abstraction levels

These interactive relations ensure a consistent view of all performance levels.

4   Practice of the Methodology

In this section, an example will be given to show the practice of the performance verification methodology. The example design is a typical supersalar CPU and the design flow is divided into three stages.

In the unit level, the performance specification is modeled as the reference design and the implementation is verified as the design under test (DUT). Performance features are expressed as properties and cover points are defined for these features. Traces generated from benchmarks are used as performance stimulus. A co-simulation environment is built as shown in Fig. 4 and performance bugs can be identified automatically.

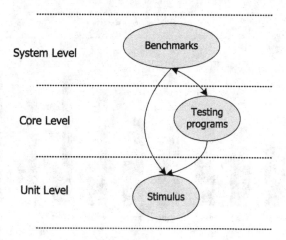

Fig. 3. Performance testing cases interaction of different abstraction levels

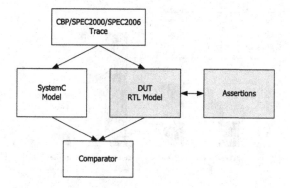

Fig. 4. Unit level performance verification with co-sim

In the core level, some micro-benchmarks are built for RTL simulation. For example, CoreMark is moderated and used as performance stimulus. The functional simulation environment can be shared for performance verification. Figure 5 shows performance testing results of various RTL verions for CoreMark. The performance increases and the miss rate decreases as the performance defects are fixed.

In the system level, FPGA prototyping systems are built and real benchmarks such as SPEC CPU can be run. The performance defects found in each level are summarized in Fig. 6.

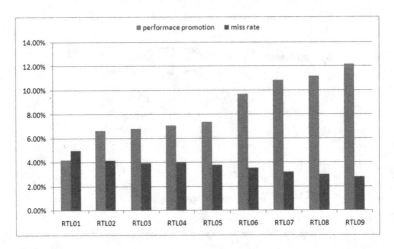

Fig. 5. Core-level performance verification with RTL simulation oriented CoreMark

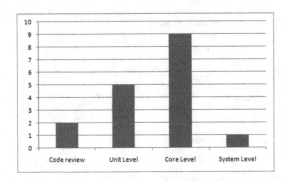

Fig. 6. Performance defects found by performance verification

5   Conclusions

In order to identify and fix the performance defects introduced during the design stages, a hierarchical performance verification methodology is proposed in this paper. Parameter sensitive performance models and coverage driven stimulus are built at the unit-level, implementation oriented performance calibration and RTL simulation based benchmarks are made at the core-level, and prototyping system and counter-based performance analysis are built in the system level. Examples show that the methodology can help fixing performance defects.

We shall refine the methodology and develop automatic tools in future works.

References

1. Noonburg, D.B., Shen, J.P.: A framework for statistical modeling of superscalar processor performance. In: Third International Symposium on High-Performance Computer Architecture, pp. 298–309. IEEE, (1997)
2. Karkhanis, T.S., Smith, J.E.: A first-order superscalar processor model. ACM SIGARCH Comput. Archit. News **32**, 338 (2004)
3. Ma, K.: Microprocessor analytical model. Ph.D. thesis, University of Science and Technology of China (2007)
4. Wang, L., Wang, Y., Li, L., Gao, J., Dou, Q.: Utilizing colored petri nets for design space exploration of asynchronous microprocessors. In: International Workshop on Reachability Problems (RP 2014), Oxford (2014)
5. Austin, T., Larson, E., Ernst, D.: Simplescalar: an infrastructure for computer system modeling. IEEE Comput. **35**, 59–67 (2002)
6. Binkert, N., Beckmann, B., Black, G., Reinhardt, S.K., Saidi, A., Basu, A., Hestness, J., Hower, D.R., Krishna, T., Sardashti, S., et al.: The gem5 simulator. ACM SIGARCH Comput. Archit. News **39**, 1–7 (2011)
7. Virtutech: Virtutech simics - a full system simulator (2004)
8. Zhang, F.X., Zhang, L.B., Hu, W.W.: Sim-Godson: a Godson processor simulator based on simplescalar. Chin. J. Comput. **30**, 68 (2007). Chinese Edition
9. Yi, J.J., Lilja, D.J.: Simulation of computer architectures: simulators, benchmarks, methodologies and recommendations. IEEE Trans. Comput. **55**, 268–280 (2006)
10. John, L.K., Eeckhout, L. (eds.): Performance Evaluation and Benchmarking. CRC Press, New York (2006)
11. Black, B., Shen, J.P.: Calibration of microprocessor performance models. Computer **31**, 59–65 (1998)
12. Desikan, R., Burger, D., Keckler, S.W.: Measuring experimental error in microprocessor simulation. In: Proceedings of the 28th Annual International Symposium on Computer Architecture, ISCA 2001, pp. 266–277. ACM, New York (2001)
13. John, L.K.: Benchmarks. In: Performance Evaluation and Benchmarking. CRC Press, pp. 27–44 (2006)
14. Hennessy, J.L., Patterson, D.A.: Computer Architecture: A Quantitative Approach, 3rd edn. Morgan Kaufmann Publisher, San Francisco (2002)

A Novel L1 Cache Based on Volatile STT-RAM

Zhang Hongguang[1](✉) and Zhang Minxuan[1,2]

[1] College of Computer, National University of Defense Technology,
Changsha 410073, People's Republic of China
{zhanghongguang14,mxzhang}@nudt.edu.cn
[2] National Key Laboratory of Parallel and Distributed Processing,
National University of Defense Technology, Changsha 410073, People's Republic of China

Abstract. Spin-transfer torque random access memory (STT-RAM) is one of the most promising substitutes for universal main memory and cache due to its excellent scalability, high density and low leakage power. Nevertheless, the current non-volatile STT-RAM cache architecture also has some drawbacks, such as long write latency and high write energy, which limit the application of STT-RAM in the top level cache design. To solve these problems, we relax the retention time of STT-RAM to explore its different write performance, and propose a novel STT-RAM L1 cache architecture implemented with volatile STT-RAM as well as its related refresh scheme. The performance of proposed design is the same as SRAM L1 cache while its overall power consumption is only 63.8% of the latter one.

Keywords: STT RAM · L1 cache · Volatile · Refresh scheme

1 Introduction

SRAM has been the mainstream technology of caches for years due to its high access speed, low dynamic power and other good features. However, with more and more cores are embedded on chip, caches need larger size. However, increasing capacity of SRAM cache leads to high leakage power, which will bring in a serious on-chip heat sink problem. So researchers are focusing on alternative substitutes for SRAM.

STT-RAM is regarded as the most promising replacement for SRAM because it owns almost all desired features of an universal memory and cache, including high storage density, fast read speed and non-volatility. However, there are two drawbacks, namely, long write latency and high write energy, which limit the application of STT-RAM in L1 cache design. In [2–4, 6, 10], there are some efficient schemes proposed to overcome the two drawbacks when applying STT-RAM in cache design, such as relaxing the non-volatility and hybrid cache design.

To overcome the two problems, we propose to relax the non-volatility of STT-RAM to gain a significant optimization in performance and power consumption. In addition, we design the related refresh scheme to improve the cache's reliability. We simulate the proposed L1 cache architecture on GEM5 simulator, and collect the simulation results to analysis its overall performance.

W. Xu et al. (Eds.): NCCET 2016, CCIS 666, pp. 32–39, 2016.
DOI: 10.1007/978-981-10-3159-5_4

2   STT-RAM Features

The basic storage cell of STT-RAM is magnetic tunnel junction (MTJ) shown in Fig. 1. There are two magnetic layers in a MTJ, namely, free layer and reference layer. They are isolated by an oxide layer. The magnetic direction of reference layer is fixed, however, that of free layer can be switched by current. If the directions of the two layers are parallel, the MTJ is in low-resistance state; if they are anti-parallel, the MTJ is in high-resistance state.

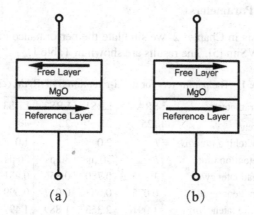

(a)   (b)

Fig. 1.   The MTJ design (1T1J). (a) High-resistance state. (b) Low-resistance state.

The MTJ's non-volatility can be analyzed quantitatively with the retention time of MTJ. We use τ to represent its retention time. τ is related to the thermal stability factor Δ and can be calculated with Eq. (1) [1].

$$\tau \approx \tau_0 exp(\Delta) \tag{1}$$

τ_0:   The attempt time and set as 1 ns.

Δ is derived from Eq. (2).

$$\Delta = \frac{E_F}{k_B T} = \frac{M_s V H_K}{2 k_B T} \tag{2}$$

M_s: The saturation magnetization.
H_k: The effective anisotropy field.
T: The working temperature.
k_B: The Boltzmann constant.
V: The volume for the STT-RAM write current.

From Eqs. (1) and (2), we can know that the data retention time of a MTJ decreases exponentially when its working temperature T increases.

According to the different T_w, MTJ has three regions, namely, the thermal activation, dynamic reverse and processional switching. We relax the MTJ's retention time to 30 μs (Δ = 10.3) and adjust the T_w to get three different design options. In this paper they are called LRS1, LRS2 and LRS3 respectively [2].

3 STT-RAM LLC Design

3.1 Performance Parameters

Based on the analysis in Chapter 2, we simulate the performance of three LRS STT-RAM designs on NVSim [5]. The results are shown in Table 1.

Table 1. The parameters for multi-retention STT-RAM cells.

Parameters	SRAM	LRS1	LRS2	LRS3
Area/F^2	125	21	22	40
Switching time/ns	/	2.0	1.5	1.0
Retention time	/	`30 μs	30 μs	30 μs
Read latency/ns	1.125	0.780	0.856	0.981
Read energy/nJ	0.075	0.083	0.087	0.099
Write latency/ns	1.091	2.363	1.889	1.497
Write energy/nJ	0.059	0.177	0.180	0.197
Leakage power/mW	24.8	1.74	1.99	1.81

From Table 1, we find that if we relax the retention time of MTJ to μs level, its access speed is almost the same with SRAM. The gap between their performance is not very large, however, the area of LRS3 is much larger than the other two designs.

Based on the above analysis, the LRS2 STT-RAM has a better overall performance and it is used in our cache design.

3.2 L1 Cache Architecture

In 2 GHz processor system, LRS2's read latency is 2 cycles, and its write latency is 3 cycles while both the two parameters of SRAM are 3 cycles. However, the retention time of LRS2 is only 30 us, which is shorter than the write interval of many blocks in L1 cache. It means that many data will be invalid if we do not take any measures.

So we propose to add two counters, namely, the refresh-counter and the access-counter, for every LRS2 block in L1 cache. The refresh-counter is used to monitor the duration time that the data have been stored in volatile blocks. We divide the retention time of STT-RAM to N_R, which is the maximum value of refresh-counter. Generally, we set $N_R = 15$ for 32 KB L1 cache. The maximum value of the access-counter is 8. So the refresh-counter is 4 bits, and the access-counter is 3 bits. The architecture is shown as Fig. 2.

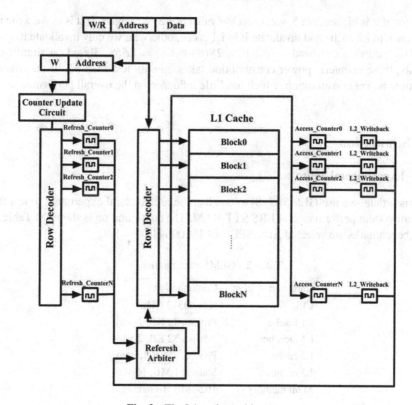

Fig. 2. The L1 cache architecture

All counters are controlled by a global clock, whose period is $T_{gc} = \tau/N_R$. The access-counter is used to record the read access number in recent 5 T_{gc} because most data in L1 are accessed again shortly since it is written into a block. If one block is not accessed in 5 T_{gc}, we think that it will no longer be accessed again in its life span. The L2_Writeback bit is used to monitor that if the last write operation is a writeback operation from L2 cache. If it is, we set its value to 1, otherwise set it to 0.

To complete the refresh operation, the data stored in a LRS block will be extracted to the buffer firstly, then is written back to the block again. If a write request comes during this process, we stop the refresh process and execute the write operation; if a read request comes, it gets data form the buffer directly and does not need to wait for the completion of refresh process. The duration of the whole process is about 5 cycles 2 GHz CPU system, which is much smaller than the retention time of LRS2 STT-RAM, so it is not necessary to consider the refresh duration in the calculation of N_R and T_{gc}.

At the end of T_{gc}, all counters are increased by 1. Both the refresh-counter and the access-counter of a LRS2 block will be reset to 0 if a write access is executed, however, the access-counter will also be reset to 0 for a read access. When a refresh-counter reaches N_R, we detect the value of access counter, if it is lower than 5, we continue the refresh process; if it is higher than 5, we detect the value of L2_Writeback. If it is 0, we write its data back to L2 cache and invalidate it in L1 cache, otherwise we only invalidate it.

The hardware overhead is (4 bits × 2)/(64 bytes) = 1.56%. Based on simulation results, these counters' power consumption takes up only less than 6% of the overall dynamic power consumption, which has little influence on the overall performance.

4 Simulation

4.1 Experimental Setup

In this article, we use GEM5 [7, 8] to conduct the architectural experiment to test the overall system performance of LRS STT-RAM. The configuration is shown in Table 2. The benchmarks are selected from SPEC CPU 2006 [10].

Table 2. GEM5 configuration

Computer system	Configuration
CPU	X86, O3, 2 GHz
L1 Icache	Private, 32 KB, 2-way
L1 Dcache	Private, 32 KB, 2-way
L2 cache	Private, 256 KB, 8-way
L3 cache	Shared, 1 MB, 16-way
Main memory	1024 MB, 1-channel

4.2 Architectural Simulation

The performance is measured by instructions per cycle (IPC), and the results are shown as Fig. 3. It can be seen that LR3 owns the best performance (at 100.5%) while LRS1's performance is the lowest one (at 99.1 %). The IPC of LRS2 is the same with SRAM.

The leakage power consumption results are shown as Fig. 4. It can be seen that the leakage power of LRS3 is the highest one, at 18.6% on average, however, the LRS1 share the lowest one, at 13.9%. The LRS2's leakage power is at 16.0%. The leakage power consumption is doubled because of the introduction of the refresh-buffer. However, the total value is still much less than that of SRAM cache.

The dynamic power consumption results are shown as Fig. 6, which includes the refresh energy. We find that the dynamic power of LRS3 is also the highest, at 101.1%, which is followed by LRS2, at 87.3%. The dynamic power of LRS1 is the lowest one, at 80.4% (Fig. 5).

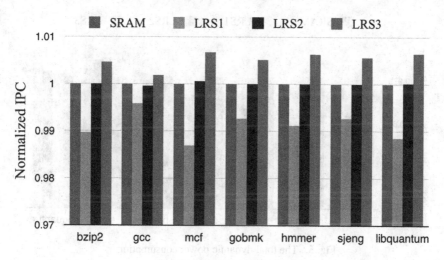

Fig. 3. The IPC test results

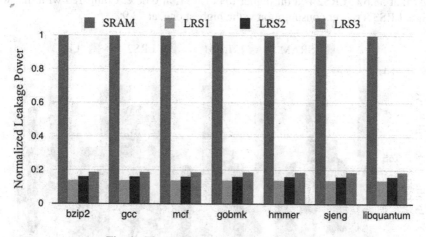

Fig. 4. The total leakage power consumption

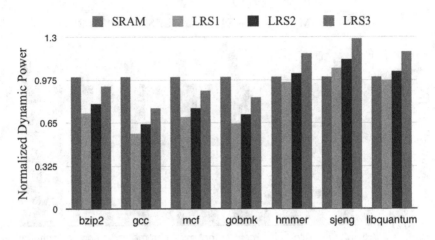

Fig. 5. The total dynamic power consumption

The overall power consumption shown in Fig. 6 is the sum of leakage and dynamic power consumption. It is clear that LRS1's power consumption is only the half of SRAM, at 58.6%. LRS2 is a bit higher than LRS1, at 63.8%. Compared with the two design, LRS3's power consumption is the highest one, at 73.9%.

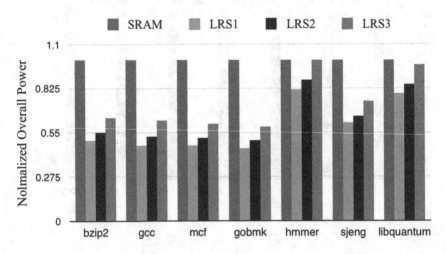

Fig. 6. The overall power consumption

5   Conclusion

In this paper, we propose a novel L1 cache architecture based on volatile STT-RAM to improve the reliability and save energy. Our simulation results show that the proposed volatile STT-RAM L1 cache has the same overall performance with SRAM, while having only 63.8% power consumption. In addition, the total on-chip area of proposed L1 cache can be saved by 64.8% ideally.

Acknowledgements. The project is sponsored by National Science and Technology Major Project, "The Processor Design for Super Computer" (2015ZX01028) in China and the Excellent Postgraduate Student Innovation Program (4345133214) of National University of Defense Technology.

References

1. Jog, A., Mishra, A. K., et al.: Cache revive: architecting volatile STT-RAM caches for enhanced performance in CMPs. In: IEEE Design Automation Conference, pp. 243–253 (2012)
2. Sun, Z., Bi, X., et al.: STT-RAM cache hierarchy with multiretention MTJ design. IEEE Trans. Very Large Scale Integr. Syst. **22**(6), 1281–1294 (2014)
3. Smullen, C., Mohan, V., et al.: Relaxing non-volatility for fast and energy-efficient STT-RAM caches. In: IEEE Symposium on High-Performance Computer Architecture, pp. 50–61 (2011)
4. Li, J., Shi, L., et al.: Low-energy volatile STT-RAM cache design using cache-coherence-enabled adaptive refresh. ACM Trans. Des. Autom. Electron. Syst. **19**(1), 1–23 (2013)
5. NVSim. http://www.rioshering.com/nvsimwiki/index.php
6. Li, Q., Li, J., et al.: Compiler-assisted STT-RAM-based hybrid cache for energy efficient embedded systems. IEEE Trans. Very Large Scale Integr. Syst. **22**(8), 1829–1840 (2014)
7. Binkert, N., Beckmann, B., et al.: The gem5 simulator. ACM SIGARCH Comput. Architect. News **39**(2), 1–7 (2011)
8. Gem5. http://gem5.org
9. Ahn, J., Yoo, S., et al.: Write intensity prediction for energy-efficient non-volatile caches. In: IEEE International Symposium on Low Power Electronics and Design, pp. 223–228 (2013)
10. Standard Performance Evaluation Corporation. http://www.spec.org

A New DVFS Algorithm Design for Multi-core Processor Chip

Chengyi Zhang[✉], Jiming Wang, Minxuan Zhang, and Xiangdi Wu

National University of Defense Technology,
Changsha, Hunan, People's Republic of China
chengyizhang@nudt.edu.cn

Abstract. With the development of the CMOS process, beyond 3 billion of transistors are integrated on chip. But the increasing power density becomes a serious problem making the performance improvement slow down. Therefore, how to optimize the power consumption of multi-core processor is a crisis in processor design. This paper proposes a dual-threshold adaptive DVFS algorithm to dynamically control the processor voltage and frequency. Comparing with traditional single-threshold algorithm, experimental results show that dual-threshold adaptive DVFS can save more power with no obviously performance reduction. The performance of most benchmarks is beyond 90% of the original performance, while the power optimization can be up to 35%.

Keywords: DVFS · Dual-threshold · Power · Multi-core

1 Introduction

Since 1965 the integrated circuit has been developing at speed of Moore's law, resulting in that more and more transistors can be integrated on chip. To leverage this huge amount of transistor resources, the processor architecture was getting more and more complex to explore the instruction-level-parallelism (ILP). But ILP has limitation [1]. To continue to increase the processor performance and eliminate the power wall, multi-core design was proposed to explore thread-level-parallelism [2]. However, multi-core design eventually leads to the contradiction between processor performance and power consumption. For example, power of many general-purpose processors has reached 100 W, even Intel Xeon E7 V3 processor's maximum power is up to 165 W. In addition, the high power density will greatly increase the cost of cooling and package, and decrease the reliability of the system. Figure 1 shows some of Intel processors' power consumption. We can see that Intel is also suffering a bottleneck of power increase and clock frequency increase.

To remove the power wall of multi-core design, we need the combined power optimization method from process, circuit design, architecture, operating system, compiler and applications [3–6]. Many studies show that the lower level we make our effort to optimize the power, the more return we can get from the work. Currently the main way to reduce power consumption includes Dynamic Power Management (DPM) [7] and Dynamic Voltage Frequency adjustment (DVFS) [8]. In recent years, due to the use of the on-chip voltage regulator, DVFS can significantly improve the

© Springer Nature Singapore Pte Ltd. 2016
W. Xu et al. (Eds.): NCCET 2016, CCIS 666, pp. 40–51, 2016.
DOI: 10.1007/978-981-10-3159-5_5

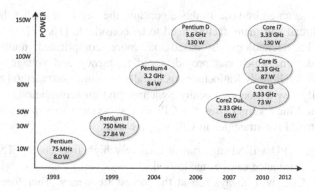

Fig. 1. The processor power consumption trend

processor power when running light-weight workloads, based on fine-grained scaling algorithm. But current DVFS algorithms are not very efficient because the jitter around the adjustment threshold. We try to find a more efficient algorithm for DVFS based on a SCP multi-core processor, which is a true silicon designed by NUDT.

2 Related Work

DVFS and the related algorithm have been researched for nearly 20 years. However, recent studies show that DVFS is still playing an important role in the modern system [9]. When the processor is running with full workload, inappropriately scaling the voltage and frequency of the processor will bring certain performance loss, resulting in final increased energy consumption. Therefore, an outstanding DVFS algorithm should ensure the efficient reduction of both power and energy.

There are two ways to dynamically regulate the voltage and frequency:

- DVFS algorithm based on profile.
  In this way, a profile is prepared in advance. The information of a certain program in the profile includes energy consumption, run time based on a certain voltage and frequency. The information are usually collected in the last runtime or assigned by the user. When the program runs again, the scheduler will refer to the profile to scale the voltage or frequency or both to match the requirement of current machine state [10–12].
- DVFS algorithm based on performance counter.
  This approach usually requires the use of a number of different performance counters within the processor. Processor runs the program and updates the performance counters at real-time. Then, according to these counters, the scheduler can dynamically scale the voltage and frequency based on certain algorithm [13–15].

At present, many processors adopt multi-core and multi-thread structure, so there are often multiple threads running at the same time. Heuristically, we can scale down the voltage and frequency of cores which are executing non-critical threads, and scale up the voltage and frequency of cores which are executing critical threads, to achieve the same effect as an entire task. In this algorithm, the key is to predict the execution time of each thread and many factors need to be considered [16, 17].

Some DVFS technology is based on more complicated multi-clock and multi-voltage design, which can provide rapid frequency and voltage switch. [18] proposed a GRLS (Globally Ratiochronous Locally Synchronous) method based on the GALS (Globally Asynchronous Locally Synchronous) implementation.

The current Linux kernel uses the CPUfreq subsystem to support the dynamic frequency control. Five strategies in CPUfreq include:

- Performance: CPU will always run at relatively high frequencies. Therefore, the processor performance can be maximized.
- Powersave: CPU will always run at the lowest frequency. Therefore, the power consumption of the processor can be minimized.
- Userspace: This is the CPUfreq to provide users with a way to manually select the frequency. The user can adjust the frequency.
- Ondemand: In this mode, CPU will automatically collect CPU utilization and adjust the operation frequency. When the CPU utilization goes to an upper threshold or a lower threshold, the frequency is scaled up or down to the highest or lowest frequency. By default, the upper threshold is 80% and the lower threshold is 50%.
- Conservative: This strategy also scales the CPU frequency according to CPU utilization, but more conservatively. When the CPU utilization goes to an upper threshold or a lower threshold, the frequency is scaled up or down step by step, instead of scaling directly to the highest or lowest frequency.

This paper proposes a dual-threshold DVFS algorithm, DTPA (Dual-Threshold Power Adaption) based on SCP. Comparing with single-threshold adjusting algorithm which is now commonly used, DPTA can save more power while ensuring performance.

3 SCP Platform

3.1 Low Power Function in SCP

SCP multi-core processor uses a variety of low power design technologies, including clock gating, power gating and DVFS, etc. There are 16 cores in SCP. Each core can be standby by gating its clock and be shut down by gating its supply power. Every four cores, so called a cluster, can scale its operating frequency separately. The 16 cores can scale its supply voltage together.

SCP provides two ways to regulate frequency. One is PLL-based, which adjusts the root clock of PLL. Another way is clock-gating-based, which adjust the clock frequency by clock gating to generate equivalent slower clock. PLL-based regulation has a longer switch time, not suitable for frequent regulation. Clock-gating-based regulation has shorter switch time, but can only scale the frequency down based on the PLL-generated clock. SCP frequency regulation framework is shown in Fig. 2, consisting of three parts: latch, shift register and the equivalent logic AND.

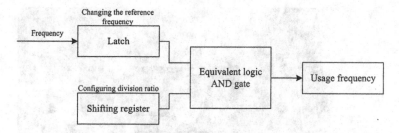

Fig. 2. SCP internal clock structure

Basic frequency and voltage regulation structure is shown in Fig. 3, which consists of three parts: CPU, CPLD and VR chip. When the configuration registers for voltage regulation are set, CPU will automatically suspend the clock and trigger a set of signals to CPLD to request voltage regulation. The CPLD coverts these signal to VR configuration signals to set the VR to the right voltage and send back an ACK to CPU when VR is ready. Then the CPU will restart the clock and continue to run at target frequency and voltage.

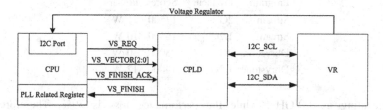

Fig. 3. Basic frequency and voltage regulation mode

3.2 SCP Experimental Environment

The experimental development board is shown in Fig. 4. It provides one SCP chip, 32 GB DDR3-1600 memory, 1 TB HDD, one network card and one graphic card, etc. It runs Linux with the kernel version 3.14.

4 DVFS Algorithm for SCP Platform

When SCP executes different programs, the power consumption varies obviously. So, it's necessary to scale the CPU's frequency as workload changes.

We tested Dhrystone and Stream benchmarks at different frequencies to collect the power consumption data. Dhrystone is compute-intensive program, while Stream is memory-intensive program.

As Table 1 shows, the power of executing Stream at 1.2 GHz is decreased by 52% compared with that of executing at 2.0 GHz, while the performance loss is only 5.7%. However, the power of executing Dhrystone at 1.2 GHz is decreased by 60% compared

Fig. 4. SCP multi-core processors experiment platform

Table 1. Performance and power consumption of Stream and Dhystone at different frequencies

Program	Frequency	Scores	Power
Stream	2G	17500	21 W
Stream	1.2G	16500	10 W
Dhrystone	2G	23000	30 W
Dhrystone	1.2G	14000	12 W

with executing at 2.0 GHz, while the perfomance loss is 39%. Therefore, for memory-intensive program, scaling down the frequency is useful to optimaize the power consumption with a acceptable performance loss, but for computing-intensive program, scalling down the frequency has no value.

Most of the current frequency scaling algorithm are based on the measure of CPU utilization. But considering only the CPU utilization to scale the frequency is not enough. Therefore, we tested the different frequency running memory intensive program (stream) and contrast of computation intensive program (Dhrystone) as Table 2 shows.

Table 2. Power consumption and utilization ratio of Stream and Dhrystone

Base frequency	Stream	Dhrystone	CPU utilization
1.2G	10 W	12 W	Over 98%
1.5G	12 W	17 W	Over 98%
1.8G	15 W	23 W	Over 98%
2.0G	21 W	30 W	Over 98%

When the two programs is running, the utilization rate of CPU are all beyond 98%, but there are obvious gap between the power consumption. The higher the running frequencies are, the greater the power gaps are. With the decrease of frequency, the power gap is gradually reduced, but the CPU utilization remains very high. Therefore, using only the CPU utilization to adjust the frequency will result in the highest frequency at last. In fact, we need not continuously increase the frequency. In SCP DVFS algorithm, we not only consider the CPU utilization, but also consider a realtime power consumption measument.

In SCP, the voltage and frequency are regulated on chip level. At the same time, the frequency of each cluster can be adjusted by clock-gating-based method, which can regulate the frequency more faster than PLL-based method. So SCP DVFS combines these two frequency regulation mechods. In this paper, the proposed DVFS algorithm has two regulation stages, one is clock-gating-based using a first level threshold, the other is PLL-based using a second level threshold. The voltage is not regulated when using clock-gating-based frequency scaling, but it must be regulated to match the frequency when using PLL-based frequency scaling, especially for frequency scaling up. Besides the two level of threshold, we use another threshold to trigger power management, it is CPU utilization. Based on many experiment results, we set the optimal power consumption threshold for each basic frequency as shown in Table 3.

Table 3. Power thresholds at different frequencies

Basic frequency	1.8G	1.5G	1.2G
Power consumption threshold	16 W	12 W	0 W

Power threshold is defined at the current PLL frequency. If the current power consumption is higher than the power threshold listed in Tabel 3, then scale up the PLL frequency. When combined with the two level threshold adjustment, the overall DTPA (double threshold power adaption) DVFS algorithm framework is shown in Figs. 5 and 6.

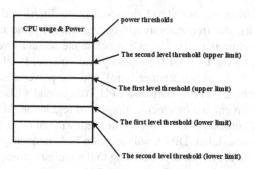

Fig. 5. DVFS regulatory framework with power consumption threshold

When DTPA algorithm is applied to SCP, the CPU frequency adjustment consists of 6 parts. When the CPU utilization is between upper limit and lower limit of the first level threshold, the CPU will hold the current frequency. Once the CPU utilization goes between the first level threshold(upper limit) and the second level threshold

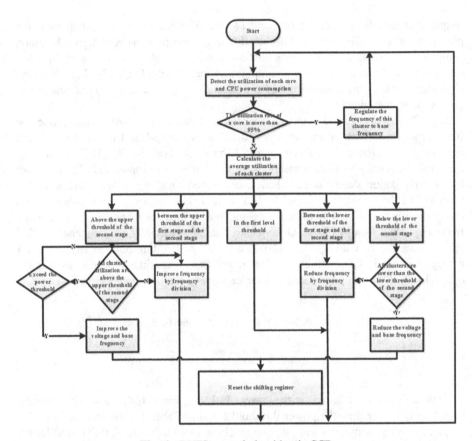

Fig. 6. DVFS control algorithm in SCP

(upper limit) or between the first level threshold(lower limit) and the second level threshold(lower limit), the frequency needs be regulated by the clock-gating-based regulation. If all the clusters utilization rate is below the second level threshold(lower limit), then scale down the CPU PLL frequency and voltage. If all cluster utilization exceeds the second level threshold(upper limit), and the power consumption is more than the power threshold, DTPA increases CPU voltage and PLL frequency. Otherwise, the frequency is regulated by clock-gating-based regulation. In the scenario of no workload, DTPA will quickly scale down the frequency to the lowest value acceptable. If a new program is scheduled, DPTA will scale up PLL frequency to a stable value, then dynamically scale the frequency according to the aforementioned framework. The adjuestment cycle is set to every 0.5 s. At each PLL frequency, the frequency can be generated by clock-gating is shown in Table 4.

Table 4. Equivalent frequency under different PLL frequency

PLL frequency	Equivalent frequency by clock-gating
2.0G	2.0G/1.8G/1.6G
1.8G	1.8G/1.62G/1.44G
1.5G	1.5G/1.35G/1.2G
1.2G	1.2G/1.08G/0.96G

5 Energy Consumption and Performance Analysis

We have done some tests for DPTA algorithm on the SCP prototype board to determine the key parameters with running some typical programs, such as UnixBench, parsec3.0 and video player.

In determining the two-level thresholds and the power consumption threshold of DTPA algorithm, we run parsec3.0 and collect results in Fig. 7.

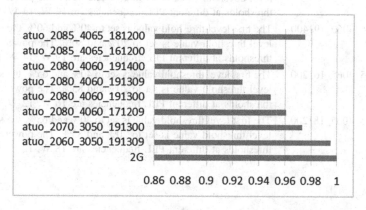

Fig. 7. Normalized energy consumption of parsec in different scenarios

We firstly run parsec with 2G PLL frequency and calculate the total energy consumption, which is shown in Fig. 9 as normalized 1. The other scenarios of energy consumption are shown in percentage of 2G scenario. The threshold configuration of each scenario is listed in Table 5.

As we can see from Fig. 9, with the same configuration of the two-level thresholds, different power thresholds configuration will have different effects on the final energy consumption. The greater the power consumption threshold is, the more the total energy consumes. With the same power threshold set, different utilization threshold configurations result in different energy saving. According to the test results in Fig. 9, we set the lower limit of the first threshold value is 40%, the upper limit is 65%, and the upper and lower limit of the second threshold value are 85% and 20% respectively. The power thresholds at different PLL frequencies are 16 W, 12 W and 0 W. With this configuration, the total energy consumption of parsec can be reduced by nearly 10%.

Table 5. Analysis of threshold in DTPA

Scenario	Description of threshold configuration
2G	SCP operating at 2G frequency
atuo_2060_3050_191309	The first level threshold value is set to 30% and 50%, the second level threshold value is set to 20% and 60%. The power thresholds at different PLLfrequencies are 19 W, 13 W, 9 W
atuo_2070_3050_191300	the first level threshold value is set to 30% and 50%, the second level threshold value is set to 20% and 70%. The power thresholds at different PLL frequencies are 19 W, 13 W, 0 W
atuo_2080_4060_171209	The first level threshold value is set to 40% and 60%, the second level threshold value is set to 20% and 80%. The power thresholds at different PLL frequencies are 17 W, 12 W, 9 W
atuo_2080_4060_191300	The first level threshold value is set to 40% and 60%, the second level threshold value is set to 20% and 80%. The power thresholds at different PLL frequencies are 19 W, 13 W, 0 W
atuo_2080_4060_191309	The first level threshold value is set to 40% and 60%, the second level threshold value is set to 20% and 80%. The power thresholds at different PLL frequencies are 19 W, 13 W, 9 W
atuo_2080_4060_191400	The first level threshold value is set to 40% and 60%, the second level threshold value is set to 20% and 80%. The power thresholds at different PLL frequencies are 19 W, 14 W, 0 W
atuo_2085_4065_161200	The first level threshold value is set to 40% and 65%, the second level threshold value is set to 20% and 85%. The power thresholds at different PLL frequencies are 16 W, 12 W, 0 W
atuo_2085_4065_181200	The first level threshold value is set to 40% and 65%, the second level threshold value is set to 20% and 85%. The power thresholds at different PLL frequencies are 18 W, 12 W, 0 W

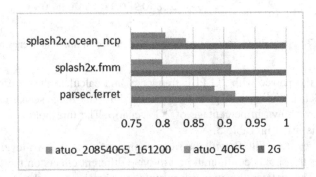

Fig. 8. Energy consumption of DTPA and single-threshold algorithm

Furthermore, we also test the widely used single-threshold algorithm comparing with DTPA, and the results are shown in Figs. 8 and 9, where the atuo_4065 represents the scenario of single-threshold DVFS algorithm with threshold value set as 65% and 40%. The performance of both scenarios is very close. However, single-threshold

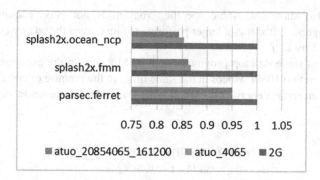

Fig. 9. Performance of DTPA and single threshold algorithm

DVFS consumes more energy than DTPA. Combining the effect of both performance and energy consumption, DTPA is more efficient than the traditional single-threshold method.

We also test UnixBench to evaluate DTPA algorithm, also taking the 2G scenario as a normalized base. Figure 10 shows that, DTPA algorithm can almost keep the performance more than 90%, while reducing the energy consumption more than performance loss. Especially for the "file_copy" program, the energy consumption is reduced by more than 35%, while keeping the performance on around 90%. Dhrystone is a compute-intensive program. At run time, the CPU utilization rate is almost 100%, so the optimization of this kind of program is difficult. As we can see from Fig. 10, DTPA can also gain a positive result that performance loss is lower than energy saving.

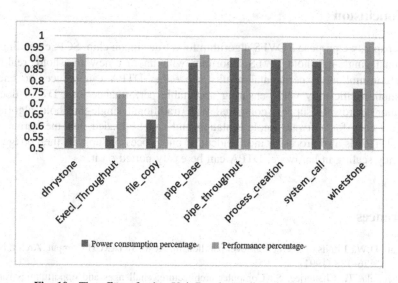

Fig. 10. The effect of using UnixBench to adjust the DTPA program

Results also show that some specific program is not good enough, such as "Execl_Throughput". It shows a larger performance loss, even the energy consumption is also reduced by half.

We also test some desktop programs, such as Mplayer. In the experiment, we use Mplayer to open two 1080P videos at the same time. In the premise of ensuring smooth play, DTPA can reduce energy consumption by over 35% as shown in Fig. 11.

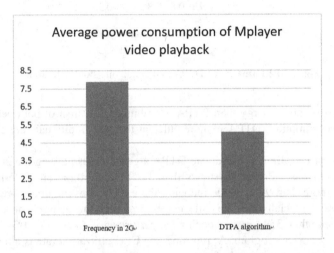

Fig. 11. Comparison of power consumption in video playback

6 Conclusion

In this paper, we propose a DVFS algorithm for a true silicon chip, SCP, extending the traditional single-threshold DVFS algorithm with another new threshold, real-time power consumtion. Experimental results show that DTPA can reduce the energy consumption efficiently while ensuring acceptable performance loss. DTPA doesn't need more hardware support compared with traditional single-threshold algorithm. DTPA is easy for software implementation and can be loaded into the kernel as a driver. DTPA is also processor independent. If one processor supports the voltage and frequency scaling in hardware, DTPA can be easily ported on it.

References

1. Wall, D.W.: Limits of instruction-level parallelism. ACM SIGARCH Comput. Archit. News **26**(4), 176–188 (1991)
2. Agerwala, T., Chatterjee, S.: Computer architecture: challenges and opportunities for the next decade. IEEE Micro **25**(3), 58–69 (2005)

3. Teodorescu, R., Torrellas, J.: Variation-aware application scheduling and power management for chip multiprocessors. ACM SIGARCH Comput. Archit. News **36**(3), 363–374 (2008). IEEE Computer Society
4. Lee, C., Lee, J.K., Hwang, T., et al.: Compiler optimization on VLIW instruction scheduling for low power. ACM Trans. Des. Autom. Electron. Syst. (TODAES) **8**(2), 252–268 (2003)
5. Pangjun, J., Sapatnekar, S.S.: Low-power clock distribution using multiple voltages and reduced swings. IEEE Trans. Very Large Scale Integr. (VLSI) Syst. **10**(3), 309–318 (2002)
6. Yi, H., Yang, X.: Optimizing the configuration of dynamic voltage scaling points in real-time applications. In: Paliouras, V., Vounckx, J., Verkest, D. (eds.) PATMOS 2005. LNCS, vol. 3728, pp. 79–88. Springer, Heidelberg (2005). doi:10.1007/11556930_9
7. Brooks, D., Martonosi, M.: Dynamic thermal management for high-performance microprocessors. In: Proceedings of PCA-7, pp. 171–82, January 2001
8. Pouwelse, J., Langendoen, K., Sips, H.: Dynamic voltage scaling on a low-power microprocessor. In: Proceedings of the 7th Annual International Conference on Mobile Computing and Networking, pp. 251–259. ACM (2001)
9. Le Sueur, E., Heiser, G.: Dynamic voltage and frequency scaling: the laws of diminishing returns. In: Proceedings of the 2010 International Conference on Power Aware Computing and Systems, pp. 1–8. USENIX Association (2010)
10. Kimura, H., Sato, M., Imada, T., et al.: Runtime DVFS control with instrumented code in power-scalable cluster system. In: 2008 IEEE International Conference on Cluster Computing, pp. 354–359. IEEE (2008)
11. Ge, R., Feng, X., Cameron, K.W.: Performance-constrained distributed DVS scheduling for scientific applications on power-aware clusters. In: Proceedings of the 2005 ACM/IEEE conference on Supercomputing, p. 34. IEEE Computer Society (2005)
12. Kong, J., Choi, J., Choi, L., et al.: Low-cost application-aware DVFS for multi-core architecture. In: Third 2008 International Conference on Convergence and Hybrid Information Technology, pp. 106–111. IEEE Computer Society (2008)
13. Eyerman, S., Eeckhout, L.: A counter architecture for online DVFS profitability estimation. IEEE Trans. Comput. **59**(11), 1576–1583 (2010)
14. Bircher, W.L., John, L.: Predictive power management for multi-core processors. In: Varbanescu, A.L., Molnos, A., Nieuwpoort, R. (eds.) ISCA 2010. LNCS, vol. 6161, pp. 243–255. Springer, Heidelberg (2011). doi:10.1007/978-3-642-24322-6_21
15. Wei, D., Fei, F.Q., Kun, H., et al.: VB-DVFS: a new algorithm for power efficiency of CMP with GALS. In: 2010 17th IEEE International Conference on Electronics, Circuits, and Systems (ICECS), pp. 297–300. IEEE (2010)
16. Cai, Q., González, J., Rakvic, R., et al.: Meeting points: using thread criticality to adapt multi-core hardware to parallel regions. In: Proceedings of the 17th International Conference on Parallel Architectures and Compilation Techniques, pp. 240–249. ACM (2008)
17. Wu, Q., Martonosi, M., Clark, D.W., et al.: A dynamic compilation framework for controlling microprocessor energy and performance. In: Proceedings of the 38th Annual IEEE/ACM International Symposium on Microarchitecture, pp. 271–282. IEEE Computer Society (2005)
18. Chabloz, J.M., Hemani, A.: Distributed DVFS using rationally-related frequencies and discrete voltage levels. In: 2010 ACM/IEEE International Symposium on Low-Power Electronics and Design (ISLPED), pp. 247–252 (2010)

Application Specific Processors

A Novel Low-Power and High-PSNR Architecture Based on ARC for DCT/IDCT

Yiliu Feng[✉], Jianfeng Zhang, and Hengzhu Liu

National University of Defense and Technology, Changsha, Hunan, China
endlessfyl@gmail.com

Abstract. Discrete cosine transform (*DCT*) and its inverse (*IDCT*) play a key role in image and video systems. In this paper, we propose an efficient DCT/IDCT architecture based on adaptive recoding coordinate rotation digital computer (*ARC*), which has been validated on an FPGA platform. Compared to the state-of-the-art DCT, the proposed architecture dissipates 8.2% less power and improves PSNR by 3.21 dB while maintaining nearly the same area and speed. The proposed architecture uses 37.6% less hardware resources, saves 31.6% in power dissipation, provides a 2.15 times speed-up and improves PSNR slightly when compared with the newest DCT/IDCT architecture.

Keywords: ARC · CORDIC · DCT · FPGA · IDCT · PSNR

1 Introduction

Recent years have experienced a significant demand for low-power implementations of algorithms in image and video processing systems, especially like discrete cosine transform *(DCT)* and inverse discrete cosine transform (*IDCT*). The reason is that DCT and IDCT are one of the most computationally intensive transforms in image and video compression standards, which have been demonstrated to provide perfect energy packing for images [1] and are very close approximation of the optimal Karhunen-Loeve transform (*KLT*) [2], such as JPEG [3], MPEG [4] and HEVC [5].

Hence, many fast algorithms are proposed to reduce the computational complexity of computing DCT/IDCT based on three different methods: multiplier-based algorithms [6], distributed arithmetic (*DA*) based algorithms [7] and coordinate rotation digital computer (*CORDIC*) based algorithms [8–12]. As the multiplier has high hardware complexity, which restricts the computation speed, and the ROM size increases exponentially with the transform length for DA-based DCT, it is an efficient way to implement DCT and IDCT based on CORDIC, which only requires shifters and adders. Huang et al. [9–11] presented a radix-2 unified DCT and IDCT algorithm based on unfolded CORDIC, but it consumes too many hardware resources and dissipates too much power. Lee et al. [12] discussed a low-power DCT based on look ahead COR-DIC, while the peak signal-to-noise ratio (*PSNR*) is reduced.

In this paper, we propose an efficient multiplier less unified DCT and IDCT architecture based on adaptive recoding CORDIC (*ARC*) [13] combined with the conventional CORDIC [14]. ARC accelerates the vector rotation and improves the

W. Xu et al. (Eds.): NCCET 2016, CCIS 666, pp. 55–68, 2016.
DOI: 10.1007/978-981-10-3159-5_6

accuracy with no performance penalty, and the post-processing of DCT/IDCT is correlated with the scale factor of the conventional CORDIC. Therefore, compared to existing DCT and unified DCT/IDCT architectures, the proposed one has outstanding performance. The proposed architecture has been synthesized on Xilinx Virtex-5 LX150T to verify the correctness and performance.

The rest of this paper is organized as follows: In Sect. 2, we discuss the efficient unified DCT and IDCT architecture. The vector rotation schemes are described in Sect. 3. Section 4 analyzes the simulation and comparison results. Conclusions are drawn in Sect. 5.

2 Efficient Unified DCT/IDCT Architecture

As a 2-D DCT is commonly calculated by first applying a 1-D DCT over the rows followed by another 1-D DCT applied to the columns of the input matrix [12], 1-D DCT is the kernel processing element. Meanwhile, both DCT and IDCT are used in image and video systems, and then designing a unified efficient architecture for 1-D DCT and IDCT is very important. In this paper, we propose a novel unified architecture for 1-D DCT and IDCT based on CORDIC.

The N-point 1-D DCT transforms a real data sequence from time domain $\{x(n), n = 0, 1, 2, \ldots, N-1\}$ to frequency domain $\{y(n), n = 0, 1, 2, \ldots, N-1\}$, which is defined as

$$y(k) = \sqrt{\frac{2}{N}} * c(k) * \sum_{n=0}^{N-1} x(n) * \cos\left[\frac{(2n+1)k\pi}{2N}\right], (k = 0, 1, \ldots, N-1) \quad (1)$$

Where $c(0) = 1/\sqrt{2}$ and $c(k) = 1$ for $k = 0, 1, \ldots, N-1$. As the 8-point DCT is commonly used in image and video standards [3–5], we can decompose the 8-point DCT into four parts. First, the 8-point input signals are preprocessed and represented as follows:

$$\begin{cases} a_0 = x(0) + x(7) \\ a_1 = x(0) - x(7) \end{cases}, \begin{cases} a_2 = x(1) + x(6) \\ a_3 = x(1) - x(6) \end{cases}$$
$$\begin{cases} a_4 = x(2) + x(5) \\ a_5 = x(2) - x(5) \end{cases}, \begin{cases} a_6 = x(3) + x(4) \\ a_7 = x(3) - x(4) \end{cases} \quad (2)$$

Then, the outputs of the 8-point DCT can be written as:

$$\begin{bmatrix} y(0) \\ y(4) \end{bmatrix} = \frac{1}{\sqrt{8}} \times \begin{bmatrix} 1 & 1 \\ 1 & -1 \end{bmatrix} \times \begin{bmatrix} a_0 + a_6 \\ a_2 + a_4 \end{bmatrix} \quad (3)$$

$$\begin{bmatrix} y(2) \\ y(6) \end{bmatrix} = \frac{1}{2} \times \begin{bmatrix} c_2 & -s_2 \\ s_2 & c_2 \end{bmatrix} \times \begin{bmatrix} a_0 - a_6 \\ a_4 - a_2 \end{bmatrix} \quad (4)$$

$$\begin{bmatrix} y(1) \\ y(7) \end{bmatrix} = \frac{1}{2} \times \begin{bmatrix} c_1 & -s_1 \\ s_1 & c_1 \end{bmatrix} \times \begin{bmatrix} a_1 \\ -a_7 \end{bmatrix} + \frac{1}{2} \times \begin{bmatrix} c_3 & s_3 \\ -s_3 & c_3 \end{bmatrix} \times \begin{bmatrix} a_3 \\ a_5 \end{bmatrix}$$

$$= \frac{1}{2} \times \begin{bmatrix} c_1 & -s_1 \\ s_1 & c_1 \end{bmatrix} \times \begin{bmatrix} a_1 \\ -a_7 \end{bmatrix} + \frac{1}{\sqrt{8}} \times \begin{bmatrix} c_3 & -s_1 \\ s_1 & c_1 \end{bmatrix} \times \begin{bmatrix} 1 & 1 \\ -1 & 1 \end{bmatrix} \times \begin{bmatrix} a_3 \\ a_5 \end{bmatrix}$$

$$(5)$$

$$\begin{bmatrix} y(5) \\ y(3) \end{bmatrix} = \frac{1}{2} \times \begin{bmatrix} c_3 & s_3 \\ -s_3 & c_3 \end{bmatrix} \times \begin{bmatrix} a_7 \\ a_1 \end{bmatrix} - \frac{1}{2} \times \begin{bmatrix} c_1 & -s_1 \\ s_1 & c_1 \end{bmatrix} \times \begin{bmatrix} a_3 \\ a_5 \end{bmatrix}$$

$$= \frac{1}{\sqrt{8}} \times \begin{bmatrix} c_1 & -s_1 \\ s_1 & c_1 \end{bmatrix} \times \begin{bmatrix} 1 & 1 \\ -1 & 1 \end{bmatrix} \times \begin{bmatrix} a_7 \\ a_1 \end{bmatrix} - \frac{1}{2} \times \begin{bmatrix} c_1 & -s_1 \\ s_1 & c_1 \end{bmatrix} \times \begin{bmatrix} a_3 \\ a_5 \end{bmatrix}$$

$$(6)$$

in which $c_m = \cos(m\pi/16)$ and $s_m = \sin(m\pi/16)$. As the rearranged 8-point DCT is presented as vector rotation matrices, it can be realized by CORDIC. For Eqs. (4), (5) and (6), we can put the constant scale factors into CORDIC to save area and power, and reduce the truncation and quantization errors.

Figure 1 shows the data flow of the DCT architecture, which consists of three adder arrays (*Adder_1, Adder_2, and Adder_3*), two processing elements (*PE_1, PE_2*) and the DCT/IDCT mode controller. The Adder_1 and Adder_2 consist of four adders and four subtractors, and two adders and two subtractors, respectively. The Adder_3 is made up of one adder, one subtractor and two constant scale factor $1/\sqrt{8}$ compensation logics. The ARC rotation ARC_1, the rotation angle of which is $\pi/8$, and the scale

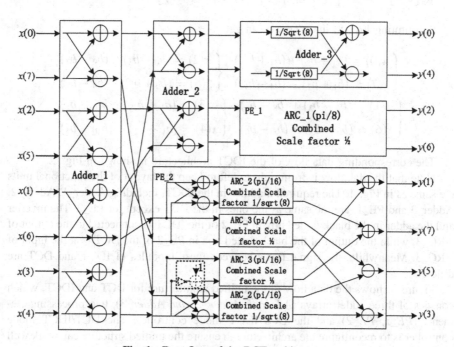

Fig. 1. Data flow of the DCT architecture.

factor is combined with the constant value $1/2$, builds the PE_1. The PE_2 consists of one inverter, five adders, four subtractors, two identical ARC_2 rotators, whose rotation angle is $\pi/16$ and the scale factor is combined with $1/2$, and two ARC_3, the rotation angle of which is also $\pi/16$, but the scale factor is combined with $1/\sqrt{8}$. According to Eqs. (5) and (6), the two outputs of ARC_2 scaled by $1/\sqrt{8}$ pass to the following adder and subtractor to rotate the results by $-3\pi/16$. The inverter and the following constant adder in the black dotted box are to get the 2's complementary of.

In the meantime, the 8-point IDCT is represented as:

$$x(n) = \sqrt{\frac{2}{N}} \times \sum_{n=0}^{N-1} c(k) \times y(k) \times \cos\left[\frac{(2n+1)k\pi}{2N}\right], (n = 0, 1, \ldots, N-1) \quad (7)$$

We can also use the decomposition method. First, the input $\{y(n), n = 0, 1, 2,\ldots, N-1\}$ are proprocessed and expressed as

$$\begin{cases} \begin{bmatrix} b_1 \\ b_0 \end{bmatrix} = \frac{1}{\sqrt{8}} \times \begin{bmatrix} 1 & 1 \\ -1 & 1 \end{bmatrix} \times \begin{bmatrix} y(0) \\ y(4) \end{bmatrix}, & \begin{bmatrix} b_3 \\ b_2 \end{bmatrix} = \frac{1}{2} \times \begin{bmatrix} c_2 & -s_2 \\ s_2 & c_2 \end{bmatrix} \times \begin{bmatrix} y(6) \\ y(2) \end{bmatrix} \\[12pt] \begin{bmatrix} b_5 \\ b_4 \end{bmatrix} = \frac{1}{2} \times \begin{bmatrix} c_1 & -s_1 \\ s_1 & c_1 \end{bmatrix} \times \begin{bmatrix} y(7) \\ y(1) \end{bmatrix}, & \begin{bmatrix} b_7 \\ b_6 \end{bmatrix} = \frac{1}{2} \times \begin{bmatrix} c_1 & -s_1 \\ s_1 & c_1 \end{bmatrix} \times \begin{bmatrix} y(3) \\ y(5) \end{bmatrix} \\[12pt] \begin{bmatrix} b_9 \\ b_8 \end{bmatrix} = \frac{1}{\sqrt{8}} \times \begin{bmatrix} c_1 & -s_1 \\ s_1 & c_1 \end{bmatrix} \times \begin{bmatrix} 1 & 1 \\ -1 & 1 \end{bmatrix} \times \begin{bmatrix} y(7) \\ y(1) \end{bmatrix} \\[12pt] \begin{bmatrix} b_{11} \\ b_{10} \end{bmatrix} = \frac{1}{\sqrt{8}} \times \begin{bmatrix} c_1 & -s_1 \\ s_1 & c_1 \end{bmatrix} \times \begin{bmatrix} 1 & 1 \\ -1 & 1 \end{bmatrix} \times \begin{bmatrix} y(3) \\ y(5) \end{bmatrix} \end{cases} \quad (8)$$

Substituting Eq. (8) into (7), we can get

$$\begin{cases} x(0) = (b_1 + b_2) + (b_4 + b_{11}) \\ x(7) = (b_1 + b_2) - (b_4 + b_{11}) \end{cases}, \begin{cases} x(2) = (b_0 + b_3) + (b_9 - b_7) \\ x(5) = (b_0 + b_3) - (b_9 - b_7) \end{cases} \\ \begin{cases} x(1) = (b_0 - b_3) + (b_8 - b_6) \\ x(6) = (b_0 - b_3) - (b_8 - b_6) \end{cases}, \begin{cases} x(3) = (b_1 - b_2) + (b_{10} - b_5) \\ x(4) = (b_1 - b_2) - (b_{10} - b_5) \end{cases} \quad (9)$$

The corresponding data flow of the IDCT architecture is shown in Fig. 2.

Note that the dataflow is from right to left to keep the layout of the functional units the same as in Fig. 1. The required modules in the IDCT, including Adder_1, Adder_2, Adder_3 and PE_1, are the same as the ones in the DCT except for PE_2. The inverter and the adder in the black dotted box in PE_2 of the IDCT is connected to the output of ARC_3, while the output of the black dotted box in PE_2 of the DCT is at the input of ARC_3. Meanwhile, the signal flows between these modules of IDCT and DCT are different.

Figure 3 shows the data flow of the unified architecture for DCT and IDCT, which consists of three adder arrays (*Adder_1, Adder_2, and Adder_3*), two processing elements (*PE_1, PE_2*) and the DCT/IDCT mode controller. The DCT/IDCT mode controller is to reconfigure the architecture to ensure the unified structure can work well

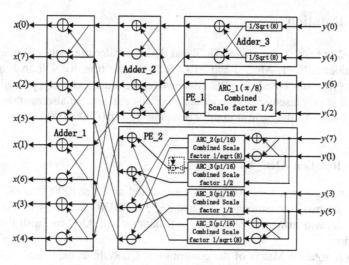

Fig. 2. Data flow of the IDCT architecture.

for DCT mode and IDCT mode, the signals of which are illustrated as the purple arrows. The inverter in the PE_2 marked with black dotted arrows are the DCT and IDCT data flows respectively, and the blue arrows are the signals which can either be DCT or IDCT data flows.

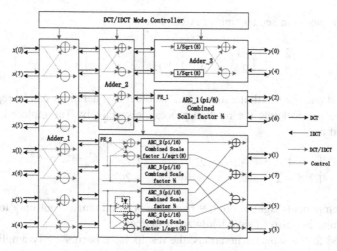

Fig. 3. Data flow of unified DCT and IDCT.

3   ARC Rotation

As discussed in Sect. 2, the unified DCT and IDCT architecture requires three different vector rotation: ARC_1, ARC_2 and ARC_3. In this Section, we will analyze how to realize these rotations based on ARC. Meanwhile, the scale factor compensation for in the Adder_3 is also discussed. To conduct a fair comparison, we also assume the word length is 12-bit, and the natural number 1 equals 12'b010000000000.

3.1   First Rotation ARC_1

The rotation angle $\pi/\sqrt{8}$ of ARC_1 is represented as 12'b010000000000. We first implement the two conventional $i = 2$ and $i = 3$ CORDIC iterations to diminish the rotation angle, and then use $i = 7$ and $i = 8$ iterations of ARC to finish the residual angle rotation.

The basic rotation Matrix of the conventional CORDIC is expressed as

$$\begin{bmatrix} x_{i+1} \\ y_{i+1} \end{bmatrix} = \begin{bmatrix} 1 & -2^{-i} \\ 2^{-i} & 1 \end{bmatrix} \times \begin{bmatrix} y_i \\ x_i \end{bmatrix} \tag{10}$$

and the basic iteration of ARC is written as

$$\begin{bmatrix} x_{i+1} \\ y_{i+1} \end{bmatrix} = \begin{bmatrix} 1 - 2^{-2i+1} & -2^{-i+1} \\ -2^{-i+1} & 1 - 2^{-2i+1} \end{bmatrix} \times \begin{bmatrix} y_i \\ x_i \end{bmatrix} \tag{11}$$

Therefore, the iteration sequencing of ARC_1 is

$$\begin{bmatrix} 1 & -2^{-2} \\ 2^{-2} & 1 \end{bmatrix}, \begin{bmatrix} 1 & -2^{-3} \\ 2^{-3} & 1 \end{bmatrix}, \begin{bmatrix} 1 & -2^{-6} \\ 2^{-6} & 1 \end{bmatrix}, \begin{bmatrix} 1 & -2^{-7} \\ 2^{-7} & 1 \end{bmatrix} \tag{12}$$

where the first and the fourth iterations, and the other two iterations can be replaced by two iterations to accelerate the rotation process, respectively. The replaced iterations are illustrated as

$$\begin{bmatrix} 1 & -2^{-2} - 2^{-7} \\ 2^{-2} + 2^{-7} & 1 \end{bmatrix}, \begin{bmatrix} 1 & -2^{-3} - 2^{-6} \\ 2^{-3} + 2^{-6} & 1 \end{bmatrix} \tag{13}$$

where the components right shifting 9 bits have been eliminated not only to simplify the architecture, but also to save hardware resources.

Compared to the separate iterations, the results have been slightly amplified after operated by Eq. (13). However, we can compensate for the rounding errors in the scale factor compensation units.

As the scale factor $\cos(\arctan(2^{-2}) \times \cos\tan(2^{-3}))$ of conventional CORDIC needs to be scaled by $1/2$, it is hard for hardware implementation. We propose an adder and shifter-based approximation to approach the new scale factor, the method is shown in Algorithm 1.

The scale factor k_i of ARC_1, the required accuracy R_Accuracy and the initial value of the achieved accuracy A_Accuracy are first set. For lines 5–9, we propose five different approximation expressions to approach the scale factor, and each part of the proposed expressions has the same critical path delay as the required iterations depicted in Eq. (13). As the scale factor is always smaller than natural number 1, lines 5–9 cover all the cases of two separate parts multiplication. The reason for using two parts multiplication to approximate the scale factor is that only one separate part cannot satisfy the required accuracy. Then, the approximation expression which has the smallest error is computed and set to the calculated accuracy in line 10. Third, the C_Accruacy is assigned to the A_Accuracy and the corresponding values consisted of the approximation expression are stored under the condition that if the C_Accuracy is smaller than the R_Accuracy and the A_Accuracy in lines 11–16. After opeated by lines 1–20, we can get the best approximation expression and the corresponding values of its components, the accuracy of which is highest for all tested values.

Algorithm 1 Scale Factor Approximation

Initialization:
Set $k\_1 = 1/(2 \times \sqrt{(1+2^{(-4)}} \times \sqrt{(1+2^{(-6)}))})$; R_Accuracy= $2^{(-10)}$; A_Accuracy=0;
Iteration:
1: for m = 1 to 10 do
2:   for n = 1 to 10 do
3:     for k = 1 to 10 do
4:       for l = 1 to 10 do
5:         A_1=$(1+2^{(-m)}+2^{(-n)}) \times (1+2^{(-k)}-2^{(-l)})$
6:         A_2=$(1+2^{(-m)}+2^{(-n)}) \times (1-2^{(-k)}-2^{(-l)})$
7:         A_3=$(1+2^{(-m)}-2^{(-n)}) \times (1+2^{(-k)}-2^{(-l)})$
8:         A_4=$(1+2^{(-m)}-2^{(-n)}) \times (1-2^{(-k)}-2^{(-l)})$
9:         A_5=$(1-2^{(-m)}-2^{(-n)}) \times (1-2^{(-k)}-2^{(-l)})$
10:          Set C_Accuracy = Minimum($|k\_1 - A\_i|, i \in [1,5]$)
11:          if C_Accuracy < R_Accuracy then
12:            if C_Accuracy < A_Accuracy then
13:              A_Accuracy = C_Accuracy;
14:                q = i; w = m; r = n; t = k; s = l;
15:            end if
16:          end if
17:        end for
18:      end for
19:    end for
20: end for
21: return A_Accuracy, q, w, r, s, t;

The A_Accuracy, the corresponding values and the type of the approximation expression are returned in line 21. After using Algorithm 1, the scale factor k_1 is represented as:

$$k_1 = 1/2 * \cos(\arctan(2^{-2}) \times \cos\tan(2^{-3}))$$
$$= \frac{1}{2 \times \sqrt{1+2^{-4}} \times \sqrt{1+2^{-6}}} \tag{14}$$
$$\cong (1 - 2^{-1} + 2^{-6}) \times (1 - 2^{-4} - 2^{-8})$$

To compensate for the rounding errors in Eq. (13), we scale the approximation Eq. (14) into $(1 - 2^{-1} + 2^{-6}) \times (1 - 2^{-4} - 2^{-8})$ after using Matlab to verify the accuracy of the results.

Figure 4 shows the data flow of ARC_1, which only consist of shifters and adders, and the "−" symbols placed near the arrows represent subtractions A pipeline balancing method is proposed to implement the architecture, which is divided into four stages. The first two stages are to execute the required iterations, and the scale factor compensation is implemented in the remaining stages. We have split the bigger shifter in evert stage into two subshifters: one has the same right shifting bits as the smaller shifter and the other executes the rest bits shifting, which means that the bigger shifter can be realized based on the smaller shifting to save hardware resources. The critical path delay of each stage is two shifts and two additions.

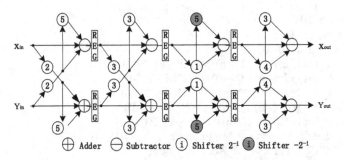

Fig. 4. Data flow of ARC_1

3.2 First Rotation ARC_2

As mentioned in Sect. 2, ARC_2 actually need to rotate the input vector by $-3\pi/16$. Hence, we combine ARC_2 with one adder and one subtractor to fulfill the rotation, and the scale factor of ARC_2 needs to multiply $1/\sqrt{8}$. Due to the scaling-free property of ARC, if ARC_2 only adopts ARC, it would require extra resources to execute the scale factor compensation. Hence, we combine the conventional CORDIC with ARC to implement $\pi/16$ rotation, and then the constant value $1/\sqrt{8}$ compensation can be combined with the scale factor of the conventional CORDIC.

As $\pi/16$ is expressed as 12'b000011001001, the conventional i = 3 iteration is first implemented, and then the i = 5, i = 8 and i = 10 iterations of ARC are executed. Meanwhile, we can also put the conventional i = 3 iteration and ARC i = 10 iteration into one iteration, and the rest are also rearranged into one iteration to get an area efficient architecture. The new iterations are expressed as:

$$\begin{bmatrix} 1 & -2^{-3}-2^{-9} \\ 2^{-3}+2^{-9} & 1 \end{bmatrix}, \begin{bmatrix} 1 & -2^{-4}-2^{-7} \\ 2^{-4}+2^{-7} & 1 \end{bmatrix} \qquad (15)$$

where the components right shifting over 10 bits which equals machine zero have been eliminated. Compared to the separate iterations, the results of Eq. (15) have also been slightly amplified.

After using the scale factor k_2 of ARC_2 to replace the k_1 in Algorithm 1, the k_2 is represented as:

$$\begin{aligned} k_2 &= 1/\sqrt{8} \times \cos(\cos \tan(2^{-3})) \\ &= \frac{1}{\sqrt{8} \times \sqrt{1+2^{-6}}} \\ &\cong (1-2^{-1}-2^{-3}) \times (1-2^{-4}-2^{-9}) \end{aligned} \qquad (16)$$

Using the same method as ARC_1, the approximation Eq. (16) is scaled into to compensate for the errors introduced in Eq. (15). The data flow of the ARC_2 is shown in Fig. 3, which is also divided into four stages to keep the critical path delay constant with ARC_1. The required iterations are realized in the first two stages, and the remaining stages are to execute the scale factor compensation. Meanwhile, the bigger shifters are also split into two subshifters to save area (Fig. 5).

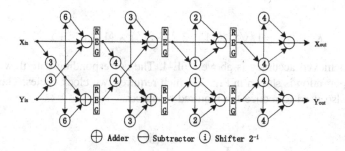

$\oplus$ Adder $\ominus$ Subtractor (i) Shifter 2^{-i}

Fig. 5. Data flow of ARC_2

3.3 First Rotation ARC_3

The rotation angle of ARC_3 is the same as ARC_2, but the scale factor is different, which only needs to be scaled by $1/2$ through right shifting the results one bit.

Hence, we only adopt ARC $(i = 4, i = 5, i = 8, i = 11)$ to design ARC_3, and the $i = 8$ and $i = 11$ iterations combined with $1/2$ are put together into one iteration. The rotation sequencing of ARC_3 is

$$\begin{bmatrix} 1-2^{-7} & -2^{-3} \\ 2^{-3} & 1-2^{-7} \end{bmatrix}, \begin{bmatrix} 1-2^{-9} & -2^{-4} \\ 2^{-4} & 1-2^{-9} \end{bmatrix}, \begin{bmatrix} 2^{-1} & -2^{-8} \\ 2^{-8} & 2^{-1} \end{bmatrix} \qquad (17)$$

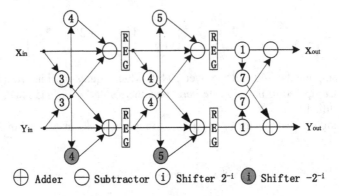

Fig. 6. Data flow of ARC_3

which is realized by three stages as illustrated in Fig. 6. As ARC_3 does not need scale factor compensation, all the stages are to execute the required iterations. We also split the bigger into two sub-shifters to reduce area.

3.4 Scale Factor Compensation for Adder_3

The scale factor in the Adder_3 is $1/\sqrt{8}$. After operated by Algorithm 1, it is approximated as:

$$K_{Adder\_3} = 1/\sqrt{8} \cong (1 - 2^{-1} - 2^{-5}) \times (1 - 2^{-2} + 2^{-8}) \tag{18}$$

where the achieved accuracy is above 1.6E-4. The corresponding date flow the scale factor compensation is shown in Fig. 7, which requires two clock cycles. The splitting scheme is also used to reduce the required resources.

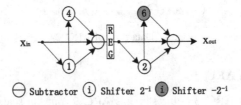

Fig. 7. Scale factor compensation for Adder_3

4 Performance Evaluation and Comparison

In this section, we compare our design with the state-of-the-art DCT discussed in [12] and the newest unified DCT and IDCT architecture presented in [10]. Meanwhile, as there are some different architectures proposed in [10, 12], we only focus on the common architectures, which can process 8-point concurrently and do not save the hardware resources at the expense of PSNR.

4.1   Area Comparison

As the Lee architecture only works in DCT mode, we synthe-size both the Huang and the proposed architectures under DCT mode and DCT/IDCT mode, respectively. The required hardware resources of the three different architecture are all shown in Table 1. For DCT mode, compared with the Lee architecture, the proposed architecture uses 52 and 1 more Slice Registers and LUT-FF pairs respectively, but requires 52 less Slice LUTs. Compared with the Huang architecture, due to the proposed vector rotation schemes, no matter working in which mode, the proposed architecture uses less hardware resources. Taking Slice Registers under DCT/IDCT mode as an example, the required number of the proposed architecture is reduced by 37.6%.

Table 1. Area, speed and power comparisons.

Comparison	Lee. [12]	Huang. [10]		Proposed arch.	
Mode	DCT	DCT	DCT/IDCT	DCT	DCT/IDCT
Slice registers	992	1506	1714	1044	1070
Slice LUTs	1172	1526	1812		1502
LUT-FF pairs	1216	1660	2019	1120 1217	1517
CPD (ns)	3.16	3.05	3.2	3.08	3.23
Latency	6	13	113	6	6
PTime(ns)	18.96	39.65	41.6		19.38
T (M samples/s)	2532	2623	2500	18.48 2597	2477
Power(mW)	98	148	212	90	145

4.2   Speed Comparison

We compare the speed in terms of critical path delay, latency, processing time and throughput. As shown in Table 1, CPD means Critical Path Delay, PTime means Processing Time, T means Throughput. The latencies of the Lee, the Huang and the proposed architectures 6, 13 and 6, respectively. For DCT mode, the critical path delays of the three different architectures are 3.16 ns, 3.05 ns and 3.08 ns, respectively. After the pipelines set up, the throughput of the Lee, the Huang and the proposed architectures are 2532(M $samples/s$), 2623(M $samples/s$) and 2597(M $samples/s$), respectively, which means the throughput of the proposed architecture is slightly lower than the Huang architecture, but exceeds the Lee architecture. The processing time is defined as how long the pipeline needs to finish a complete computation, which equals the critical path delay times and latency. The processing time of the Lee and Huang are 18.96 ns and 39.65 ns, respectively, but the proposed architecture only requires 18.47 ns. For DCT/IDCT mode, compared to the Huang architecture, even the critical path delay and throughput of the proposed architecture are slightly worse, the processing time provides a factor of 41.6/19.38 = 2.15-fold improvement because of its less latency.

4.3 Accuracy Comparison

We first investigate the accuracy of the rotation because they have an impact on the PSNR [16] of the full DCT and IDCT blocks.

We use bit error ratio (BER) to compare the accuracy of the proposed rotation elements with the Huang CORDIC [12] and the Lee CORDIC [10]. Taking the rotation angle $-3\pi/16$ as an example, a pseudorandom sequence of 1000 vectors lying evenly in the convergence range $[0, 2^8 - 1)$ is generated. We use these vectors as the inputs of the proposed ARC_2, Huang CORDIC and Lee CORDIC, the corresponding BERs of rotation of the three different architectures are shown in Fig. 8. The BERs of the proposed ARC_2 are the smallest, which are below $3E - 4$, while the BERs of the Huang CORDIC are the biggest and exceed $2E - 3$, and the BERs of the Lee CORDIC approximately equal $1E - 3$. The reason that ARC_2 has improved BERs is that it uses ARC combined with conventional CORDIC to implement the rotation elements and the proposed scale factor approximation scheme.

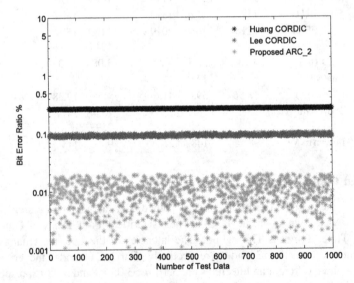

Fig. 8. BER comparison

Using PSNR to evaluate the performance of the three different DCT architectures, including the Lee architecture [10], the Huang architecture [12] and the proposed architecture, we generate 500 8 × 8 test matrices to obtain the average PSNR. The PSNRs of the Lee, the Huang and the proposed architectures are 43.16 dB, 45.98 dB and 46.37 dB, respectively, which means that the PSNR of the proposed architecture exceeds the Lee architecture is improved by 3.21 dB. The reason for the improved PSNR is that the BERs of rotation elements of the proposed architecture are lower than the rotation elements in the Lee architecture. Compared with the Huang architecture, the PSNR of the proposed architecture is also higher. The reason is not only the proposed novel architecture, which shortens the required number of iterations to reduce the errors, but also the rotation elements based on the efficient ARC combined with conventional CORDIC, which have higher accuracy.

4.4 Power Comparison

We use the Xpower tool [15] to estimate the power dissipation of the Lee, the Huang and the proposed architectures. The method used is to build a harness that can connect to all of the inputs and outputs of the circuit. Xpower is used to estimate the power of the device with and without the measured circuit in the harness. The difference between the two versions is the power dissipation of the circuit of interest. This approach is described in more detail in [18]. Since the power estimation is a function of the toggle rate of the signals, we set the toggle rate of the signals to 12.5% to bracket the estimated power dissipation.

As illustrated in Table 1, for DCT mode, the three different architectures dissipate 98 mW, 148 mW and 30 mW, respectively, which means the proposed architecture dissipates 8.2% and 39.2% less power than the Lee and the Huang architectures, respectively. For DCT/IDCT mode, the Huang and the proposed architectures consume 212 mW and 145 mW, respectively, which means the dissipated power of the proposed architecture is reduced by 31.6%.

5 Conclusion

This paper has presented an Improved FPGA implementation of DCT/IDCT architecture based on ARC. An efficient architecture for DCT/IDCT is first described. For the different vector rotations, we adopt ARC and conventional CORDIC combined with different scale factors to simplify the architecture and improve the accuracy. The result demonstrate that the proposed architecture has the best PSNR and dissipate the least power. Compared with the Lee architecture, both the throughput and the processing time of the proposed architecture are also slightly better. Compared with the Huang architecture, all of the required hardware resources, the latency and the processing time are highly reduced with a little loss in critical path delay and throughput.

Acknowledgments. This work is supported by Xilinx. We also would like to thank Jianfeng Zhang and the reviewer for their revisions and suggestions.

References

1. Rao, K.R., Yip, P.: Discrete Cosine Transform: Algorithms, Advantages. Applications. Academic press, New York (2014)
2. Clarke, R.: Relation between the Karhunen Loèvet and cosine transforms. Commun. Rada Signal Process. IEE Proc. F **128**(6), 359–360 (1981)
3. Wallace, G.K.: The JPEG still picture compression standard. IEEE Trans. Consum. Electron. **38**(1), xviii–xxxiv (1992)
4. Le Gall, D.: MPEG: a video compression standard for multimedia applications. Commun. ACM **34**(4), 46–58 (1991)
5. Ahmed, A., Shahid, M.U.: N point DCT VLSI architecture for emerging HEVC standard. VLSI Des. **2012**, 6 (2012)
6. Li, C.-Y., et al.: A probabilistic estimation bias circuit for fixed-width booth multiplier and its DCT applications. IEEE Trans. Circuits Syst. II Express Briefs **58**(4), 215–219 (2011)
7. Yu, S., Swartziander, E.: DCT implementation with distributed arithmetic. IEEE Trans. Comput. **50**(9), 985–991 (2001)
8. Xiao, L., Huang, H.: A novel CORDIC based unified architecture for DCT and IDCT. In: 2012 International Conference on Optoelectronics and Microelectronics (ICOM). IEEE (2012)
9. Huang, H., Xiao, L.: CORDIC based fast radix-2 DCT algorithm. IEEE Sig. Process. Lett. **20**(5), 483–486 (2013)
10. Huang, H., Xiao, L.: CORDIC based fast algorithm for power-of-two point DCT and its efficient VLSI implementation. Microelectron. J. **45**(11), 1480–1488 (2014)
11. Huang, H., Xiao, L., Liu, J.: CORDIC-Based Unified Architectures for Computation of DCT/IDCT/DST/IDST. Circ. Syst. Sig. Process. **33**(3), 799–814 (2014)
12. Lee, M.W., Yoon, J.H., Park, J.: Reconfigurable CORDIC-based low-power DCT architecture based on data priority. IEEE Trans. Very Large Scale Integr. (VLSI) Syst. **22**(5), 1060–1068 (2014)
13. Zhang, J., et al.: Adaptive recoding CORDIC. IEICE Electron. Express **9**(8), 765–771 (2012)
14. Meher, P.K., et al.: 50 years of CORDIC: algorithms, architectures, and applications. IEEE Trans. Circ. Syst. I Regul. Pap. **56**(9), 1893–1907 (2009)
15. Xilinx, X.E.U.G., Xilinx power tools tutorial (2010). 2012
16. Zhang, J., Chow, P., Liu, H.: An efficient FPGA implementation of QR decomposition using a novel systolic array architecture based on enhanced vectoring CORDIC. In: 2014 International Conference on Field-Programmable Technology (FPT). IEEE (2014)

Microsecond-Level Temperature Variation of Logic Circuits and Influences of Infrared Cameras' Parameters on Hardware Trojans Detection

Yongkang Tang[1,2(✉)], Jianye Wang[1], Shaoqing Li[2], Jihua Chen[2], and Binbin Yang[2]

[1] Academy of Air-defense and Anti-missile, Air Force Engineering University, Changle East Road 1, Xi'an 710043, China
yokydang@163.com
[2] School of Computer, National University of Defense Technology, Sanyi Street, Changsha 410073, China
sqli@163.com
http://www.springer.com/lncs

Abstract. Currently, hardware Trojans have posed a serious threat to the integrated circuit security. A novel approach using chips' infrared radiation to detect Trojans on a second scale was proposed in 2014. However, the temperature differences can be distinguishable on a microsecond scale between the normal areas in normal chips and the corresponding infected areas in chips with Trojans. As a result, the second-level detection can influence the detection accuracy reversely because of the temperature balance. On the other hand, infrared cameras' ability to detect Trojans is determined by three parameters. They are the noise equivalent temperature difference (NETD), the pixel size and the frame frequency. It will be of benefit to Trojans detection using infrared cameras, if we determine the influences of the three parameters on detection. In this paper, we utilize finite element analysis to simulate the microsecond-level temperature variations of a fixed pixel-size silicon substrate while logic circuits on this size silicon substrate vary and operate under different challenges. Then, we find that the distinguishable time between different cases is on a microsecond scale according to a normal NETD. Based on our simulation results, an increasing step size (ISS) approach is proposed to capture dies' microsecond-level infrared maps accurately using the low frame frequency infrared cameras. Finally, we analyze the temperature variations while a fixed logic circuit under a fixed challenge is operating on the different pixel-size silicon substrates. Based on the results, we get the link between NETD and the pixel size on the Trojan detection.

Keywords: Hardware Trojan · Finite element analysis · Infrared camera's parameters · Increasing step size approach

This work was supported by the National Natural Science Foundation of China (NSFC, grants no. 61471375).

W. Xu et al. (Eds.): NCCET 2016, CCIS 666, pp. 69–80, 2016.
DOI: 10.1007/978-981-10-3159-5_7

1   Introduction

In the current integrated circuit (IC) industry, the Graphic Database System (GDS) II files are usually outsourced to third-party foundries because IC designers lack their own manufacturing equipment. Therefore, original chips are vulnerable to Trojans' unwanted activities, such as bypassing or disabling the security fence of a system, leaking confidential information, deranging, or destroying entire chips [1]. Academia has proposed various approaches to detect or to prevent these threats, including side channel analysis [3,4], reverse engineering [6], function and structure analysis [7,8] and design-for-test [2,5]. Side channel analysis is one of the most effective methods because it is easy to be implemented. It does not occupy the area of layouts and does not harm the chips' operation. Traditionally, the main side channel signals are power and route-delay. However, these signals are difficult for testers to achieve 2-dimension detection. In [1], Abdullah and Hu, et al. used the infrared radiation as the side channel signal and captured dies' infrared maps by an infrared camera. They achieved Trojan detection and location at the same time. Their experimental evaluations reveal that their proposed methodology can detect very small Trojans with 3–4 orders of magnitude smaller power consumptions than the total power usage of the chip. However, their infrared maps is captured for 30 s and averaged over time [1], and such a long time can have reverse influences on detection accuracy. Dies' temperature can vary significantly on a microsecond scale after logic circuits start to operate. Besides, dies are easy to be heated to temperature balance, if logic circuits work for a long time.

In this paper, we utilize finite element analysis to analyze the microsecond-level temperature variation of a fixed pixel-size silicon substrate on which logic circuits vary and operate under different challenges. Then, we propose an increasing step size (ISS) approach to capture infrared maps accurately using low frame frequency infrared cameras. Finally, we discuss the link between NETD and the pixel size on detecting a fixed logic circuit on various pixel-size silicon substrates. Our results can provide testers an approach to choose a proper infrared camera for their Trojan detection.

2   Preparation

2.1   Pre-analysis

The infrared cameras' ability on Trojans detection is mainly limited by their three performance parameters. They are NETD, the pixel size and the frame frequency.

NETD determines the fastest time for infrared cameras to identify the temperature difference of substrates on which logic circuits are various in structure and workload, after logic circuits start to operate. There is also a direct link between the pixel size and t(NETD). t(NETD) is the time for the temperature between substrates within a pixel size reaching to a NETD difference. The larger the pixel size is, the slower the temperature rises. The detected substrates will also be influenced seriously by the heat from around logic circuits because of the heat conduction, if chips operate for a long time. Generally, the frame frequency is much smaller than $\frac{1}{t(NETD)}$. Therefore, it is difficult for testers to capture the infrared maps accurately after logic circuits work.

2.2   Assumptions

(1) The static power is ignored because it is relatively steady under the modern common processes, and the transient power is mainly responsible for the temperature variation.

(2) The physical parameters of silicon, including the specific heat, density and the thermal conductivity, are fixed during temperature rising.

(3) The channel between the source and the drain in a MOS is considered as a surface because its thickness can be ignored, compared with the thickness of a silicon substrate.

(4) The environmental noise and the measurement noise in the actual thermal maps captured by an infrared camera are Gaussian white noises. There are many sophisticated algorithms to mitigate these noises. Therefore, we don't consider the influences of the two noises in our simulation.

(5) The initial temperature of a silicon substrate in our simulation is 25°C. We consider that the temperature difference of different substrates is effective when this difference of their farthest points is a NETD. Currently, the NETDs of the popular infrared cameras range from 20 mK to 40 mK. In our experiment, the NETD is 30 mK.

(6) The temperature (heat conduction) influence of logic circuits around on the detected substrates is the same when the logic circuits on the detected substrates vary and operate under different workloads. The temperature difference of the detected substrates caused by various logic circuits operating for several microseconds under different workload is on the micro-Kelvin scale. Therefore, the difference of temperature gradient between detected substrates and substrates around in different cases can be ignored.

3   Surface Heat Flux of Source-Drain Resistance

The amount of the surface heat flux of source-drain resistances in logic circuits determines the temperature variation rate of substrates, so it has an influence on t(NETD). For the NAND in Fig. 1a, its input A is period pulses and its input B is '1'. Therefore, M_4 PMOS is off but M_1 NMOS is on. M_3 PMOS and M_2 NMOS are switched alternatively. Figure 1c shows the NAND's RC equivalent model. The positions of four MOSs in NAND layout are shown in Fig. 1b.

If A is '0' and B is '1', M_3 PMOS is on but M_2 NMOS is off. The current flows from power source to C_L through M_3R_P (as shown in Fig. 2a). Part of the energy is transformed into the heat of M_3R_P, and residual energy is stored in C_L. If A is '1', the states of M_3 PMOS and M_2 NMOS are opposite. The current

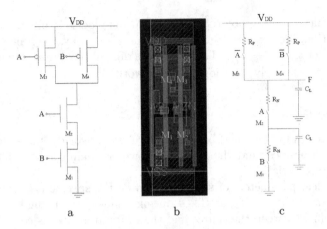

Fig. 1. NAND's logic circuit, NAND's layout and NAND's RC equivalent model

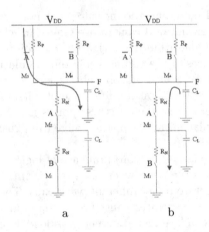

Fig. 2. MOSs' states and current flow in NAND under different input A

flow is shown in Fig. 2b. The energy stored in C_L is changed into the heat of M_2R_N and M_1R_N.

While A is '1' and B is '1', the voltage of F rises from 0 to V_{DD}. The transient energy provided by the power source and that stored in C_L are given by the following equations.

$$E_{VDD} = \int_0^\infty i_{VDD}(t)V_{DD}dt = V_{DD}\int_0^\infty C_L\frac{dV_{out}}{dt}dt = C_LV_{DD}\int_0^{V_{DD}} dV_{out} = C_LV_{DD}^2$$

$$E_C = \int_0^\infty i_{VDD}(t)V_{out}dt = \int_0^\infty C_L\frac{dV_{out}}{dt}V_{out}dt = C_L\int_0^{V_{DD}} V_{out}dV_{out} = \frac{C_LV_{DD}^2}{2}$$

The two equations indicate that the transient energy is only determined by the load capacitance of logic circuits and the voltage of power source. The link among the transient energy provided by the power source, that stored in C_L, and that transformed into the heat of M_3R_P is described by $E_{VDD} = E_C + Q_{M_3R_P}$, so the heat of M3$R_P$ is $Q_{M_3R_P} = E_{VDD} - E_C = \frac{C_L V_{DD}^2}{2}$.

While A is '0' and B is '1', the voltage of F declines from V_{DD} to 0. The transient energy in C_L is consumed by M_2R_N and M_1R_N. The relationship between M_2R_N and M_1R_N is $M_2R_N = M_1R_N$, so the heat of M_2R_N and M_1R_N is $Q_{M_2R_N} = Q_{M_1R_N} = \frac{E_C}{2} = \frac{C_L V_{DD}^2}{4}$.

If the frequency of period pulses to A is $f_{0 \to 1}$, the heat power of M_3 PMOS is $P_{M3} = \frac{C_L V_{DD}^2}{2} f_{0 \to 1}$, and the heat power of M_2 NMOS and M_1 NMOS is $P_{M1} = P_{M2} = \frac{C_L V_{DD}^2}{4} f_{0 \to 1}$.

Assume that the gate areas of PMOSs and NMOSs in this NAND are S_{PMOS} and S_{NMOS} separately, so the surface heat flux of M_3 PMOS is

$$SHF_{M_3} = \frac{P_{M_3}}{S_{PMOS}} \tag{1}$$

, and the surface heat fluxes of M_2 PMOS and M_1 NMOS are

$$SHF_{M_2} = SHF_{M_1} = \frac{P_{M_2}(P_{M_1})}{S_{NMOS}} \tag{2}$$

It is similar to give the surface heat fluxes of any logic circuits such as NOR and NOT under different challenges.

4   Experiment Simulation and Results

We choose a 2-input NAND, a 2-input NOR and a NOT from a 40 nm process library. Their parameters are shown in Table 1.

Table 1. Parameters of logic circuits from a 40 nm process library

Types	V_{DD}(V)	C_L(fF)	S_{PMOS}(μm^2)	S_{NMOS}(μm^2)
NAND	0.9	30.69	0.0122	0.0132
NOR	0.9	35.55	0.0248	0.0104
NOT	0.9	33.11	0.0124	0.0104

The physical parameters of silicon are in Table 2. Readers must note that, to accelerate the simulation, the thickness of the virtual substrate in our experiments is 20 μm. Our previous experimental evaluation revealed that the t(NETD) is also on the microsecond scale when the thickness of substrate is standard. Therefore, we address our theory with the 20 μm-thickness substrate.

Table 2. Physical parameters of silicon substrate

C (J/(kg ·°C))	ρ (g/cm^3)	K (W/m)	Thickness (μm)
703	2.35	150	20

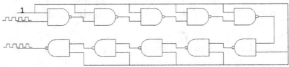

Fig. 3. NAND chain

4.1   Simulation of Trojans

The Same Logic Circuit Under Different Workloads. The NAND chain in Fig. 3 is to imitate the originally pure logic circuits. Its input A is period pulses with 1 GHz, and its input B is '1'.

The surface heat fluxes of MOSs in NAND are presented in Table 3. We use ABAQUS to simulate the temperature variations of the substrate. The temperature distributions of the time when the farthest point reaching to 25.03 °C, 2 μs and 3 μs are shown in Fig. 4. From the figures, it is easy to find the temperature conducting process. The temperature of substrate farthest point rises along with the time, ranging from 25 to 26.31 in 3 μs.

25.03°C(490ns)   2μs   3μs

Fig. 4. Temperature distributions of the virtual substrate under NAND chain

To find the temperature differences in different workloads, we simulate the temperature variations of this NAND chain operating under 750 MHz input A, 500 MHz input A and 250 MHz input A. The surface heat fluxes of NAND under these various challenges are presented in Table 3. The results are shown in Fig. 5.

From Fig. 5b, c and d, it is easy to find that the t(NETD)s are around 790 ns.

Different Logic Circuits Under the Same Workload. First, we use a NOR to take the place of the last NAND of the chain in Fig. 3 (as shown in Fig. 6a). The surface heat flux of NOR is presented in Table 4. The temperature variation of NOR-NAND chain under 1 GHz is shown in Fig. 7a. In this condition, the temperature of substrate farthest point varies from 25 to 26.18 in 3 μs.

Table 3. Surface heat fluxes of NAND(W/μm^2)

Types	M$_4$ PMOS	M$_3$ PMOS	M$_2$ NMOS	M$_1$ NMOS
1 GHz	0	1.02×10^{-3}	4.71×10^{-4}	4.71×10^{-4}
750 MHz	0	7.64×10^{-4}	3.53×10^{-4}	3.53×10^{-4}
500 MHz	0	5.09×10^{-4}	2.35×10^{-4}	2.35×10^{-4}
250 MHz	0	2.55×10^{-4}	1.18×10^{-4}	1.18×10^{-4}

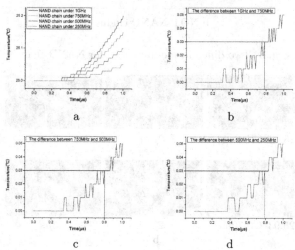

Fig. 5. Temperature differences of NAND chain under different workload

Second, we add a NOT to the end of the original NAND chain (as shown in Fig. 6b). The surface heat flux of NOT is presented in Table 4. The temperature variation of NOT-NAND chain under 1 GHz workload is shown in Fig. 7b, and the temperature of substrate farthest point ranges from 25 to 26.46 in 3 μs.

Compare the temperature variations of three different logic circuit chains (as shown in Fig. 8), it is easy to find that the temperature difference between NOR-NAND chain and NAND chain is less than a NETD during 1 μs but the difference at 2 μs is 80 mK. Therefore, the distinguishable time point locates between 1 μs and 2 μs. Similarly, it can also be convinced that the distinguishable time of NOT-NAND chain and NAND chain is between 1 μs and 2 μs.

Table 4. Surface heat fluxes of NOR and NOT(W/μm^2)

Types	M$_4$ PMOS	M$_3$ PMOS	M$_2$ NMOS	M$_1$ NMOS
NOR	0	0	0	0
NOT	-	-	1.08×10^{-3}	1.29×10^{-3}

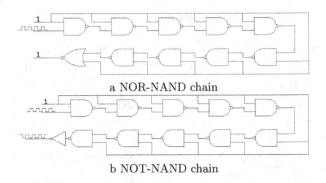

a NOR-NAND chain

b NOT-NAND chain

Fig. 6. Two different modifications for NAND chain

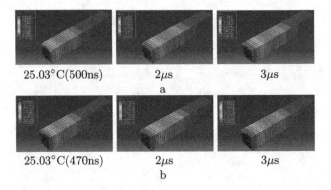

25.03°C(500ns)   2μs   3μs

a

25.03°C(470ns)   2μs   3μs

b

Fig. 7. Temperature distributions of silicon substrate under NOR-NAND chain and NOT-NAND chain

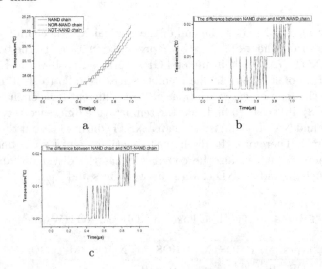

a

b

c

Fig. 8. Temperature differences among NAND chain, NOR-NAND chain and NOT-NAND chain

The experimental results reveal that NETD determines the distinguishable time t(NETD). The larger NETD is, the longer t(NETD) is. If NETD is larger, it is also easier for the temperature of detected substrates to be affected by logic circuits around.

The Approach to Capture Microsecond-Level Infrared Data. The above analysis indicates that the most effective time to detect the different logic circuits is on microsecond scale. Generally, the frame frequency F of infrared cameras ranges from several hundred hertz to a thousand hertz. Therefore, F and t(NETD) satisfy the following inequality

$$F \ll \frac{1}{t(NETD)} \tag{3}$$

That is why infrared cameras cannot capture the microsecond-level temperature variations of detected substrates accurately. To solve this problem, we propose a novel increasing step size (ISS) approach (as shown in Fig. 9). The algorithm is shown in Table 5.

Table 5. The algorithm to capture the optimal infrared data

Steps	
Step1	Infrared cameras operate steadily, i=1
Step2	Trigger logic circuits to work for t(NETD)
Step3	Logic circuits are stopped to wait for $\frac{1}{F}$ + i × t(NETD), triggered again to work for t(NETD)
Step4	i = i+1
Step5	If i = N, output N groups of infrared data. Otherwise, go to step3
Step6	Select the infrared data whose detected areas' temperature is highest

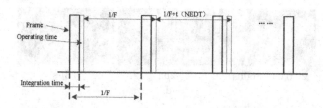

Fig. 9. Increasing step size algorithm

The integration time of the infrared cameras is adjustable from nanosecond scale to millisecond scale. Therefore, it can be set as same as t(NETD) to gain the optimal infrared data.

The number of infrared data that should be captured in every test is $N = \frac{1/t(NETD)}{F}$, and the total time for every test is $t = \frac{1/t(NETD)}{F^2}$.

It is almost impossible to trigger detected logic circuits and infrared equipment to work at the same time. The worst case is that an experiment needs N times to capture the effective infrared data.

One may argue that there is accumulated heat during a test. This heat can lead to inaccurate results because the total operation time of logic circuits is N × t(NETD).

However, according to inequality (3),

$$t(NETD) \ll \frac{1}{F} < \frac{1}{F} + i \times t(NETD) \tag{4}$$

Therefore, the time for heat dissipation is much longer than that for operation every time, and the accumulated heat is near to zero.

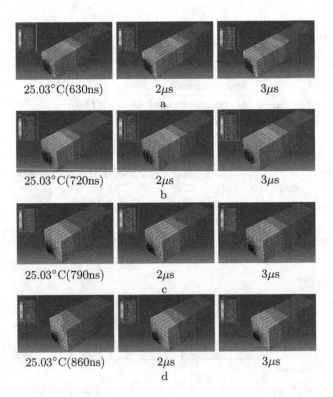

25.03°C(630ns)   2µs   3µs

a

25.03°C(720ns)   2µs   3µs

b

25.03°C(790ns)   2µs   3µs

c

25.03°C(860ns)   2µs   3µs

d

Fig. 10. Temperature distributions of silicon substrate under different pixel sizes

4.2   Simulation of Different Pixel Sizes

Different infrared cameras have various pixel sizes. Pixel sizes can have influence on t(NETD). The larger the pixel size is, the longer t(NETD) is. Therefore, the logic circuits around the detected substrate will also have more serious influences on the temperature variation of the detected substrate.

We simulate different pixel sizes which are 2-fold, 3-fold, 4-fold and 5-fold than the size of the detected logic circuit. The logic circuit is the NAND chain in Fig. 3 under the 1 GHz workload. The temperature variations of different pixel sizes and the temperature differences of them are shown in Figs. 10 and 11 respectively. From Fig. 10, we can find that the speed of temperature conducting in the substrate is slowing down with the substrate area (pixel size) increasing.

From Fig. 11, it is easy to find that the temperature rising trend sees a marked drop while pixel size increases. Therefore, to meet a certain test demand, the larger the pixel size is, the lower NETD is. Namely, the link between NETD and the pixel size is

$$NETD \propto \frac{1}{S_{pixel}} \tag{5}$$

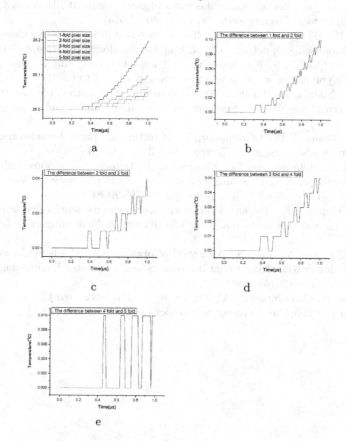

Fig. 11. Temperature differences among different pixel sizes

5 Conclusions

In this paper, in the light of using infrared cameras to detect Trojans, we propose an innovational approach by using finite element analysis to simulate and compare the microsecond-level temperature variations of various logic circuits operating under different workloads. The simulation results indicate that the detectable difference appears on the microsecond scale. To capture this microsecond-level difference accurately using low frame frequency infrared cameras, the ISS approach is proposed. Our simulation results also reveal that t(NETD) is inverse proportional to NETD and the pixel size. In addition, we find the inverse proportional link between the pixel size and NETD when testers detect a fixed size Trojan. All the results provide testers an approach to choose a proper infrared camera for their Trojan detection.

References

1. Abdullah, N.N., Hu, K.Q., Farinaz, K., et al.: Novel techniques for high-sensitivity hardware Trojan detection using thermal and power maps. IEEE Trans. Comput.-Aided Des. Integr. Circuits Syst. **32**, 1792–1805 (2014)
2. Tang, Y.K., Wang, J.Y.: Built-in self-monitor-based finite state machines Trojans detection and self-lock defence. IET J. Eng. (2016). doi:10.1049/joe.2016.0012
3. Agrawal, D., Baktir, S., Karakoyunlu, D.: Trojan detection using IC fingerprinting. In: IEEE Symposium on Security and Privacy, pp. 296–310 (2007)
4. Jin, Y.E., Makris, Y.: Hardware Trojan detection using path delay fingerprint. In: IEEE International Workshop on Hardware-Oriented Security and Trust, pp. 51–57 (2008)
5. Kelly, S., Zhang, X.H., Tehranipoor, M.: Detecting hardware Trojan using on-chip sensors in an ASIC design. J. Electron. Test **31**(1), 11–26 (2015)
6. Wang, X.X., Tehranipoor, M., Plusqeullic, J.: Detecting malicious inclusions in secure hardware: challenges and solutions. In: IEEE International Workshop on Hardware-Oriented Security and Trust, pp. 15–19 (2008)
7. Cha, B., Gupta, S.K.: Trojan detection via delay measurement: a new approach to select paths and vectors to maximize effectiveness and minimize cost. In: EDAA (2013)
8. Chen, X.M., Liu, Y., Li, S.S.: A method of obtaining ASIC schematic using scan chain. In: International Industrial Informatics and Computer Engineering Conference, pp. 985–990 (2015)
9. Rabaey, J.M., Chandrakasan, A., Nikolic, B.: Digital Integrated Circuits: A Design Perspective. Publishing House of Eelctronics Industry, Beijing (2010)

BFDir: A Space-Efficient Coherence Directory Based on Bloom Filter

Jicheng Chen, Yaqian Zhao[✉], Hongzhi Shi, and Yihan Li

State Key Laboratory of High-End Server and Storage Technology,
Inspur Group Company Limited, Beijing, China
{chenjch,zhaoyaqian,shihzh,liyihan}@inspur.com

Abstract. Directory-based coherence is widely used in modern CMP systems. As the number of cores increases, it is increasingly deemed as the only candidate for on-chip cache coherence maintaining. However, limitations of traditional coherence directory pose serious challenges to deal with the ever-increasing size of the system. The hardware overhead and redundant message broadcasting problems dramatically degrade the scalability and performance of the system. In this paper, a space-efficient coherence directory BFDir is proposed. The directory dramatically reduces the directory size as the share list is shortened by Bloom filter. Also, it does not incur message broadcasting as that in limited directories. The evaluation results show, for 32-core CMP systems, compared to full-map directory, 59% overhead of share list can be avoided at the expense of 2.77% performance loss on average; compared to 16-bit coarse directory, 22% overhead of share list can be avoided at the expense of 0.16% average performance loss on average; compared to 8-bit coarse directory, 48% invalid messages are saved and the performance is improved by 2.31%.

Keywords: CMP · Cache coherence directory · Bloom filter · Space-efficient

1 Introduction

CMP processors, which contain multiple processing cores on a single chip have become popular design choice for high-performance processors. Currently, 8-core CMPs are commonplace on the mobile processor and server processor markets. Cores integrated in a single processor will continue to increase with the development of semiconductor technology, and tens or maybe hundreds of cores may be integrated in future CMP processors. In CMP systems, the shared memory programming paradigm is the key component to exploit the performance. To support the paradigm, the cache coherence across all cores in the system has to be maintained with cache coherence protocol (abbreviated as CC protocol).

Basically, all CC protocols fall into two categories: snooping and directory-based protocols. The snooping protocol is often used in CMP systems with few cores (such as IBM Power6 [1]) as it does not scale well with the increase of core number. The directory-based protocols use a hardware structure (called directory) to record coherence

© Springer Nature Singapore Pte Ltd. 2016
W. Xu et al. (Eds.): NCCET 2016, CCIS 666, pp. 81–93, 2016.
DOI: 10.1007/978-981-10-3159-5_8

information to avoid the message broadcasting in snooping protocols, but the hardware cost of the directory grows as the square of the number of cores.

In this paper, we propose a space-efficient coherence directory BFDir to reduce the hardware overhead of the directory structure and avoid the message broad-casting in snooping protocol. In the directory implementation, each core of the system is mapped to multiple positions of the share list by several hash functions. BFDir has two advantages. Firstly, mapping one core to multiple positions in the share list reduces the size of the share list and thus saves the directory space significantly. Secondly, as the share list records all potential sharers of a memory block, it will never overflow and no broadcasting thus exists, which will benefit the performance of the system.

2   Related Work

The basic idea of directory protocol is to establish a directory that maintains a global view of the coherence state of each block. Each entry of the directory has a share list to record which core has a valid copy of a memory block. Full-map directory is a typical implementation of coherence directory, in which each entry is allocated to each memory block in the memory and each bit of the share list is assigned to one core of the system [2]. It is simple, but its share list is redundant [3]. To reduce the length of share list, many directory designs are proposed, such as limited directory [4], linked directory [5–7] and coarse directory [8].

A limited directory only records fixed number of sharer pointers (for example 5 sharers). Its drawback is pointer overflow. When the number of sharers of a memory block exceeds the pointer number, extra operations (such as broadcasting messages to all other cores) have to be executed. Moreover, as the number of cores grows, the share list overflows tend to occur more frequently, which degrades the performance significantly. In linked directory, share information is distributed to a number of small-scale local directory. It compresses the share list, but increases the implementation complexity. Coarse directory reduces the size of share list by a set-associative structure. However, it yields redundant message broadcasting, since each bit of the share list represents a set tag.

During the last few years, some proposals that compressed tagless or sharing patterns have been presented to optimize the design of directory. Jason et al. proposed the Tagless Coherence Directory (TL), a scalable directory structure based on a grid of Bloom filters [9]. SPACE [10] stores the sharing patterns table instead of share list. SPATL [11] combines Tagless and SPACE. Lei et al. presented an area-efficient coherence directory which uses hybrid representation of share list [12]. These methods has made more changes to the directory structure and cache coherence protocol, although they significantly reduce the directory overhead.

Compared with these existing works, our proposal has several advantages. Firstly, only tiny modifications are made to the directory structure, which facilitates the management of the directory and reduces the overhead. Secondly, it is easy to match the coherence protocol with the directory. Lastly, our directory can scale well as the system grows to include more cores and processors.

3 The Methodology

In the section, we will first describe the idea of BFDir, and then explain why it is a good candidate to implement share list of coherent directory. Lastly, we describe the directory design and the protocol operations related to the directory.

3.1 Bloom filter

The bloom filter is a space-efficient, probabilistic data structure, designed to test whether an element is a member of a set [13]. It is implemented with a binary-array, and multiple hash functions as shown in Fig. 1. Each of the functions hashes some element of the target set to one position of the array. An element is determined to be a member of the set only when all the positions where it maps in the array are set.

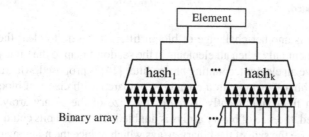

Fig. 1. A sample implementation of bloom filter.

Bloom filter is a good candidate to implement an efficient coherence directory due to two facts:

– Firstly, it is a space-efficient data structure. It is possible to map n cores (processors) to m-bit binary array, where n can be much larger than m. For example, if n equals 32 and the number of hash functions is 2, 10-bit array is enough to record the sharers ($C_{10}^2 = 45 > 32$).
– Secondly, using bloom filter can avoid the overflow of the share list, and thus get rid of the time-consuming message broadcasting.

The disadvantage of bloom filter is mapping conflict, which can result in false sharing and error removing.

– False sharing occurs when an element is not a member of the set but the query returns true. Figure 2 shows a simple example of false sharing in Bloom filter, where the elements C0, C1 and C2 are mapped to position (0, 4), (2, 4) and (0, 2) respectively. When C1 and C2 are sharers, the position 0, 2, 4 are set to 1. The query for sharers will return C0, C1 and C2, while C0 is not a real sharer. Fortunately, the false sharing only affects the performance but not the correctness of the protocol. Hence, in typical coherence protocol implementations, such as the classical MESI protocol, false sharing is allowed. Moreover, the false sharing can be reduced and the side effect can be mitigated by sophisticated design of the hash function and choosing a proper size of the array.

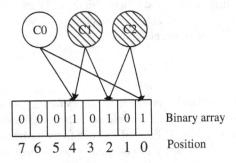

Fig. 2. An example of false positive in bloom filter. E0, E1 and E2 are elements, and E1 and E2 are in the set and shaded.

- Error removing is another challenge of bloom filter. It is safe to clear the bit and remove the element only when all elements in the set don't map to the same position. To safely remove an element, counting bloom filter [14] is proposed, which replaces each bit of the binary array with a counter. Compared with classical bloom filter, counting bloom filter significantly increases the size of the binary array. If 2-bit counters are used, the size of binary arrays is doubled. The added bits could be better utilized to increase the size of the binary arrays which reduce the mapping conflicts.

3.2   Directory Design Based on Bloom Filter

The coherence directory based on bloom filter (BFDir) contains two state bits and the share list based on bloom filter, as shown in Fig. 3. The share list provides a space-efficient structure which uses multiple different hash functions to map one core to several bits of the share list. In the BFDir, the design of the hash functions is critical and it can be implemented in the following three ways.

- With hard-wired logic. The function of the logic is to produce k numbers smaller than m, where k and m are the number of the hash functions and size of the share list respectively. Every time a core becomes a sharer, feed it to the logic and generate k numbers which are used to index into the share list and set the corresponding bits to 1. The hard-wired logic implementation is quite efficient and the latency is small. The drawback is that the logic cannot be programmed and it is impossible to change the mapping to fit the need of the system.
- As a lookup table. Each entry of the table is related to a core and k bits of it are set to 1. Every time a core becomes a sharer, the table is looked up and the entry related to the core is located and the k positions indicated by the entry are set to 1. The drawback of this method is that the hardware cost to implement a lookup table is high. Also, the lookup process can be time-consuming and the latency is large. The advantage is that the mapping can be changed.

– With registers. It is possible to use one or several registers to store the positions where each core is mapped. Every time a core becomes a sharer, the register or register block related to the core is used to set the share list. This implementation can be very time-efficient and flexible. The mapping can be easily changed by writing new values to the registers. The limitation is that enough registers must be provided to record the mapping, which may not be a problem as the FPGA chip used to implement the directory controller usually have plenty of register resources.

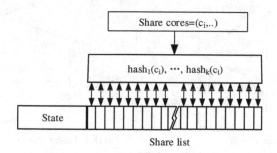

Fig. 3. The coherence directory based on bloom filter.

The size of the share list is also important. If it is too small, the probability of false sharing is high, which degrades the performance; if it is too large, the hardware cost of the directory structure increases. Suppose there are n cores in the system, the share list is m-bit long and k hash functions are used in the Bloom filter implementation. In such system, the condition $C_m^k \geq n$ must be satisfied; otherwise, more than one cores have identical mapping.

3.3 Protocol Operations

As a BFDir only records which cores probably share the requested block, share list may have many false sharers. To handle them, we use a lazy way, in which the share list is left unchanged until one core asks for an exclusive permission. The cost to lazily update the share list is that redundant messages needs to be sent, which may increase traffic in the interconnection network and yield negative impact on the performance. However, our evaluation shows that the performance loss is acceptable.

• Read Requests
  When the directory controller receives a read request, the directory controller corresponding to the block can be in one of three states:
  – The share list records no sharers for the requested block. This is to say, no core holds a valid copy of the block. The directory controller forwards the request to memory. The requester is added to the share list after receiving data.
  – The share list records only one sharer for the requested block. That is to say, the block is in E/M state and only one core (termed as owner) holds a valid copy. The directory controller forwards the request to the owner. The requester is added to the share list after receiving data from owner.

- The share list records more than one sharers for the requested block. The directory controller returns the valid copy to the requester and adds the requester to the share list. As shown in Fig. 4(c), there may be false sharer as the new sharer added.

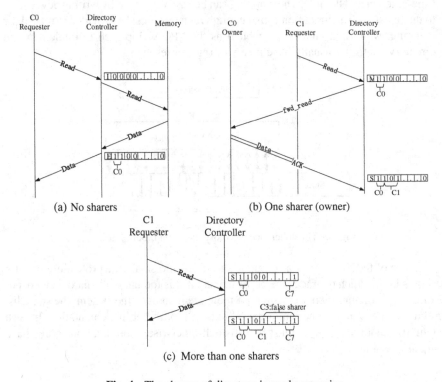

(a) No sharers   (b) One sharer (owner)

(c) More than one sharers

Fig. 4. The change of directory in read processing

- **Write Requests**
  When a core (the writer) needs to write a block, it issues a request to the directory. Once the write request arrives the directory controller, there are three cases:
  - The share list records no sharers for the block. The directory controller asks the memory to provide the data directly to the writer and records the writer in the share list.
  - The share list records exactly one sharer (the owner) for the block. The directory controller forwards the request to the owner. The owner provides the data to the writer and invalidate the local copy. After the writer received data, the directory controller deletes the owner from share list and adds the writer to the share list.
  - The share list records more than one sharers for the block. The directory controller returns the data to the writer and sends invalid messages to all sharers. After the writer received data, the directory controller deletes all sharers and adds the writer to the share list.

As shown in Fig. 5(c), error removing never happens in BFDir, since all sharers are deleted in each writing process. So that classical bloom filter rather than counting bloom filter is used to design the share list. However, false sharing may exist in BFDir, and leads to redundant invalid messages. To reduce the occurrence of false sharing, the probability that each bit of the share list is mapped to 1 should be equal. Therefore, the hash functions in BFDir should satisfy the following conditions:

(1) $C_m^k \geq n$

(2) $P\left(hash_j^l(c_i) = 1\right) = \dfrac{n \times k}{m}, \; i = 1, 2, \ldots, n; j = 1, 2, \ldots, k; l = 1, 2, \ldots, m$

Where n is the number of cores, k is the number of hash functions, m is the length of share list, much smaller than n. Since there is a power increase of C_m^k with m, hash function space grows larger as n increases, with the result that the probability of false sharing will be reduced, and the system performance will be improved.

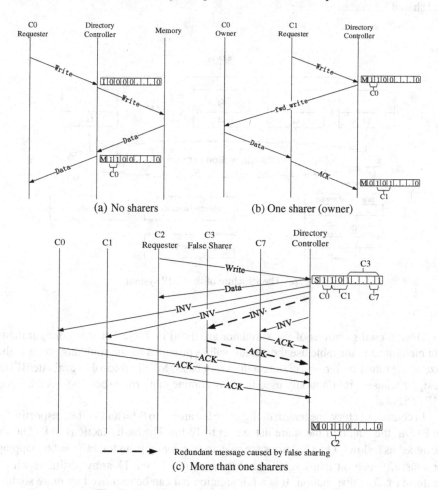

(a) No sharers   (b) One sharer (owner)

(c) More than one sharers

Fig. 5. The change of directory in write processing

4   Evaluation

In this section, we evaluate the performance of BFDir with typical parallel benchmarks. The performance is compared with those collected in a full-map directory and a coarse directory implementation respectively.

4.1   Experimental Setup

The quantitative evaluation is performed on an extensively modified version of gem5 simulation toolkit [15]. In the paper, we modified the Ruby model to support coherence protocol based on BFDir implementation. The structure of the CMP system used in the evaluation is depicted in Fig. 6, in which all cores have private L1 data/instruction caches and shared L2 cache.

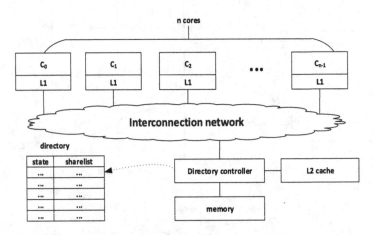

Fig. 6. The structure of the CMP system.

Overall configurations of the simulator are listed in Table 1. Other configurations not mentioned in the table use the default values provided by the simulator, such as the size of the router buffer. We choose a directory based MESI protocol to evaluate BFDir design because it is commonly used in many commercial processors, such as the Xeon MP series.

In coarse directory, the length of the share list are set to 8-bit and 16-bit, respectively. In BFDir, the length of the share list are set to 12-bit. The hash functions in BFDir are designed as follows: (1) 32 options are selected randomly from total $C_{12}^2 = 66$ mapping options; (2) each bit maps some set element to one of the 12 array positions with a uniform random distribution. It is a fair solution but can be improved by more sophisticated design.

Table 1. Simulator configurations in the evaluation

Item	Value	Item	Value
Number of CPUs	32	Cache line size	64 KB
ISA	Alpha	L1 data cache size	64 KB
CPU model	Timing	L1 instruction cache size	32 KB
Simulation mode	FS mode	Associativity of L1 cache	4 ways
Frequency of CPU	1 GHz	L1 access latency	1 cycle
Topology of network	Crossbar	L2 Cache size	256 KB
CC protocol	MESI	Associativity of L2 Cache	8 ways
Memory size	4 GB	L2 access latency	8 cycles
Memory access latency	100 cycles	Cache replace Policy	PSEUDO LRU

4.2 Benchmarks

The benchmarks used in the evaluation is from SPLASH-2 [16] and PARSEC [17] benchmark suite, which are probably the most commonly used suite for scientific studies of parallel machines with shared memory. All the benchmarks are compiled to alpha ISA with gcc cross-compiler. And O3 optimization option is used in the compilation.

The simulation ticks (referred as ST) and number of invalid messages for memory blocks in NP/I (Not Present or Invalid) state (refer to as N_{inv}) of the four directory implementations are collected for all the benchmarks respectively. The performance loss of directory A is evaluated as

$$P_l = \frac{ST_A}{ST_{FM}} - 1 \qquad (1)$$

Table 2. Benchmarks

Benchmark		Description	Problem Size
SPLASH-2	FFT	Performs 1D fast Fourier transform using six-step FFT method	262, 144 data points
	radix	An integer radix sort	n524288
	barnes	Imlements the Barnes-Hut method to simulate the interaction of a system of bodies.	16348
	ocean_ns	Studies the role of eddy and boundary currents in influencing large-scale ocean movements (contiguos partitions)	130 * 130
	ocean_sq	Studies the role of eddy and doundary currents in influencing large-scale ocean movements (non_contiguos partitions)	130 * 130
	Cholesky	Performs blocked Cholesky Factorization on a sparse matrix	Tk15.o
PARSEC	Bodytrack	Body tracking of a person	1000
	ferret	Content similarity search server	Small size

Where ST_A and ST_{FM} denote the simulation ticks when directory A and full-map directory are adopted respectively. The relative number of invalid messages of directory A is defined as

$$RN_{inv-A} = N_{inv-A} / N_{inv-FM} \qquad (2)$$

Where N_{inv-A} and N_{inv-FM} denote Ninv when directory A and full-map directory are adopted respectively (Table 2).

4.3   Performance Results

From Table 3, it can be seen that there are 64 M memory blocks. Therefore, the total size of directory is 272 MB in full-map directory, 80 MB in 8-bit coarse directory, 144 MB in 16-bit coarse directory, and 122 MB in BFDir. Compared to full-mapped directory, BFDir saves 160 MB directory space, which accounts for 59% of the total overhead of the full-map directory structure.

Table 3. Comparison of the size of directory

	Share list (bits)	Directory entry (bits)	Total size of directory (MB)
Full-map directory	32	34	272
8-bit Coarse directory	8	10	80
16-bit Coarse directory	16	18	144
BFDir	12	14	112

As shown in Fig. 7, the performance loss of BFDir compared to full-map directory is mostly within 4% in the 32-core system. For ferret, the performance loss of BFDir is negligible, only 0.907%, less than that of 16-bit coarse directory. While for ocean_ns, the performance loss is relative large, about 4.599%. This is due to the fact that during the execution, there are many data sharings among cores and the Write-after-Reads are frequent which incurs a lot of redundant invalid messages and increases network congestion and enlarges the latencies of data accesses. So the performance loss of coarse directory is also large. From Fig. 7, it is also clear that, the performance loss varies for different programs, such as cholesky and ocean_sq. This is due to the fact that, each program has its own data access pattern, which mostly relies on the characteristics of the algorithm the program implements and how the algorithm is programmed. Overall, BFDir with 12 bits share list is comparable to coarse directory with 16 bits share list in performance. This means that BFDir can avoid more unnecessary message broadcasting than coarse directory.

Figure 8 shows the relative number of invalid messages during the execution of the benchmarks. It is noted that, Fig. 8 depicts the relative number of invalid messages for blocks in NP/I state only, which are rare in full-map directory, so the ratio seems quite significant. Compared to full-map directory, both BFDir and coarse directory incur redundant invalid messages. For BFDir, the number of relative invalid messages is below 9, except for cholesky; for 16-bit coarse directory, the number of relative invalid messages is below 8, except for cholesky; while for 8-bit coarse directory, the number is much larger,

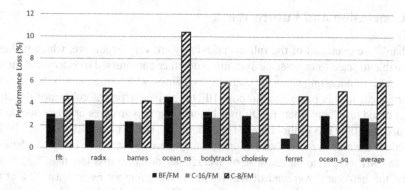

Fig. 7. Comparison of performance loss to full-map directory. BF, C-16, C-8 and FM represent BFDir, 16-bit coarse directory, 8-bit coarse directory and full-map directory respectively.

even larger than 19. Compared to 8-bit coarse directory, our BFDir reduces 46% invalid messages with 41% improvement on the size of directory, while 16-bit coarse directory reduces 55% invalid messages with 83% improvement on the size of directory. Using BFDir implementation can dramatically reduce blind message broadcasting. This is the reason why BFDir achieves better performance, as shown in Fig. 7.

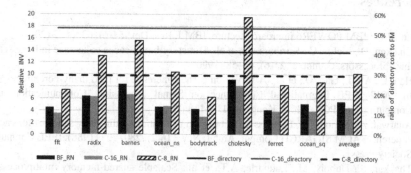

Fig. 8. Comparison of relative invalid messages and directory cost to full-map directory

By comparing the results in Figs. 7 and 8, it is shown that reducing the number of redundant messages broadcasting can benefit to improve system performance. However, besides the number of invalid messages for blocks in NP/I state, there are many factors affecting performance, such as the characteristics of the algorithm the program implements. Therefore, performance loss and relative number of invalid messages may have different changes, as presented by ferret.

On average, our BFDir nearly half the number of redundant invalid messages and performance loss in 8-bit coarse directory, and slightly increase the number of redundant invalid messages and performance loss in 16-bit coarse directory. The results confirm the motivation for pursuing better performance by reducing redundant messages.

5   Conclusion and Future Work

The hardware overhead of the full-map directory are very expensive, which makes it impossible to scale to large-scale systems. And other compressed directories incur lots of message broadcasting when the share list overflows, which significantly degrades the performance. In this paper, we propose BFDir, a space-efficient coherence directory design based on bloom filter. BFDir uses bloom filter to map cores or processors in the system to multiple bits of the share list and shorten its size. The results show that BFDir can reduce the hardware overhead of the full-map directory structure by at least 59% for 32-core CMP system at the expanse of average performance loss less than 2.77%, and reduce the hardware overhead of the 16-bit coarse directory by at least 22% at the expanse of performance loss less than 0.16%. Also, it avoids 46% redundant invalid messages and improves 2.31% performance compared to 8-bit coarse directory.

There are several work to do in the future. Firstly, the hash function should be designed more sophisticated. Secondly, more experiments will be carried out to observe the performance of BFDir in terms of scalability, area, and power consumption. Thirdly, current evaluations are carried on systems that use MESI protocol, other coherence protocol such as MOESI will also be studied.

References

1. Le, H.Q.: IBM POWER6 microarchitecture. IBM J. Res. Dev. **51**(6), 639–662 (2007)
2. Chaiken, D., Fields, C., Kurihara, K., et al.: Directory-based cache coherence in large scale multiprocessors. Computer **23**(6), 49–58 (1990)
3. Han, L., An, J., Gao, D., et al.: A survey on cache coherence for tiled many-core processor. In: 2012 IEEE International Conference on Signal Processing, Communication and Computing (ICSPCC), Hong Kong, pp. 114–118 (2012)
4. Agarwal, A., Simoni, R., Hennessy, J., et al.: An evaluation of directory schemes for cache coherence. ACM SIGARCH Comput. Archit. News **16**(2), 280–298 (1988). IEEE Computer Society Press
5. Thakkar, S., Dubois, M., Laundrie, A.T., et al.: Scalable shared-memory multiprocessor architectures. Computer **23**(6), 71–74 (1990)
6. Thapar, M., Delagi, B., Flynn, M.: Linked list cache coherence for scalable shared memory multiprocessors. In: Proceedings of 1993 Seventh International Parallel Processing Symposium, Washington, DC, USA, pp. 34–43. IEEE Computer Society (1993)
7. Alnaes, K., Kristiansen, E.H., Gustavson, D.B., et al.: Scalable coherent interface. In: Proceedings of the 1990 IEEE International Conference on Computer Systems and Software Engineering (CompEuro 1990), pp. 446–453. IEEE (1990)
8. Gupta, A., Weber, W., Mowry, T.: Reducing memory and traffic requirements for scalable directory-based cache coherence schemes. In: Scalable Shared Memory Multiprocessors, pp. 312–321 (1995)
9. Zebchuk, J., Qureshi, M.K., Srinivasan, V., et al.: A tagless coherence directory. In: 42nd Annual IEEE/ACM International Symposium on Microarchitecture (MICRO-42), pp. 423–434. ACM, New York (2009)
10. Zhao, H., Shriraman, A., Dwarkadas, H.: SPACE: sharing pattern-based directory coherence for multicore scalability. In: International Conference on Parallel Architectures and Compilation Techniques, pp. 135–146 (2010)

11. Zhao, H., Shriraman, A., Dwarkadas, S., et al.: SPATL: honey, I shrunk the coherence directory. In: International Conference on Parallel Architectures and Compilation Techniques, pp. 33–44 (2011)
12. Fang, L., Liu, P., Hu, Q., et al.: Building expressive, area-efficient coherence directories. International Conference on Parallel Architectures and Compilation Techniques, pp. 299–308. IEEE (2013)
13. Bloom, B.H.: Space/time trade-offs in hash coding with allowable errors. Commun. ACM 13(7), 422–426 (1970)
14. Fan, L., Cao, P., Almeida, J., Broder, A.Z.: Summary cache: a scalable wide-area web cache sharing protocol. IEEE/ACM Trans. Netw. 8(3), 281–293 (2000)
15. Binkert, N., Beckmann, B., Black, G., Reinhardt, S.K., et al.: The gem5 simulator. ACM SIGARCH Computer Arch. News 39, 1–7 (2011)
16. Woo, S.C., Ohara, M., Torrie, E., Singh, J.P., Gupta, A.: The SPLASH-2 programs: characterization and methodological considerations. In: Proceedings of the 22nd International Symposium on Computer Architecture, vol. 23, no. 2, pp. 24–36 (1995)
17. Bagrodia, R., Ameyer, R., Takai, M.: Parsec: a parallel simulation environment for complex systems. IEEE Comput. 31(10), 77–85 (1998)

FPGA-Based High Throughput TDMP LDPC Decoder

Ruochen Liao[✉], Yuzhuo Fu, and Ting Liu

School of Microelectronics, Shanghai Jiao Tong University, Shanghai 200240, China
liaorc@sjtu.edu.cn

Abstract. In this paper, a high-throughput decoder architecture for quasi-cyclic low density parity check (QC-LDPC) codes is presented. Using the Normalized Min-Sum algorithm and the turbo-decoding message-passing algorithm, the proposed design expanded degree of parallelism to improve the throughput at a cost of hardware resource usage. Based on the proposed architecture, we implemented a (8176, 7154) Euclidian geometry-based QC-LDPC code decoder on a Xilinx Kintex7 (XC7K325T-2) board. The FPGA implementation results show that the decoder can achieve a total decoding throughput of 1.6 Gbps at the clock frequency of 105Mth at 10 iterations.

Keywords: Low-density parity-check · Turbo-decoding message-passing · Normalized min-sum · FPGA

1 Introduction

Low-Density Parity-Check (LDPC) codes were discovered by Gallager in 1962 [1]. Later in late 1990s, LDPC codes were rediscovered by MacKay and shown to approach Shannon capacity [2]. With excellent error control capacities, LDPC codes have been considered for emerging wireless communication standards, such as IEEE802.16e, IEEE802.11n, and DVB-S2 etc.

The original approach for LDPC decoders is known as Gallager's two-phase message-passing (TPMP) algorithm. Since TPMP algorithm need to decode iteratively using sum-product algorithm [1] at a high cost of calculation complexity, variations such as the min-sum algorithm and normalized min-sum algorithm [3] are also widely used. Previous works focused on the hardware implementations of TPMP algorithm with all kinds of architectures (e.g. fully parallel, partially parallel, and serial) have been proposed. However, the convergence speed of these methods are slow, which is troublesome in high-throughput applications. To address this problem, turbo-decoding message-passing (TDMP) algorithm [4] has been proposed. A single iteration in TPMP algorithm is divided into sub-iterations to accelerate convergence speed. The throughput is increased since less number of iterations is needed at the same bit error rate (BER).

The proposed architecture aims to expand degree of parallelism of a TDMP LDPC decoder. We take advantage of pipelining and parallel processing in the proposed high-throughput FPGA decoder. In additional with configurable depth of the block RAM in FPGA design, which allows the high bandwidth of message passing. Furthermore, the design carefully deals with the choosing of degree of parallelism to avoid data conflict

© Springer Nature Singapore Pte Ltd. 2016
W. Xu et al. (Eds.): NCCET 2016, CCIS 666, pp. 94–101, 2016.
DOI: 10.1007/978-981-10-3159-5_9

when introducing pipelining. In result, the proposed decoder greatly improved parallel level in processing comparing with others. The improvement helps the decoder to achieve a high-throughput under a low clock frequency.

2   Previous Works

In this section, previous works with FPGA-based hardware designs are listed.

Chen Xiaoheng, Kang Jinyu and Lin Shu built a (8176, 7156) LDPC decoder with two specific optimizations called vectorization and folding [5]. With their efforts on taking advantage of configurable embedded memory in FPGA, the decoder achieved a total throughput of 713.8 Mbps at 15 iterations.

Wang Zhongfeng proposed a (8176, 7156) LDPC decoder based on Xilinx field programmable gate array Virtex-II 6000 [6]. The decoder employed an efficient nonuniform quantization scheme to reduce the size of memories storing soft messages. The results showed that Wang's work achieved a maximum decoding throughput of 172 Mbps at 15 iterations.

Xiang Bo in his work at 2011 implemented decoders for multiple LDPC code length ranging from 576 to 2304 [7]. Xiang's main effort was to include pipelining, block interleaving and nonzero sub-matrix reordering into his decoding technic. By Xiang's reordering feature, memory conflict was reduced when using pipeline in LDPC decoder. Xiang's best result achieved 955 Mbps at 10 iterations with a clock frequency of 214 MHz.

Previous works on LDPC decoder using TDMP algorithm share a common problem, which is that they all need a relatively high clock frequency to achieve a high throughput. For TDMP algorithm introduces potential memory conflict when processing multiple rows parallely, the dilemma between frequency and throughput appears. Our work aims at analysing the best degree of parallelism in TDMP algorithm. Therefore the proposed decoder reaches a high throughput at a relative low clock frequency.

3   High-Throughput Parallel LDPC Decoder Architecture

3.1   Decoding Algorithm

The proposed decoder uses the same algorithm as the one in work [8], which is the min-sum turbo decoding message passing algorithm. With TDMP algorithm, the convergence speed is faster than its opponent TPMP algorithm. By using min-sum algorithm, the calculation complexity of updating log-likelihood ratios is reduced.

3.2   Decoder Overview

In this section, the overview architecture of the proposed decoder will be shown. And the function of each part will be introduced.

Generally, the proposed LDPC decoder consist of four main parts. Four parts and the interconnects are shown in Fig. 1.

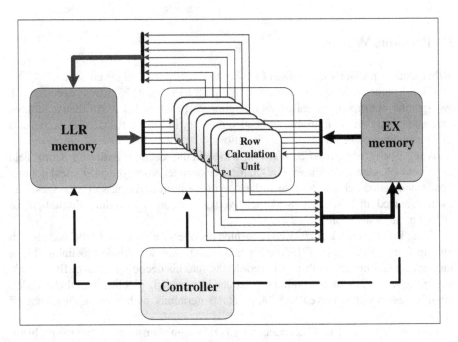

Fig. 1. LDPC decoder overview

The function of each part:

- LLR memory: The log-likelihood ratio memory. This module stores log-likelihood ratio of all the check nodes. This module also deals with the input and output data flow.
- EX memory: The extrinsic information memory. This module stores the extrinsic information passing from check nodes to variable node.
- Controller: The control module of decoder. This module generates read and write addresses for all the memories.
- Row calculation Unit: The row information update module. This is the main calculation module of the decoder, which does all the computation process and update the log-likelihood ratio and extrinsic information of each row in every iteration. The proposed parallel and pipeline structure is implemented in this part. Figure 2 shows that we implemented a number of P row calculation units in total, which means P rows of check nodes can be calculating in parallel.

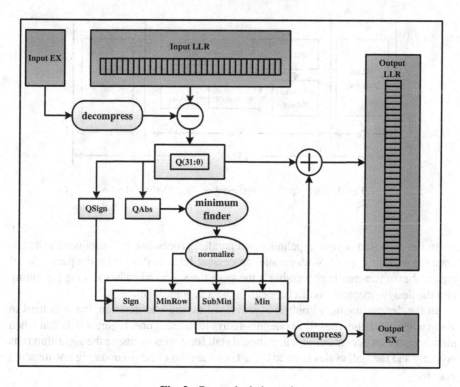

Fig. 2. Row calculation unit

3.3 Parallel Decoder Core Architecture

This is the structure for a single row calculation unit in Sect. 3.2.

Basically the update process is divided into three stages. The first stage deals with the data reading and decompression of extrinsic information. The second stage handles the main calculation process of check node unit (CNU). The last stage compresses the data and stores the updated data back to memory.

3.4 Parallel Decoder Core Architecture

During updating one log-likelihood ratio, three steps are needed by LDPC decoder: read original data from memory, calculate new log-likelihood ratios and extrinsic information, write back the updated data to memory. In Fig. 3, read or write cycle is assumed to be T_c (T_c also stands for time of a clock cycle), and the delay of calculation module is assumed to be X ns. Thus the cycle delay of updating one data is,

$$T_{path} = \left\lceil \frac{2T_c + X}{T_c} \right\rceil \tag{1}$$

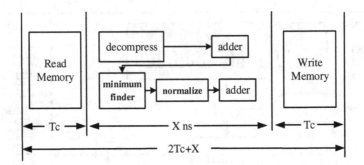

Fig. 3. Delay path for updating one log-likelihood ratio

In the proposed design, pipelining and parallel processing are introduced to accelerate the decoding speed. With parallel processing feature, P is set for the parameter of the number of sub-matrix processing at the same time. And when introducing pipelining into the design, memory conflict appears to be a new problem.

In the design, memory conflict is prevented during one iteration, but it is hard to avoid when algorithm runs form one sub-matrix to the next one. Figure 4 tells that when memory conflict occurs our pipeline should stall for cycles to ensure the algorithm runs properly and the stall cycles is set to T_{stall}. Then the total cycles of updating one iteration T_{total} is,

$$T_{total} = 2N_{iter}\left(T_{stall} + \left\lceil \frac{511}{P} \right\rceil\right) + T_{path} - 1 \tag{2}$$

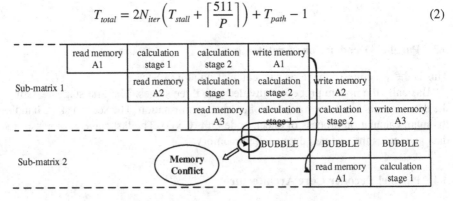

Fig. 4. Potential memory conflict in pipelining

Since we want to avoid memory conflict during one iteration, the offset distance in one sub-matrix should be taken into consideration. We define $offset_1$ and $offset_2$ to be the distance between 1's in one sub-matrix and define a parameter L,

$$L = \min(offset_1 - offset_2, 511 - (offset_1 - offset_2)) \tag{3}$$

For (8176, 7154) LDPC code, $L \geq 104$. Thus to avoid memory conflict, we need

$$T_{path} P \leq L \tag{4}$$

On the other hand, $Throughput = \dfrac{f_{clk} len}{T_{total}}$. And apparently, $len = 7136$ in (8176, 7154) code.

The design needs a total throughput no less than 1.6 Gbps. Therefore, with the analysis above, we get one solution that $P = 26$, $f_{clk} \approx 100$ MHz, $T_{path} = 4$, $T_{stall} = 3$.

3.5 Quantization

Since quantization of log-likelihood ratios affects the memory usage of LDPC decoder and the path delay of data processing, it is reasonable to choose a shorter quantization mode for our design (Table 1).

Table 1. Coding gain analysis

Coding gain (dB)		Iteration						Resource util. (Slice)
		5	6	7	8	9	10	
Quantization	Float	7.17	7.24	7.24	7.24	7.30	7.32	/
	7bit [2, 4]	7.12	7.20	7.17	7.22	7.24	7.25	45346
	6bit [2, 3]	7.00	7.08	7.05	7.10	7.11	7.13	39741
	5bit [2, 2]	6.69	6.74	6.78	6.78	6.78	6.79	33118

When processing with 10 iterations, 5bit quantization results in a 6.79 dB coding gain, only 0.4 dB worse than a float number decoder. But with 5bit quantization, the slice resource utilization will drop 26.9%. Since a 6.79 dB coding gain is enough for our case, we choose a 5bit quantization.

4   Implementation and Performance Evaluation

4.1   Implementation Platform

The decoder is implemented on a Xilinx Kintex7 (XC7K325T-2FFG900) board under development environment Xilinx Vivado. The design can meet the timing constraint to run under 105 MHz. To test the function of our decoder, we used a host computer and the PCI-E interface to control the decoder and transmit data with it.

Considering the data transmission speed would not match the design throughput of our LDPC decoder, we add additional input and output FIFO to our decoder to test its highest performance (Fig. 5).

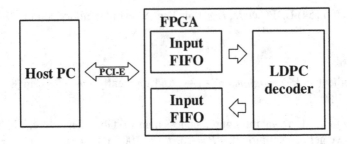

Fig. 5. System overview for decoder testing

4.2 Implementation Result and Resource Utilization

We prototyped the proposed high-throughput LDPC decoder architectures on Xilinx Kintex7 (XC7K325T-2FFG900) device. The prototype is verified under a 1e10 bits LDPC data decoding test. We also tested our design in variety working frequency. All the FPGA resource utilization result after implementation is given in Table 2.

Table 2. FPGA resource utilization

Clock frequency	75 MHz	85 MHz	95 MHz	105 MHz
FF	165067	165067	175649	175650
LUT	132214	132222	151501	152761
BRAM	221	221	221	221

4.3 Comparison with Other Works

Table 3 shows the throughput result of proposed design and some of previous works. Comparing with other woks, the proposed design greatly improves degree of parallelism and achieves a total throughput of 1.6 Gbps only requiring a clock frequency of 105 MHz. To have a more reasonable comparison, we introduce this so called Normalized Throughput, which is defined as,

Table 3. Comparision

Parameter	Wang [6]	Xiang [7]	Chen [5]	Proposed
FPGA	Virtex-II 6000	CMOS	XC4VLX-160	XC7K325T
Clock frequency (MHz)	193	214	212.2	105
Degree of parallelism	2	2	4	26
Iteration	15	10	15	10
Throughput (Mbps)	199.2	728	713.8	1628.8
Normalized Throughput (Mb)	15.5	34.0	50.5	155.1
FPGA utilization (slice)	23052	-	17857	38213

$$T_{pN} = T_p \times N_{iter}/f_{clk} \tag{5}$$

Comparison between Normalized Throughput takes iteration number and frequency into consideration. According to the result table, the proposed decoder has 3 times of Normalized Throughput comparing with others.

5 Conclusion

We present a high-throughput (8176, 7154) LDPC decoder with expansion of degree of parallel. Our work takes the advantage of pipelining and parallel processing to implement TDMP algorithm. When compared with previous works on LDPC decoder, our result achieves a two-times improvement in normalized throughput, which indicate the proposed architecture have a high throughput in low clock frequency system. Another main contribution of this work is to give an analysis on the selecting of best degree of parallelism for the (8176, 7154) LDPC code. The same method can also be applied to other LDPC codes to design large parallel high-throughput decoders.

Acknowledgements. This work is supported by the National Science Foundation of China (Grant No. 61373032, Grant No. 61472244) and Innovation Program of Shanghai Municipal Education Commission (Grant No. 14ZZ018).

References

1. Gallager, R.G.: Low-density parity-check codes. IRE Trans. Inf. Theory **8**(1), 21–28 (1962)
2. MacKay, D.J.C.: Good error-correcting codes based on very sparse matrices. IEEE Trans. Inf. Theory **45**(2), 399–431 (1999)
3. Fossorier, M.P.C., Mihaljević, M., Imai, H.: Reduced complexity iterative decoding of low-density parity check codes based on belief propagation. IEEE Trans. Commun. **47**(5), 673–680 (1999)
4. Mansour, M.M.: A turbo-decoding message-passing algorithm for sparse parity-check matrix codes. IEEE Trans. Sign. Process. **54**(11), 4376–4392 (2006)
5. Chen, X., et al.: Memory system optimization for FPGA-based implementation of quasi-cyclic LDPC codes decoders. IEEE Trans. Circuits Syst. I Regul. Pap. **58**(1), 98–111 (2011)
6. Wang, Z., Cui, Z.: Low-complexity high-speed decoder design for quasi-cyclic LDPC codes. IEEE Trans. Very Large Scale Integr. Syst. **15**(1), 104–114 (2007)
7. Xiang, B., et al.: An 847–955 Mb/s 342–397 mW dual-path fully-overlapped QC-LDPC decoder for WiMAX system in 0.13 m CMOS. IEEE J. Solid-State Circuits **46**(6), 1416–1432 (2011)

A Dynamic Multi-precision Fixed-Point Data Quantization Strategy for Convolutional Neural Network

Lei Shan[✉], Minxuan Zhang, Lin Deng, and Guohui Gong

School of Computer Science, National University of Defense Technology,
Changsha, China
ssl12999@163.com

Abstract. In recent years, deep learning represented by Convolutional Neural Network (CNN) has been one of the hottest topics of research. CNN inference process based models have been widely used in more and more computer vision applications. The execution speed of inference process is critical for applications, and the hardware acceleration method is mostly considered. To relieve the memory pressure, data quantization strategies are often used in hardware implementation. In this paper, a dynamic multi-precision fixed-point data quantization strategy for CNN has been proposed and used to quantify the floating-point data in trained CNN inference process. Results shows that our quantization strategy for LeNet model can reduce the accuracy loss from 22.2% to 5.9% at most, compared with previous static quantization strategy, when 8/4-bit quantization is used. When 16-bit quantization is used, only 0.03% accuracy loss is introduced by our quantization strategy with half memory footprint and bandwidth requirement comparing with 32-bit floating-point implementation.

Keywords: CNN · Fixed-point · Data quantization

1 Introduction

Deep learning has received much more focus than ever and ignited tremendous research enthusiasm on Artificial Intelligence (AI) in recent years. State-of-the-art computer vision(CV) researches use deep learning model in image classification achieved great success, especially models based on Convolutional Neural Network (CNN) has led to great advances in image classification accuracy. In 2012, Hinton [1] and his students applied CNN based model in Image-Net [2] Large-Scale Vision Recognition Challenge (ILSVRC), and achieved world best result by the top-5 accuracy of 84.7% in classification task. Since then CNN has become the most accurate

L. Shan—The research is supported by Specialized Research Fund for the Doctor Program of Higher Education of China with Grant No. 20124307110016, and by National Natural Science Foundation of China with Grant No. 61176030.

W. Xu et al. (Eds.): NCCET 2016, CCIS 666, pp. 102–111, 2016.
DOI: 10.1007/978-981-10-3159-5_10

model in image recognition. In the following years, new CNN based models improved
the accuracy to 88.8% [3], 93.3% [4], and 96.4% [5] in ILSVRC 2013, 2014, and 2015.

Although CNN based methods achieved state-of-the-art performance, the computation and memory resource requirements of CNN are much larger than traditional
methods. Even the inference process of CNN consumes large amount of computation
and bandwidth resources. While most CNN based applications use the inference process of off-line trained model, this problem will be an obstruction to the study and
application of CNN. To address this problem, many researchers have proposed various
CNN inference process acceleration techniques. Hardware acceleration was mostly
used and optimization techniques from either computing or memory access aspects
were proposed.

When using hardware implementation to accelerate CNN inference process, most
techniques were proposed to accelerate the computation part. However, with the
increasing scale of CNN models, higher and higher resolution image input, and large
amount of intermediate data to transfer and store, memory capacity and bandwidth will
meet great challenge. Especially when CNN deployed on embedded hardware platform, like FPGA and AISC, with limited on-chip memory capacity and limited off-chip
memory bandwidth.

To address this problem, fixed-point data quantization is a good way to relieve the
memory capacity and bandwidth pressure. Fixed-point data quantization means using
shorter fix-point numbers to represent floating-point ones in the original system. It will
reduce the requirement of both on-chip memory capacity and off-chip memory bandwidth. However, using shorter data representation will introduce truncation error, leads
to accuracy loss.

In this paper, we proposed a dynamic multi-precision fixed-point data quantization
strategy and a work flow for the whole CNN inference process. Our strategy aims to
minimize the truncation error introduced by converting from floating-point data to short
fixed-point data. We employ dynamic multi-precision fixed-point data quantization for
every CNN layer and every inner-layer computation. We experiment the strategy on
MINST dataset by LeNet [10] model, but our quantization strategy is also suitable for
other CNN models.

2   Related Work

Shorter fixed-point representation of data can also significantly reduce memory footprint and computation resources. Consequently, most of previous CNN accelerators
used fixed-point data quantization.

In [6], Vanhoucke et al. quantified weights and output of activations into 8-bit.
They proposed quantization errors tend to propagate sub-linearly and not cause
numerical instability, but didn't present the detail of quantization error analysis. Most
of previous work adopted the 16-bit data quantization strategy. In [7], Chen et al.
showed that using 16-bit numbers instead of 32-bit ones only introduced 0.26% more
error rate on MNIST dataset. In [8], 16-bit numbers were used in the inference process
while 32-bit numbers were used in training process, and results on MNIST dataset
showed that there was only 0.01% accuracy reduction.

Previous data quantization strategies are mostly static, data in every CNN layer is quantified into same bit width and same precision. In [9], Qiu et al. emphasized data quantization is rather important and propose a dynamic-precision data quantization strategy, data precision is dynamic for different layers and feature map sets while static in one layer to minimize the truncation error of each layer. Their work shows only 0.4% accuracy loss is introduced by our data quantization flow for the very deep VGG16 model when 8/4-bit quantization is used. But they just use dynamic-precision on the layer level, not the whole CNN including inner-layer computation level.

3   Data Quantization

Data quantization in CNN means using fixed-point data to represent the original floating-point data, including input image data, floating-point trained weights and bias data, intermediate data of each layer and output data, then converting the original floating-point CNN model to fixed-point CNN model. In this section, we will introduce the method of converting floating-point data to fixed-point data.

3.1   Fixed-Point and Floating-Point

The radix point position of a fixed-point number is fixed, while floating-point number is not fixed. A floating-point number takes at least 32 bits width in computer, while a fixed-point number can take less bit width, such as 16 bits, 8 bits, even 4 bits. So fixed-point numbers can save much more memory capacity and bandwidth resource when stored and transferred.

The representation range of floating-point numbers is narrow, while the representation precision is high. For example, a floating-point number can represent an arbitrary number in [−1.0, 1.0]. On the contrary, the representation range of fixed-point numbers is wide, while the representation precision is low. For example, a 16-bit fixed-point number can represent an integer number in [−32768, 32767], the representation precision is only one. So using shorter fixed-point numbers represent float-point ones will generate truncation error, leads to precision loss.

3.2   Q-Value of Fixed-Point Number

The Q-value is assigned by programmer to indicate the radix point position of a fixed-point number. With Q-value a fixed-point number can represent either an integer number or a decimal number. Table 1 lists 16 Q-values of 16-bit fixed-point number and the Decimal Range and the representation precision of each Q-value. Table 1 shows different Q-value represented fixed-point number has different Decimal Range and representation precision. When the Q-value is larger, the Decimal Range is smaller while the representation precision is higher. On the contrary, When the Q-value is smaller, the Decimal Range is larger while the representation precision is lower. So Decimal Range and representation precision is a pair of contradictions and a fixed-point

Table 1. Q-presentation of 16-bit fixed-point number

Q Presentation	Decimal Range	Precision
Q15	$-1 \leq X \leq 0.9999695$	$2-15$
Q14	$-2 \leq X \leq 1.9999390$	$2-14$
Q13	$-4 \leq X \leq 3.9998779$	$2-13$
Q12	$-8 \leq X \leq 7.9997559$	$2-12$
Q11	$-16 \leq X \leq 15.9995117$	$2-11$
Q10	$-32 \leq X \leq 31.9990234$	$2-10$
Q9	$-64 \leq X \leq 63.9980469$	$2-9$
Q8	$-128 \leq X \leq 127.9960938$	$2-8$
Q7	$-256 \leq X \leq 255.9921875$	$2-7$
Q6	$-512 \leq X \leq 511.9804375$	$2-6$
Q5	$-1024 \leq X \leq 1023.96875$	$2-5$
Q4	$-2048 \leq X \leq 2047.9375$	$2-4$
Q3	$-4096 \leq X \leq 4095.875$	$2-3$
Q2	$-8192 \leq X \leq 8191.75$	$2-2$
Q1	$-16384 \leq X \leq 16383.5$	$2-1$
Q0	$-32768 \leq X \leq 32767$	20

number representation must trade-off between them. The Q-presentation of other bit width, such as 8-bit and 4-bit, can be calculated from 16-bit Q-presentation.

The transformation between floating-point number and fixed-point number with Q-value shown in Eqs. 1 and 2 (16 bits):

$$x_q = (\text{int})x * 2^Q \tag{1}$$

$$x = (\text{float})x_q * 2^{-Q} \tag{2}$$

Where x_q is the fixed-point number, and x is represented floating-point number. For a certain fixed-point number, it's real floating-point value is function of bit width and Q-value, shown in Eq. 3:

$$V_{fixed} = f(l, Q) = \sum_{i=0}^{l-1} B_i \cdot 2^{-Q} \cdot 2^i \tag{3}$$

Where l is the bit width and B_i is the binary number at ith bit.

3.3   Computation Transformation

When a floating-point number transformed into a fixed-point number with certain length, the computation which participated in should be replaced by fixed-point computation. In real world hardware implementation, such as fixed-point DSP, FPGA and ASIC, the computation accomplished by fixed-point computation units. In this paper, we use C program simulation method to simulate fixed-point computation.

Figure 1 shows C program simulation of basic fixed-point computation. Figure 1(a) is fixed-point addition and subtraction simulation. Figure 1(b) is fixed-point multiplication simulation. Figure 1(c) is fixed-point division simulation. These simulations replaced floating-point computation by fixed-point computation.

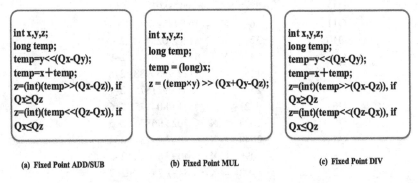

(a) Fixed Point ADD/SUB   (b) Fixed Point MUL   (c) Fixed Point DIV

Fig. 1. C program fixed-point computation simulation

For CNN, the computation of each layer is shown in Eq. 4:

$$Y = f(WX + b) \tag{4}$$

Where W is the weight matrix, b is the bias, f is the activation function, X is the input and Y is the output of the layer. These data are transform into fixed-point data with Q-value first, then the floating-point computations in Eq. 4 can be simulated by the fixed-point computation.

4 Dynamic Multi-precision Quantization

A shorter bit width is always wanted in fixed-point data quantization, because the shorter the data quantified, the less memory resources are required. But the shorter of the data, the truncation error will increase, leads to more accuracy loss. Most of previous works shorten the bit width directly, and use static fixed-point quantization strategy, which may be not effective for reducing truncation error and CNN accuracy loss when shorter bit width is adopted.

In this paper, we proposed a dynamic multi-precision fixed-point data quantization strategy and a data quantization workflow, to quantify the floating-point data in trained CNN inference process. Our strategy aims to improve the accuracy of overall CNN model when shorter bit width fixed-point data quantization is used.

4.1   Methodology

Fixed-point data quantization not only includes the quantization of data length, but also the quantization of data precision. Reducing the length of data bit width will generate larger truncation error, while improving data representation precision can reduce the error. Fixed-point data representation precision is determined by Q-value.

Unlike previous static-precision quantization strategies, in the proposed dynamic multi-precision fixed-point data quantization strategy, the Q-value of every fixed-point data transformed from floating-point data in trained CNN inference process, and every intermediate data participate in fixed-point computation which transform form floating-point computation, is dynamic for the whole CNN, including different layers and inner-layer. Every kind of fixed-point data is set to multi-precision, to minimize the truncation error of whole CNN. The method to dynamically analyze the optimal Q-value is in Eq. 5:

$$Q_d = \operatorname*{argmin}_{Q} \sum \left| V_{float} - V_{fixed}(L,Q) \right| \tag{5}$$

Where V_{float} is the float-point data value, $V_{fixed}(L,Q)$ is the fixed-point data represent value transformed by Eq. 3, By dynamically adjusting the Q-value to find the optimal Q_d, the truncation error of fixed-point data quantization can be minimized.

4.2   Quantization Workflow

The dynamic multi-precision fixed-point data quantization workflow is shown in Fig. 2, consists of three phases: the weight and bias quantization phase, interlayer input and output quantization phase, and inner-layer intermediate data quantization phase. When using the workload to search the optimal Q-value, the bit width of fixed-point data should be fixed to a certain length, such as 16/8/4-bit. The phases of workflow are introduced as follows.

The weight and bias quantization phase aims to find the optimal Q-value for weights and bias in each layer, as shown in Eqs. 6 and 7:

$$Q_d = \operatorname*{argmin}_{Q} \sum \left| W_{float} - W_{fixed}(L,Q) \right| \tag{6}$$

$$Q_d = \operatorname*{argmin}_{Q} \sum \left| b_{float} - b_{fixed}(L,Q) \right| \tag{7}$$

Where W_{float} and b_{float} is float-point weight and bias value respectively, while $W_{fixed}(L,Q)$ and $b_{fixed}(L,Q)$ is fixed-point weight and bias value respectively. In this phase, the dynamic range of weight and bias is analyzed first. Generally, weights and bias in CNN are trained in a certain numerical range. We initialize a low static Q-value for them to avoid data overflow, then we search for the optimal Q_d of each layer in the adjacent domains of the initial Q-value.

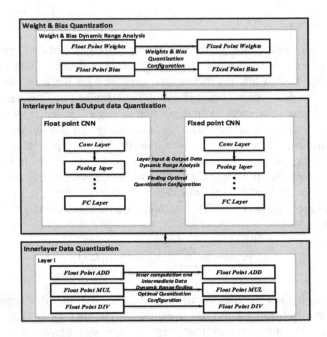

Fig. 2. Dynamic multi-precision data quantization workflow

Interlayer input and output quantization phase aims to find the optimal Q-value for input data of CNN and output feature maps of each layer, as shown in Eqs. 8 and 9:

$$Q_d = \operatorname*{argmin}_{Q} \sum \left| I_{float} - I_{fixed}(L, Q) \right| \tag{8}$$

$$Q_d = \operatorname*{argmin}_{Q} \sum \left| O_{float}^{l} - O_{fixed}^{l}(L, Q) \right| \tag{9}$$

Where I_{float} and O_{float} is float-point input value of CNN and output value of each layer respectively, while $I_{fixed}(L,Q)$ and $O_{fixed}^{l}(L,Q)$ is fixed-point input value of CNN and output value of each layer respectively. For CNN, the output of a layer is the input of the next layer. The input data of CNN is the Pixel data of images with certain numerical range, therefor can be quantified as the first phase. The relation of output and input data in each layer is defined in Eq. 4. So we can compute the theoretical dynamic range of output data layer by layer, then a greedy algorithm is used to search the optimal Q_d of output data.

After the first two data quantization phases, the fixed-point input data, weights and bias will be computed to run the fixed-point CNN model. The computation is defined in Eq. 4, and the fixed-point computation method is shown in Fig. 1. The inner-layer intermediate data in computation should be carefully quantified too. **The inner-layer intermediate data quantization phase** aims to find the optimal Q-value for inter-mediate data in each layer, as shown in Eq. 10:

$$Q_d = \operatorname*{argmin}_Q \sum \left| y_{float} - y_{fixed}(L, Q) \right| \tag{10}$$

Where y_{float} is the float-point value of intermediate data in a layer, while $y_{fixed}(l, Q)$ is the Fixed-point value. We can compute the theoretical dynamic range of intermediate data, such as AX and $AX + b$, by Eq. 3 with the quantified input data, weights and bias, and initialize a low static Q-value for them. Then a greedy algorithm is used to search the optimal Q_d of inner-layer intermediate data. Finally, the entire data quantization configuration is generated.

5   Evaluation

We explore different data quantization strategies with LeNet model on MNIST dataset. The results are shown in Table 2. The recognition accuracy is used as performance measure. We use the dynamic multi-precision(DMP) fixed-point data quantization to convert floating-point LeNet model to fix-point model, and experiment on different bit width, including 16-bit, 8-bit, and 4-bit. We arranged experiments on static fixed-point data quantization strategy as contrast set to compare the two strategies. All results are obtained under Tiny-CNN framework.

Table 2. Exploration on different data quantization strategies with CNN

Experiment	Exp1	Exp2	Exp3	Exp4	Exp5	Exp6	Exp7	Exp8	Exp9
Weights & Bias bits	Float	16	16	8	8	8	4	8/4	8/4
Input & Output data bits	Float	16	16	8	8	8	4	4	4
Intermediate data bits	Float	16	16	8	16	16	16	16	16
Weights & bias Precision	N/A	Q14	DMP	N/A	Q6	DMP	N/A	Q3	DMP
Input & Output data precision	N/A	Q14	DMP	N/A	Q6	DMP	N/A	Q6/Q3	DMP
Intermediate data precision	N/A	Q8	DMP	N/A	Q8	DMP	N/A	Q8	DMP
Accuracy	99.24%	96.59%	99.21%	N/A	96.18%	98.98%	N/A	77.21%	93.34%

[a]Weights & Bias bits "8/4" in Exp8 and Exp9 means 8-bit for weights and 4-bit for bias.
[b]N/A in Exp4 and Exp7 means "not available" when some data is quantified to 0.

In Table 2, Exp1 shows recognition accuracy is 99.24% when 32-bit floating-point data are used in trained LeNet model. We use floating-point CNN model as baseline and employ different fixed-point data quantization strategies on it. Exp2 and Exp3 use 16-bit data quantization, and employ static and dynamic multi-precision data quantization strategy respectively. The static Q-value (Q14, Q14 and Q8) chosen in Exp2 is theoretical analyzed and calculated by the different data range, and set to a low static value for them to avoid data overflow. Same method id applied to Exp5 and Exp8. Exp3 shows recognition accuracy is 99.21% when DMP strategy is employed, while only 96.59% accuracy is achieved by static strategy. We try to use 8-bit quantization for all data in Exp4 but the result is wrong for LeNet model, because some intermediate data are quantified to 0. Therefore, for LeNet model, intermediate data must be quantified to 16-bit. Exp6 shows recognition accuracy is 98.98% when DMP strategy is employed, while only 96.59% accuracy is achieved by static strategy in Exp5. We try to use 4-bit quantization for all data except intermediate data in Exp7 but the result is wrong for LeNet model, because some weights are quantified to 0. Therefore, for LeNet model, weights can be quantified to 8-bit at most. Exp9 shows recognition accuracy is 93.34% when DMP strategy is employed, while only 77.21% accuracy is achieved by static strategy in Exp8.

The comparison of dynamic multi-precision fixed-point data quantization strategy and static fixed-point data quantization is shown in Fig. 3. It shows that dynamic multi-precision strategy for is better than previous static quantization strategy, can reduce the accuracy loss from 22.2% to 5.9% at most, when 8/4-bit quantization is employed. When 16-bit quantization is used, only 0.03% accuracy loss is introduced by our dynamic multi-precision strategy with half of the memory capacity and bandwidth requirement comparing with 32-bit floating-point implementation.

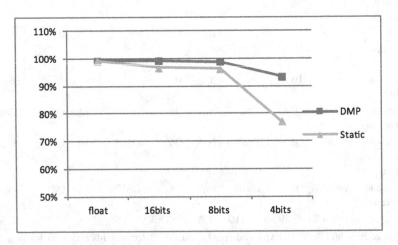

Fig. 3. Comparison of dynamic and static data quantization strategy

6   Conclusion

Although CNN inference process is computation intensive, the limited memory bandwidth is one of the bottlenecks of accelerating deep CNN models when implemented in embedded hardware. Fixed-point data quantization strategy is trade-off between the bit length of fixed-point numbers and the accuracy to relieve the memory bandwidth pressure. In this paper, we proposed a dynamic multi-precision fixed-point data quantization strategy for CNN based on comprehensive analysis of different data quantization strategies. Results shows that our quantization strategy for LeNet model is better than previous static quantization strategy, can reduce the accuracy loss from 22.2% to 5.9% at most, when 8/4-bit quantization is employed. When 16-bit quantization is used, only 0.03% accuracy loss is introduced by our quantization strategy with half memory footprint and bandwidth requirement comparing with 32-bit floating-point implementation. Our quantization strategy is also suitable for other CNN models.

References

1. Russakovsky, O., Deng, J., Su, H., Krause, J., Satheesh, S., Ma, S., Huang, Z., Karpathy, A., Khosla, A., Bernstein, M., Berg, A.C., Fei-Fei, L.: ImageNet large scale visual recognition challenge. Int. J. Comput. Vis. **115**, 211–252 (2015)
2. Krizhevsky, A., Sutskever, I., Hinton, G.E.: Imagenet classification with deep convolutional neural networks. In: NIPS, pp. 1097–1105 (2012)
3. Zeiler, M.D., Fergus, R.: Visualizing and understanding convolutional networks. In: Fleet, D., Pajdla, T., Schiele, B., Tuytelaars, T. (eds.) ECCV 2014, Part I. LNCS, vol. 8689, pp. 818–833. Springer, Heidelberg (2014)
4. Szegedy, C., Liu, W., Jia, Y., Sermanet, P., Reed, S., Anguelov, D., Erhan, D., Vanhoucke, V., Rabinovich, A.: Going deeper with convolutions. arXiv preprint arXiv:1409.4842 (2014)
5. He, K., Zhang, X., Ren, S., Sun, J.: Deep residual learning for image recognition. arXiv preprint arXiv:1512.03385 (2015)
6. Vanhoucke, V., Mao, M.Z.: Improving the speed of neural networks on CPUs. In: Deep Learning and Unsupervised Feature Learning Workshop NIPS (2011)
7. Chen, T., Du, Z., Sun, N., Wang, J., Wu, C., Chen, Y., Temam, O.: Diannao: a small-footprint high-throughput accelerator for ubiquitous machine-learning. In: ASPLOS, vol. 49, no. 4. ACM, pp. 269–284 (2014)
8. Chen, Y., Luo, T., Liu, S., Zhang, S., He, L., Wang, J., Li, L., Chen, T., Xu, Z., Sun, N., et al.: Dadiannao: a machine-learning supercomputer. In: MICRO. IEEE, pp. 609–622 (2014)
9. Qiu, J., Wang, J., Yao, S., et al.: Going deeper with embedded FPGA platform for convolutional neural network. In: ACM/SIGDA International Symposium on Field-Programmable Gate Arrays. ACM (2016)
10. LeCun, Y., Bottou, L., Bengio, Y., Haffner, P.: Gradient-based learning applied to document recognition. Proc. IEEE **86**(11), 2278–2324 (1998)

Computer Application and Software Optimization

Optimization of Two Bottleneck Programs in SAR System on GPGPU

Yang Zhang$^{(\boxtimes)}$, Zuocheng Xing, Cang Liu, Chuan Tang, Lirui Chen,
and Qinglin Wang

National Laboratory for Parallel and Distributed Processing,
National University of Defense Technology, Changsha, China
{zhangyang,zcxing,liucang,tc8831,chenlirui14}@nudt.edu.cn,
wangqinglin.thu@gmail.com

Abstract. The Synthetic Aperture Radar (SAR) system is a kind of modern high-resolution microwave imaging radar used in all-weather and all day long to provide remote sensing means and generate high resolution images of the land under illumination of radar beam. Unlike optical sensors, SAR algorithm needs a post-processing process on the data acquired to form the final image. In this article, we use the General Purpose Graphic Processing Units (GPGPU) to accelerate two of SAR algorithms, PGA (Phase Gradient Autofocus) and PDE (Partial Differential Equations), which are two computational intensive algorithms in the post-processing process for the system. Our work shows that the GPU architecture has different acceleration effects on the two algorithms. PGA can achieve an acceleration of 21.7% and PDE can get a speed up of 2.58× on GPGPU. We analyse the reasons for the results and conclude that GPU is a promising platform to accelerate the SAR system.

Keywords: SAR system · PGA · PDE · GPU · Acceleration

1 Introduction

Synthetic aperture radar (SAR) is a kind of modern high-resolution microwave imaging radar used in all-weather and all day long. It uses the principle of synthetic aperture, pulse compression technology and the method of signal processing. And make use of real aperture antenna to obtain distance and azimuth bidirectional high resolution remote sensing imaging. Unlike optical (Landsat) data, the SAR data requires extensive two-dimensional, space variant signal processing before an image is formed [1]. As we all know, it occupies an absolutely important position in imaging radars. With the widespread application of SAR, more attentions have been increasingly paid on its image post-processing technology because of its complicated process. In the SAR image post-processing, PGA algorithm and PDE algorithm are two key algorithms that are always the bottleneck operations. Our goal is to optimize the two algorithms and relieve the bottlenecks.

© Springer Nature Singapore Pte Ltd. 2016
W. Xu et al. (Eds.): NCCET 2016, CCIS 666, pp. 115–124, 2016.
DOI: 10.1007/978-981-10-3159-5_11

GPUs is well-known as its powerful computing capability and high energy efficiency. It is originally designed to exploit the concurrency inherent in graphics workloads. Now it has been widely used in high performance computing (HPC) platform as an accelerator [2–4]. As we known, it is featured with thousands of processors and few control units. For example, state-of-the-art Maxwell architecture has up to 3072 cuda cores and few megabytes on-chip memory [5]. The massive cores are used to tolerate long memory latency and to deliver high throughput.

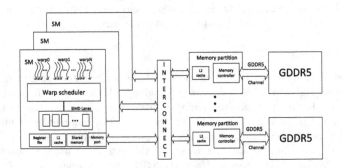

Fig. 1. Baseline architecture of our GPU.

The emerge of CUDA (Compute Unified Device Architecture) and OpenCL (Open Computing Language) programming models makes GPUs an easy platform for computing and boost its further development [6,7]. In CUDA, threads take a hierarchical structure, that is many threads are grouped into a thread block and several thread blocks constitute a thread grid. A large workload can be divided into several blocks which are further divided into a number of threads. A warp is made up of 32 threads and its threads execute in a lockstep style. Several warps are scheduled by warp scheduler for high performance. The memory also has a hierarchical structure, which includes on-chip memory such as register file, L1 cache, shared memory, L2 cache and off-chip memory such as global memory. Among them, global memory is a large but slow memory where data between different stream multi-processors (SM) can communicate and shared memory stores data which belong to the same thread block. Threads in a block run in an SIMT (Single Instruction Multiple Threads) manner and they can synchronize among themselves through barriers. Figure 1 is the baseline architecture of our GPU.

ArrayFire is a software platform which is developed by AccelerEyes for users and programmers to quickly develop data parallel programs in C, C++, Fortran, and Python [8]. ArrayFire provides simple high-level functions instead of low-level GPU APIs such as CUDA, OpenCL and OpenGL to allow scientists, sociologists and economists to take full advantage of the computation ability of GPU. Combined with friendly interface to users, automatic memory management, real-time compilation, parallel loop structure for GPU, and hardware-accelerated graphic library interface, ArrayFire becomes ideal for rapid parallel algorithm prototyping and end to end application establish. We use ArrayFire to accelerate PDE algorithm for noise reduction processing.

[1] has described the signal processing operations in a digital processor which has been built to produce images from the Seasat-A SAR data. [9] presents a new frequency scaling processing algorithm for spotlight SAR data processing. In [10], the two-dimensional exact transfer function (ETF) is calculated and range-variant phase corrections have been calculated in order to process many azimuth lines per block. [11] introduces a novel and efficient Synthetic Aperture Radar processor. The previous works mainly focus on the SAR algorithm itself. As a contrast, we put an emphasis on the simple implementation of SAR algorithm on GPU and the optimization of their performance.

The remainder of this paper is organized as follows: In Sect. 2, the CUDA programming model and arrayfire are described. Sect. 3 proposes the implementation of the two algorithms in GPU. The simulation result is presented in Sect. 4. Section 5 provides some conclusions.

2   CUDA Programming Model and Arrayfire

We use CUDA and arrayfire to optimize the programs. CUDA is a popular software model to develop applications for GPU and arrayfire is a new software which is based on CUDA to develop GPU program in an easier and faster way.

2.1   CUDA Programming Model

In 2007, Nvidia released the CUDA architecture [6]. Since then, CUDA is a mainstream of parallel programming model that is used by many fields in parallel computing. Because the majority of GPU resources are used for calculation and the execution pattern meets the SIMT model, it uses SIMT model for the development of highly parallel programs. CUDA makes GPU an easier and more powerful programming platform for parallel computing over CPU.

CUDA is a software programming model which allows programmers to exploit the parallel potential in GPU. It is a minimal extension to C and C++ and has few instructions but very fast execution. It adopts the single instruction multiple data mode. As Fig. 2 shows, kernels execute over a set of parallel threads and threads are organized in a hierarchy structure. Each block can have up to 3 dimensions and contains up to thousands of threads. Threads within one block can share the shared memory and synchronize. If the memory bandwidth is not enough, throughput will be limited by the memory copy process from CPU to GPU or vice versa. The fast on-chip resources such as registers, shared memory and constant memory can be used to reduce the off-chip memory access. Shared memory can store data on chip to reduce memory access time. By allowing data reuse between data blocks and reducing bank conflicts in shared memory, there will be less long-latency global memory accesses. In addition, there are two restrictions. Firstly, one block can only use the shared memory within one SM

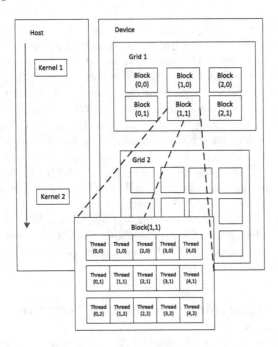

Fig. 2. CUDA programming model.

and shared memory can't be shared by blocks in different SMs. Secondly, the capacity of shared memory in each SM is limited and it is divided by multiple blocks. Thus, using excessive shared memory may reduce the number of concurrent blocks mapped onto one SM. Therefore, reasonable distribution of work over multiple cores to reduce long latency is a challenging work.

2.2 Arrayfire

Over the past decades, GPU has been more and more common over consumers and computer developers. Despite of the growing number of successful projects, the GPU software number increases slowly. That is mainly due to the difficulties in GPU programming. In the early times, the advent of CG, GLSL, HLSL and Brook stream programming marked the beginning of stream programming. They are the precursors of GPU programming. But the calculations of them need to be mapped to the graphics pipeline, which restricts their applications. After that, CUDA and OpenCL introduced a more general programmable software architecture which is easier than stream programming. However, even with these advances, it is still difficult for the average programmer to learn CUDA and OpenCL, because they are more difficult than the standard single-threaded C and C++ programming.

Some former companies are also trying to achieve this goal. One of the first such companies, Peak-Stream, has built a C/C++ runtime library functions to provide GPU developers with a rich set of tools. RapidMind has developed a flexible intermediate layer to support a variety of front-end languages and back-end hardware. These are attempts to bridge the gap between hardware and software developers. ArrayFire is the newest development platform for GPU in an attempt to bridge this gap and transplant high-level functions to the bottom hardware. Our goal is to provide more programmability and portability for the program without sacrificing performance.

3 Implementation

To accelerate the two algorithms, we need to make use of the inherent parallelism and the different memory architecture in GPU. The parallelism in GPU is a kind of lightweight parallelism and it can be assigned by programmer. When a loop is encountered in the program, we can explicitly dispatch threads as many as possible to execute the loop concurrently. For the memory part, we mainly use two kinds of memories those are the shared memory and the global memory. Global memory is persistent across kernel launches by the same application. Data stored in the global memory is also the only way to perform data exchange between different SMs. For comparison, shared memory has much higher bandwidth and much lower latency than global memory. Programmer can directly allocate the capacity of shared memory in one SM. It can be shared by multiple threads in one block but not between multiple blocks because the life time of shared memory is as long as the block's.

3.1 PGA

We use Matlab program to finish pre-simulation and acquire the results of the two algorithms. In order to carry out GPU acceleration, we first make an appropriate conversion from Matlab program to C language program. Since Matlab is a more abstract high-level language, its invoked libraries can not be reused in CUDA. So to make the programs more efficient, we rewrite and add several functions in C language from the Matlab library functions. In this process, we ensure functional coherence between C programs and Matlab programs, while maintaining the programs' correctness through the conversion. The redesigned functions in PGA are as follows.

- Calculation functions: variance computation cov(), averaging computation mean(), circulate and shift computation circshift_real(), and the sort of array.
- Transform functions: fast Fourier transformation and fast inverse-Fourier transformation.
- Fitting functions: binomial curve fitting.

   We revise and optimize the C implementation of PGA and make sure the correctness and the high efficiency. The optimization process is as follows.

- We isolate the functions which have many computations and are easy to parallel for acceleration on GPU.

- We set up local and global variable carefully. To reduce data transmission of kernel functions, we take local variable as much as possible.
- Taking the effect of computer architecture to the program's efficiency into consideration, we optimize time locality and space locality to enhance IPC (Instruction Per Cycle).

We put the optimized C programs onto GPU to make full use of its powerful computing capability and efficient storage characteristics. The CUDA code first makes a serial execution on the host CPU side. When encountering the kernel function, the code will be loaded onto the GPU for execution. By specifying the amount of threads and blocks in the kernel, we can parallelize the data process explicitly. When the kernel is finished, the data will be copied from GPU to the CPU side, where the serial execution continues. Therefore, the placement method of data and the parallelism optimization are particularly important. So we take the following steps to finish the GPU implementation.

- We migrate the C language program without parallelism directly to Nvidia's CUDA programming platform to make the program run on the CPU-GPU heterogeneous platforms, following CUDA programming syntax rules and various API interfaces. In this way, this part of program still runs on the CPU and the cost of data movement between CPU and GPU is reduced.
- When conducting fast Fourier transform, a one-dimensional plan, namely cufftHandle plan, is created, followed by a Fourier transform cufftExecC2C. CUFFT_FORWARD, as a function parameter, shows the Fourier transform is performed, while CUFFT_INVERSE indicates an inverse Fourier transform is performed.
- Use the multi-threaded feature of GPU to accelerate Fourier transform parts in the program.
- Use a variety of memory hierarchy, such as global memory, shared memory and etc., to reduce data access time and optimize memory access efficiency.

We have attempted to put all functions (the whole PGA program) into the GPU for execution. However we find the execution efficiency is low. That is because the program flow is too complicated and the too many functions with a number of parameters further complicate the program. Since each function call and access to local variables involves function stack operation, so it is easy to cause stack overflow. Although the algorithm has some parallelism, i.e., the image data can be processed in parallel blocks, in the realization of the program, we find because this process is a complex serial procedure and each block contains a number of function calls, the algorithm's parallel process is not very suitable for the GPU's lightweight thread feature.

Since we can not put all the functions in GPU, we adopt a compromise approach to place the most complex computational process, FFT and IFFT transformation, onto GPU for acceleration. Each time the algorithm needs FFT and IFFT transformation, data are moved from CPU to GPU through cudaMemcpy() and it calls the cufft library for transformation. After the calculation is completed, the results are moved from GPU to CPU by cudaMemcpy() to take the next step of the calculation. The whole process is illustrated as Fig. 3.

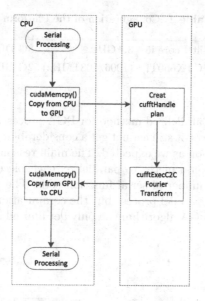

Fig. 3. Execution process of PGA.

3.2 PDE

To accelerate PDE, we use open source software to accelerate the critical parts in it. PDE contains input matrix transformation and regularization, multiple iterations of arithmetic operations and two-dimensional convolution calculation. Since the input matrix transformation, regularization and the matrix operation are not the bottlenecks, and to avoid the redundant overhead of data transfer between CPU and GPU, these operations are carried out in CPU. Two-dimensional convolution operation takes a long time and is done several iterations, so we put it to the GPU to accelerate its process and reduce latency.

Arrayfire comes with library functions to optimize two-dimensional convolution operation. First, we need to call the header file of arrayfire.h. After the procedure calls the function of convolve2(), the underlying functions will finish the copy of data to the GPU and the two-dimensional convolution operation. The convolution process includes the development of parallelism and the optimization of storage. After the calculation is completed, the results will be passed to the CPU for the following index calculation, multiplication and division.

4 Throughput Performance and Analysis

We take an image of 16k * 4k as the input of PGA and compare the results before and after acceleration. The CPU and GPU configurations are in Table 1 and the two platforms' performance are comparable. The results show that the time spent in GPU is 48.345 s, in contrast to 58.84 s on CPU. GPU can get 21.7% improvement over the CPU implementation.

Table 1. Configuration of the Platform

CPU	Intel core i5	3.4 GHz	8G DDR4
GPU	(GTX660Ti)	(1006/1084 MHz)	2G GDDR5

Although we take parallelized method for PGA processing and get good performance with less efforts, it still cannot get a considerable speed-up ratio beyond the serial implementation as we expected. The main reason is that, although the entire program has several pieces to parallelize, each piece is a complex procedure that contains a number of serial function calls. The program data can be divided into pieces for parallel process but the computational process is hard to parallelize. Therefore PGA algorithm can only get limited improvement (Fig. 4).

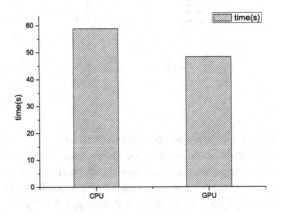

Fig. 4. The acceleration effect of PGA on GPU.

However we can get further improvement through the following method. One solution is to optimize the image processing algorithm to reduce the number of function calls, making it more suitable for GPU's characteristics. Another solution is to use other platforms for acceleration, such as MIC, which has more control logic to handle complex procedures (Fig. 5).

The input data of PDE is an image of 12k * 4k and it runs on a computer with a configuration as Table 1 shows. The running results of PDE program show that the time spent on CPU is 49.21 s, while the time spent on GPU is 19.072 s. We can achieve an acceleration of 2.58×.

It can be seen that, since the two-dimensional convolution has high parallelism inherently, we can take the parallel method to get the desired speed-up ratio. The main reason is that the algorithm itself has a high degree of parallelism, and each thread has a relatively simple calculation process. Meanwhile, there are no bottleneck operations and critical paths. This massive parallelism is suitable for parallel processing, and this also makes the optimization of on-chip

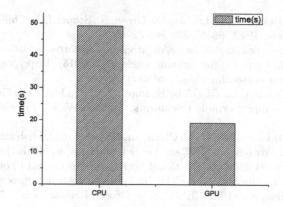

Fig. 5. The acceleration effect of PDE on GPU.

data storage possible. Thus PDE algorithm is very suitable for the acceleration on GPU platform.

5   Conclusion

In this article, we use the General Purpose Graphic Processing Units (GPGPU) to accelerate two of SAR algorithms, PGA and PDE, which are two bottleneck algorithms in the post-processing process for the system. We first inspect the characteristics of the two algorithms, those are their computing process, the parallelism of the algorithms and the memory access patterns. Then, we take distinct methods to accelerate the two algorithms. One way is to use CUDA library functions to simplify the process and to optimize the throughput of PGA, the second way is to use open source software to accelerate the critical parts of PDE. The two methods adapt to different characteristics of the two algorithms and both achieve good performance. So our work show that GPU is a promising accelerator for the SAR system. Our next work is to put the whole SAR system on GPU and to achieve better performance.

Acknowledgments. This work is supported by National Science Foundation of China (Grant No. 61170083, 61373032) and Specialized Research Fund for the Doctoral Program of Higher Education (Grant No. 20114307110001).

References

1. Cumming, I.C., Bennett, J.R.: Digital processing of SEASAT SAR data. In: IEEE International Conference on Acoustics, Speech, and Signal Processing, ICASSP 1979, vol. 4. IEEE, pp. 710–718 (1979)
2. http://www.top.500.org
3. http://www.green500.org

4. Owens, J.D., Houston, M., Luebke, D., Green, S., Stone, J.E., Phillips, J.C.: GPU computing. Proc. IEEE **96**(5), 879–899 (2008)
5. http://www.geforce.com/hardware/desktop-gpus/geforce-gtx-titan-x
6. Nvidia: Nvidia Cuda C programming guide v7.5 (2015). http://developer.nvidia.com/nvidia-gpu-computing-documentation
7. Sanders, J., Kandrot, E.: CUDA by Example: An Introduction to General-Purpose GPU Programming, Portable Documents. Addison-Wesley Professional, Reading (2010)
8. Malcolm, J., Yalamanchili, P., McClanahan, C., Venugopalakrishnan, V., Patel, K., Melonakos, J., Arrayfire: a GPU acceleration platform. In: SPIE Defense, Security, and Sensing, p. 84 030A. International Society for Optics and Photonics (2012)
9. Mittermayer, J., Moreira, A., Loffeld, O.: Spotlight SAR data processing using the frequency scaling algorithm. IEEE Trans. Geosci. Remote Sens. **37**(5), 2198–2214 (1999)
10. Eldhuset, K.: A new fourth-order processing algorithm for spaceborne SAR. IEEE Trans. Aerosp. Electron. Syst. **34**(3), 824–835 (1998)
11. Liu, B., Wang, K., Liu, X., Yu, W.: An efficient SAR processor based on GPU via CUDA. In: 2nd International Congress on Image and Signal Processing, CISP 2009, pp. 1–5. IEEE (2009)

A Channel-Level RAID5 Schema Based Physical Address in SSD

Ya Feng[✉], Yuxuan Xing, Nong Xiao, and Fang Liu

State Key Laboratory of High Performance Computing,
Department of Computer Science, National University of Defense Technology,
Changsha, People's Republic of China
fengya1991@gmail.com

Abstract. Flash-based solid state disks (SSDs) have been widely used for its high performance, low power, and concurrency features. With the increase in storage capacity, the reliability problem of SSD is becoming increasingly serious. In this paper, we implemented a technique based SSDs by constructing RAID-5 to enhance the reliability of SSD while maintaining its performance. First, we construct RAID-5 stripe based on SSD physical address which means no mapping tables to store stripe information. Second, our schema constructs dynamic stripe with log-structure to solve the inherent small write problem associated with conventional RAID-5. Third, since the correlation between data stripe, we realize garbage collection based on stripe group. Finally, we conduct extensive simulations using real-world traces and synthetic benchmarks in the SSDsim [1]. The experimental results show that we consume less than 7% of the performance and 6% of the storage consumption of SSD to achieve inner-channel RAID-5 to improve the reliability of SSD.

Keywords: Solid state disk · Redundant array of independence disk · Concurrency · Garbage collection

1 Introduction

Solid-state drivers (SSD) has a high-performance, low-power, high concurrency, and small physical size advantages based on NAND flash. To promote the further development of the SSD, manufacturers push each cell to store more bits to increase flash capacity and decrease the unit price of SSD. Following a single cell storing two bits (Multiple-Level Cell, MLC) technology is mature, flash memory products with a single cell storing three bits (Triple-Level Cell, TLC) began to appear [2]. Unfortunately, both products have significant side effects on flash endurance and reliability compared to the typical SLC (Single-Level Cell). For example, a typical SLC can tolerate 100 k P/E (program/erase) cycles, whereas MLC and TLC flash memories suffer from low endurance limits of less than 10,000 P/E cycles and 2,500 P/E cycles, respectively. This in turn exacerbates the issue of reliability in flash based products as the bit error rate (BER) is strongly correlated to the wear down of P/E cycles.

In order to ensure reliability, traditional SSD record an error correction code (ECC) in out-of-band (OOB). ECC adds extra parity bits to ensure data reliability, commonly

© Springer Nature Singapore Pte Ltd. 2016
W. Xu et al. (Eds.): NCCET 2016, CCIS 666, pp. 125–135, 2016.
DOI: 10.1007/978-981-10-3159-5_12

used the Hamming code and BCH. However, ECC has some intrinsic limitations. First, with the increase of SSD capacity, we need to add more extra ECC parity bits to ensure the reliability of SSD, and greater reliability brings more OOB ECC memory overhead and computation overhead. Next, context, page-level, block-level, and chip-level errors cannot be corrected. Hence, to address the limitations of ECC, redundant array of independent disks (RAID) has been developed in SSD. The internal structure of an SSD exhibits a hierarchical architecture. Parallelism between channels and chips provides the technical support to implement RAID into a single SSD.

In this paper, we realized a technique for providing RAID in SSD at channel level. RAID-5 technology is widely used, mainly because RAID-5 both full takes advantage of parallelism to improve performance, but also ensures data reliability through redundancy. RAID5 technology is based on the characteristics of the disk, although you can use without modification on the SSD, there are huge difference between disk and SSD on the internal structure, working principle, access method and so on. The main problem with RAID-5 is that any stripe data update will cause a corresponding parity update. Thus, the number of P/E cycles of flash memory increase rapidly and the lifespan of SSD can be shorten. To resolve the aforementioned problem, we use a dynamic RAID5 stripe based on log-structure, according to the order of the write request arrives to construct stripe. This could effectively alleviate the small write problem, and can take full advantage of SSD internal parallelism to improve read and write performance. Furthermore, the technique, which makes stripe group based on physical address, both saves memory space and speeds up the addressing. Through experiments with the SSDsim, we tested the performance of SSD with RAID-5 and analyzed the space consumption.

The reminder of the paper is organized as follows. In the next section, we discuss background and related works. Section 3 describes the design details. Section 4 evaluates and simulates the proposed scheme and Sect. 5 concludes this paper.

2   Background and Related Works

2.1   SSD Basics

Flash-based solid state disks (SSDs) have been widely used for its high performance, low power, concurrency features. SSD is a Flash chip package, providing the same access with disk interfaces. There are parallel structures in SSD. An SSD consists of multiple channels, which has a separate memory controller. Each memory controller connected to one or multiple chips. Each chips has several dies, which has its own internal read/write signal line. Each die is composed of multiple planes. Each plane consists of one or two registers and multiple blocks while each block have more than one page. Page is the smallest unit of SSD to read and write, and block is the smallest unit to erase. The natural rich internal parallelism of SSDs is the most important factors that contribute to the high performance. Yimo Du [3] raised Dual-page mode to extend the parallelism beyond plane level, exploring the parallelism among pages within a block.

SSD has three features: page-level to read and write, block-level to erase; out-of-place update; limited life. If there is no free space to write to, a cleaning operation, called garbage collection, is invoked, which migrates valid data to other space and erase invalid block. Wear-leveling strategy write data to flash evenly, so that all of flash P/E cycles is similar. In order to hide the difference between SSD and traditional disk, SSD controller implemented Flash Translation Layer (FTL). FTL mainly achieves address mapping, garbage collection and wear leveling.

2.2   RAID in SSD

Making full use of the internal parallelism in SSD can improve its performance. RAID-5 improves data reliability by redundancy, while improving performance by reading and writing in parallel. RAID-5 can trade-off between data reliability and performance, which makes RAID-5 widely used.

There are three ways to write for RAID-5:

- Full-stripe write. Making full use of parallelism to write stripe data makes no extra read and write operations. It is the most effective type of writing.
- Reconstruction write. New parity data is calculated by new data and unmodified data of stripe.
- Read-modify write. New parity data is calculated by new data, old parity data and modified data of stripe.

Obviously, data updates in RAID-5 could cause additional write overhead except full-stripe write mode, which results in performance loss.

Traditional RAID technology mainly designed for disk, without considering the characteristics of SSD. Therefore, it is difficult to take the advantages of SSDs. SSD is quite different with disk on the internal structure, working principle, access method and so on. Here are the details:

- Disks have higher performance for sequential read and write than random read and write while no significant performance for SSDs.
- Internal disk can only operate in order, while SSD does concurrently.
- SSD tolerates a limited P/E (program/erase) cycles. Bit error rates of SSD rapidly increase as the P/E cycles of flash memory progress. Bit error rates of traditional disks are not known to be correlated with the age of a disk.
- Disks do fixed point update. SSDs with non-point update generate invalid data after the update and make garbage collection. But copy of valid data will generate the write amplification effect when garbage collection.

As describe above, we need to take the characteristics of SSD into consideration when use RAID-5 technology in SSD.

2.3   Motivation

Traditional RAID-5 array constructed as shown in Fig. 1. Take five channel as an example, Stripe 0 consists of pages D0–D3 and P0, while stripe 1 consists of pages D4–D7 and P1.

Any error page can be restored by other data of stripe. The stripe map table in the controller holds the information about location or stripe. Assume data pages D1 through D4 are updated. Since the non-point update, the updated data is written to a new location which is on the same chip of the old data. Then using read-modify-write or reconstruct-write to calculate and write parity. The last step is to update stripe map table.

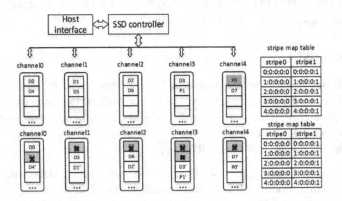

Fig. 1. Internal implementation of conventional RAID-5 in SSD

The most obvious drawback is that both read-modify-write and reconstruct-write brings extra write and read overhead which results in performance degradation and SSD life consumption. Furthermore, frequently updating parity leads to more loss where the chip parity belongs to and eventually lead to more garbage collection. All of these will reduce the SSD life.

Im Soojun [4] considered parity update overhead in RAID-5 structure for flash memory chips, proposed partial parity update method for updating parity by directly read updating data in buffer to calculate and being written to the buffer. It is possible to reduce the read operation of the update process as there are no need to read the original data in the flash memories.

Lee Sehwan [5] focused on the problem that P/E cycles of flash memory decrease as the density increased, while BER increases as the P/E cycles increased. They present a life-span reliability scheme, which dynamically managed the size of striping group to cope with the increasing error rates of flash memory as the number of P/E cycles increased.

Yu Wang [6] proposed a new data redundancy architecture called CR5M (Channel-Raid5 with Mirroring), which utilized hidden mirror chips to accelerate the performance of small writes. For small updates, different from the normal operation of data updates, CR5M only writes new data to data chip and mirror chip, which protects new data with a copy, maintaining the original stripe unchanged.

Xiaoquan Wu [7] proposed RAID-Aware SSD (RA-SSD) that could distinguish user data from parity by detecting the different access patterns from the upper RAID layer, and store them separately at different flash blocks. RA-SSD could effectively reduce the overhead of garbage collection.

3 Design and Implementation

Considering characteristics of SSD, we realized RAID-5 scheme based on the physical address of the channel-level on SSD. We mainly discuss from the viewpoint of data layout and garbage collection.

3.1 Data Layout of SSD

Controller of SSD achieves RAID-5 algorithm to complete data layout. It has the following characteristics:

- Construct RAID-5 stripe based on the physical address. Unlike traditional RAID-5 based on logical address, stripe number and stripe data is determined by the physical address.
- Form a channel-level RAID-5 with page granularity. That is, each stripe is composed of all pages with same physical address numbers in different channels.
- Constructs dynamic stripe with log-structure. We use a dynamic RAID-5 stripe based on log-structure, according to the order of the write request arrives to construct stripe. Furthermore, we append data to add or modify.

Take Fig. 2 as an example. A stripe consists of pages in the different channels which has same physical address, namely same PPN. In Fig. 2, stripe 0 is composed of D0–D3 and P0, while stripe 1 consists of D4–D7 and P1. As data is modified, the SSD controller simply writes data into flash as the order of write request arrives, then calculates parity and write to exactly location. After writing, the controller marks the old pages as obsolete. As shown in Fig. 2, the update data D1′–D4′ construct a new stripe, then controller calculates and write P2 into flash memory. This process does not generate additional overhead to read and write, and can solve the traditional RAID5 write amplification problems, improve the SSD performance, and increase the life of SSD.

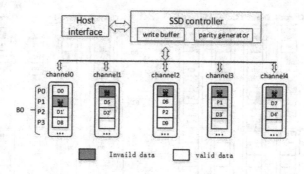

Fig. 2. Data layout of RAID-5

Furthermore, all chips are written to evenly no matter where hot data store. RAID-5 technology based on log-structure solves SSD wear imbalance which caused by frequently updating, and ultimately avoids the impact due to garbage collection.

When considering the number of write data is insufficient to form a complete band, as shown in Fig. 2, if only two page data reach at a certain time, in order to protect the data, they are directly written to the flash with log structure according to the order to arrive, while stored in buffer of SSD, waiting for more data to be written. When enough data reach, we form a complete stripe immediately, then calculate and write the parity. If the failure happens before a stripe completes, SSD controller simply read with the last stripe data after back to normal.

Firstly, the above data writing method by implementing RAID5 policy in channel-level, combines the ECC and RAID to significantly improve reliability of SSD. Next, the log-structured stripe solves effectively alleviate the small write problem, and can take full advantage of SSD internal parallelism to improve read and write performance. Finally, the technique, which makes stripe group based on physical address, both saves memory space and speeds up the addressing.

3.2 Garbage Collection

SSDs take non-point update. Updated data is written to other free pages, then the SSD controller marks the old data invalid, and finally updates FTL mapping table to complete the update. If there is no free space to write to, a cleaning operation is invoked to make free space. Because of SSD page-level for read and write, block-level for erase, SSD controller chooses the block with least valid data to migrate its valid data to other free space, then erase the block. After erasing, the block is free. In this paper, taking into account the relevance of RAID-5 stripe data, we take the global garbage collection to cleaning all the blocks in the same stripe.

The cleaning process has following features:

- Take all the blocks in same stripe as cleaning unit. As shown in Fig. 3(a), a GCG (Garbage Collection Group) is composed of physical blocks are all of the same block number, which is decided by the properties of SSD and RAID-5 stripe.

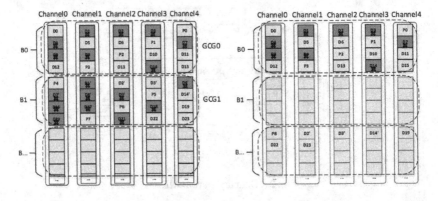

Fig. 3. Garbage Collection of SSD with RAID-5

- Global garbage collection policy. There are 256 different priority queues in memory of SSD, and every GCG mounted on one queue in accordance with the number of free block. Choose the GCG in high priority queue to be cleaning object.
- Valid data migrated by cleaning process is constructed RAID-5 stripe with log-structure.
- Only data pages are copied, the parity pages are not.

In Fig. 3, the cleaning process selects GCG1 in high priority GC queue as the victim object. Then the valid data is migrated into the SSD controller DRAM. Note here that parity pages do not migrate as valid data. In our example, only D2′, D3′, D14′, D19, D22, D23 migrate and among them D2′, D3′, D14′ and D19 form a stripe and with them, a new parity page, P8 is calculated and stored in channel 0. The last remaining valid pages store as log-structure and wait for arrival of write request. As shown in Fig. 3(b), after cleaning process, D22 and D23 store at next stripe.

4 Evaluation

For evaluation, we implemented RAID-5 data layout and garbage collection scheme on the SSD simulator. SSDsim is an event-driven, modularly structured, and highly accurate simulator for SSD which was developed by Huazhong University of Science and Technology [1, 8]. We extend the SSDsim by modifying several function modules including trace file pre-processor, read request processing module, write request processing module, mapping table, allocation algorithm, and garbage collection to support channel-level RAID-5.

Table 1 presents the simulation parameters where 10% of the SSD is utilized as over-provisioned space for cleaning operation. To compare the difference in performance, we implemented RAID-5 and RAID0 on the SSD respectively. We also compare the different numbers of channel on the RAID-5, respectively as shown in Table 2 because of the more channels, the better performance. In order to evaluate the performance of pure SSD, we chose four real-world traces and a benchmark. Table 3 describes the four traces and their characteristics [9–11].

Table 1. The Fixed Experiment Parameters

Parameters	Values
Page read	20 μs
Block write	200 μs
Block erase	1.5 ms
Transfer one byte	25 ns
Page size	2 KB
Pages per block	64
Blocks per plane	2048
Planes per die	4
Dies per chip	4
Chips per channel	1

Table 2. The Varied Experiment Parameters

Conf.	RAID0	RAID5	RAID5
SSD1	16	16	17
SSD2	8	8	9

Table 3. The Characteristics of traces

Trace name	Write ratio	Ave. size (KB)
Financil1	85%	2.32
Financil2	15%	2.89
Postmark	90%	4270
Iozone	100%	150

4.1 Real-World Workloads

Figures 4 and 5 show the performance in term of mean response time in SSD1, SSD2 configure. The y-axis denotes the mean response time of read/write. It is apparent that average response time of read operations (KB/MS) of Financil1 and Financil2 are significantly more than Postmark and Iozone, as shown in Fig. 4. The reason is that the former includes many random small write, while the latter includes huge sequential writes. Considering the characteristics, small write bring more garbage collections to reduce performance. Furthermore, Financil2 outperforms to Financil1. This is due to the fact that Financil1 has more write operation than Financil2 and write operation may cause garbage collection, which result in worse read and write performance.

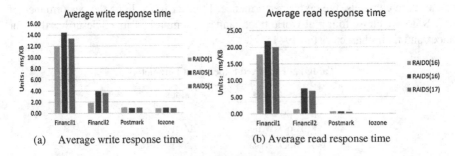

(a)   Average write response time   (b) Average read response time

Fig. 4. Performance on SSD1

For write performance of RAID-0 and RAID-5, RAID0, which does not handle parity, offers the best performance. And RAID-5 with more channels, surpasses RAID-5 with less. The reason is that RAID-0 holds no redundancy, and data is written directly

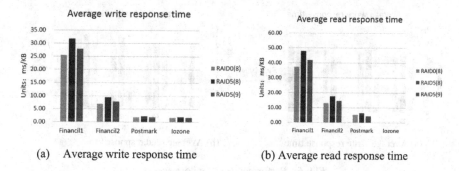

(a)   Average write response time   (b) Average read response time

Fig. 5. Performance on SSD2

to parallelization. On the contrary, RAID-5 with less channels holds parity to ensure data reliability, resulting in lower parallelism. RAID5 with 17 channels equalized RAID-0 and RAID-5, the performance is somewhere in between. In Fig. 5, RAID-5 with 16 channels decrease 20.4% average write performance and 26.8% average read performance compared with RAID-0. And RAID-5 with 17 channels decrease 5.8% average write performance and 7.3% average read performance. Similar to the simulation results with SSD2 configuration.

Therefore, RAID-5 technology in SSD results in a slight performance degradation and storage overhead increase. However, RAID-5 provides higher reliability compared to RAID-0. Equations 1 and 2 describe the reliability for RAID-0 and RAID-5. For example, assuming that the reliability of single SSD is 90%, the reliability of RAID-0 with configuration SSD1 is 18.5%, and the reliability of RAID-5 with same configuration is 51.5%. Thus, it is increased 2.78 times for RAID-5 than RAID-0. The similar calculation to configuration SSD2, we concluded that the reliability of RAID-5 was increased 1.89 times than RAID-0.

$$R_{RAIDSET} = \prod_{i=1}^{n} (R_{SSD_i}) \tag{1}$$

$$R_{RAID-5} = n \times (1 - R_{SSD}) \times R_{SSD}^{(n-1)} + R_{SSD} \tag{2}$$

4.2 Synthetic Workloads

In order to better evaluate the performance, a set of synthetic workload is also used. As shown in Figs. 6 and 7, evaluations take place under different write ratio. Figure 6 shows the performance of a random read and write workload, write ratio were 20%, 40%, 60%, 80%, the average request size of the request 4 KB. By comparing the results, RAID-5 with write ratio at 80% has the minimum gap for the performance compared with RAID-0. For example, RAID-5 with 17 channels is 7.3% lower than RAID-0, and RAID-5 with 16 channels is 15.6% lower than RAID-0.

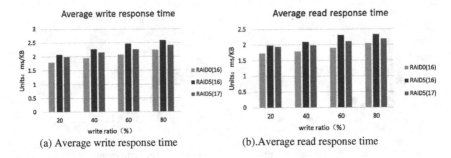

(a) Average write response time   (b).Average read response time

Fig. 6. Performance of random access

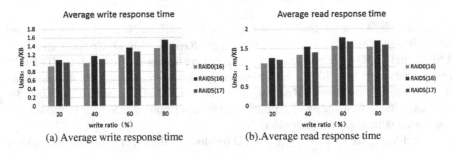

(a) Average write response time   (b).Average read response time

Fig. 7. Performance of sequential access

Figure 7 presents performance of sequential read and write workloads and write ratio were 20%, 40%, 60%, 80%. Similar to the simulation results with Fig. 6, RAID5 write ratio at 80% has the minimum gap for the performance compared with RAID-0. RAID5 with 17 channels is 6.6% lower, and RAID5 with 16 channels is 14% lower.

From Figs. 6 and 7, RAID-5 technology supporting SSD is more suitable for write-intensive applications. Meanwhile sequential access performance is better than random access for SSD.

4.3   Garbage Collection Overhead

In the SSD inside, RAID-5 improves SSD reliability by writing additional parity data which consumes storage space and reduces performance. However, parity data is not copied and migrated as valid data, there is little effect during garbage collection.

5   Conclusion

In this paper, we implemented a RAID-5 technique supporting SSDs by constructing stripe at channel-level to enhance the reliability of SSD. For SSD performance degradation and life consumption caused by frequently parity updating, we realize RAID-5 based physical address and constructed stripes with log-structure. Furthermore, taking into account the relevance of RAID-5 stripe data, we take GCG as cleaning unit to make garbage collection. Experimental results showed that we consume less than 7% of the performance degradation and 6% of the storage consumption to realize RAID-5 technology which greatly improves the reliability of SSD. There are still many issues that need to be looked into more closely. For example, constructing stripe based on physical address makes flash memory wear out at similar time. As a result, RAID arrays supporting SSDs are subject to correlated failures, which can't ensure the reliability of SSD. We are currently looking into this question.

Acknowledgments.   We are grateful to our anonymous reviewers for their suggestions to improve this paper. This work is supported by the National High-Tech Research and Development Projects (863) and the National Natural Science Foundation of China under Grant Nos. 2015AA015305, 61232003, 61332003, 61202121.

References

1. Hu, Y., Jiang, H., Feng, D., Tian, L., Luo, H., Zhang, S.: Performance impact and interplay of SSD parallelism through advanced commands, allocation strategy and data granularity. In: Proceedings of International Conference on Supercomputing (ICS), pp. 96–107 (2011)
2. Cai, Y., Erich, F.H., Onur, M., and Ken, M.: Error-patterns in MLC NAND flash memory: measurement, characterization, and analysis. In: IEEE DATE (2012)
3. Du, Y., Zhang, Y., Xiao, N.: Dual-page: exploring parallelism in MLC flash SSDs. In: Proceedings of the 6th IEEE International Workshop on Multicore and Multithreaded Architectures and Algorithms (M2A2), Paris. IEEE (2014)
4. Soojun, I., Shin, D.: Flash-aware RAID techniques for dependable and high performance flash memory SSD. IEEE Trans. Comput. **60**(1), 80–92 (2011)
5. Lee, S., Lee, B., Koh, K., Bahn, H.: A lifespan-aware reliability scheme for RAID-based flash storage. In: Proceedings of the 2011 ACM Symposium on Applied Computing, Taichung, pp. 374–379. ACM (2011)
6. Wang, Y., Wang, W., Xie, T., Pan, W., Gao, Y., Ouyang, Y.: CR5M: a mirroring-powered channel-RAID5 architecture for an SSD. In: Proceeding of Mass Storage Systems and Technologies, Santa Clara, pp. 1–10. IEEE (2014)
7. Wu, X., Xiao, N., Liu, F., Chen, Z., Du, Y., Xing, Y.: RAID-aware SSD: improving the write performance and lifespan of SSD in SSD-based RAID-5 system. In: 2014 IEEE Fourth International Conference on Big Data and Cloud Computing (BdCloud). IEEE (2014)
8. Hu, Y., Jiang, H., Feng, D., Tian, L., Luo, H., Ren, C.: Exploring and exploiting the multi-level parallelism inside SSDs for improved performance and endurance. IEEE Trans. Comput. **62**(6), 1141–1155 (2013)
9. IOzone: IOzone Filesystem Benchmark [EB/OL], 10 Dec 2014. http://www.iozone.org
10. Postmark: FreshPorts–benchmarks/postmark [EB/OL], 10 Dec 2014. http://www.freshports.org/benchmarks/postmark
11. Laboratory for Advanced System Software: 10 Dec 2014. http://traces.cs.umass.edu/index.php/Storage/Storage

Unification Protection Design for a Certain Type of Vehicle-Borne Server

Chengkuan Sun[✉], Jianping Cai, Wanli Sha, and Shangyong Liang

The Computer Department, Jiangsu Automation Research Institute,
Lianyungang, China
sck@foxmail.com,
{caijianping,shawanli,liangshangyong}@jari.cn

Abstract. The vehicle-borne environment has great influence to vehicle-borne server when it is in normal operation. In this paper, the vehicle-borne server is taken many ways to keep work normally when it is in the vehicle-borne environment such as anti-vibration design, thermal design, electromagnetic compatibility design, noise reduction design and so on. In each of the design, the methods and main structure diagram are given in this paper. A type of vehicle-borne server products is developed successfully according to this unification protection design methods. The vehicle-borne server is taken many environmental tests to make sure that it can work responsibly.

Keywords: Reinforcement server · Comprehensive protection · Automotive environment · The secondary reinforcement

1 Introduction

Currently, the vehicle-borne equipment demand for high availability of computer is becoming stronger. More data centers are deployed on vehicle-borne equipment. The vehicle-borne server products with high stability, powerful data handling capacity and many other advantages have been recognized by more and more users, vehicle-borne type server products will get greater development in the near future. At this stage, a variety of the commercial server product meets the operational needs of various industries, but for the vehicle-borne environment vehicle-borne server product is not rich. The server products which can be able to work in the vehicle-borne environment must overcome the strong vibration, which should have sufficient strength and rigidity [1]. When the vehicle-borne server's structure could not overcome the fatigue caused by mechanical force effectively, its reliability cannot be guaranteed. In addition, structure resonance will have an impact on the electrical performance of the vehicle-borne-mounted server too. In the moment, performance of computer hardware are getting more powerful, server products which are developed specifically will take long period, high cost and high risk. And therefore, the secondary reinforcement of commercial server meets the industry needs.

In the United States military equipment, the boundary between military and civilian technology is becoming more and more obscured. The concept of COTS (Commercial Off-the-shelf) that is so-called commercial reinforcement is widely used on various

© Springer Nature Singapore Pte Ltd. 2016
W. Xu et al. (Eds.): NCCET 2016, CCIS 666, pp. 136–148, 2016.
DOI: 10.1007/978-981-10-3159-5_13

products. In this article, the reinforced server is designed according this concept. To reinforce the weak link of mature commercial product so as to satisfy the specific environment and then get high-performance products is more and more popular in vehicle-borne industry. Further strengthening of the commercial product not only can save the cost of equipment research, reduce risk and shorten time, but also for companies to develop more advanced information technology products. In commercial server, the connection among the motherboards, optical drives, hard drives and other components are rigid. In vehicle-borne environment, the strong vibrations may cause poor contact and damage to the components. There is a gap between commercial servers and the vehicle-borne server in two aspects such as the chassis thermal performance and compatibility. Therefore, a commercial server consolidation, so that it can adapt to the harsh environment of strong, is an important topic in the automotive equipment field.

2 Chassis Structure and Composition

The stability of the server is an important factor to judge its overall performance. The vibration resistance performance is one of the main indicators to measure electronic equipment [2]. Therefore, the design of the vibration resistance for the server is an important part. In the vehicle-borne environment, the force on the server is varied, in which the most harmful ones to the device are vibration and shock. The failure of the electronic equipment may be caused by vibration and shock. The mainly reason is that there is no effective anti-vibration, mitigation measures and isolation systems formed in product design. In engineering, the vibration is usually divided into active and passive vibration isolation for different vibration sources. When the machine or the equipment is vibration source, active vibration isolation is that the machine or the equipment will be isolated from the support base to reduce the impact to its foundation. As we known, passive vibration is that the vibration source is from the underlying movement, measures will be taken to isolate the equipment and foundation in order to reduce the impact on the device [3]. In this design, the vehicle-borne server will be fixed in the vehicle-borne cabinet, and thus passive vibration isolation mode will be taken.

As shown in Fig. 1, this type of vehicle-borne server is made up by chassis and core components. All of the core components are supplied by commercial suppliers. The main chassis is made of frames, front panel, and rear panel and rail components. There are two frames in the frame called within frame and outer frame. Front panel and rear panel are fixed by screws to outer frame. To ensure the tightness between the panel and the frame, all the contacts between them are installed with conductive seal. The left and right sides of the front panel is provided with a handle for easy mobility. Two rails are fitted on both sides of the chassis's housing. The connection between the rail and the housing is rigid by screws. In order to facilitate debugging and maintenance, a debugging door is obligated on left of the front panel. There are all so many conductive seals between the debugging door and the front panel. High reliability connectors are fitted on rear panel connectors. This type connector has a strong performance on anti-shock and vibration, anti-electromagnetic interference shielding. Circular vents are opened on front and rear panel of the chassis. The internal fans forced convection in the

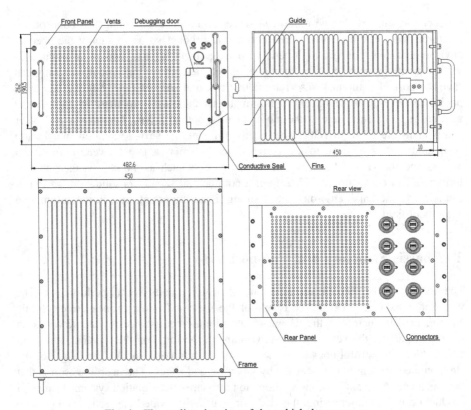

Fig. 1. The outline drawing of the vehicle-borne server

chassis, and the air can through the vents from front panel to rear panel. Heat dissipation inside the chassis is very effective.

3   Anti-vibration Design

3.1   Within Framework Design

The vehicle-borne server which is designed in this article is fitted in automotive cabinet. The installation of the vehicle-borne server in the cabinet is limited. It cannot be installed on the outer surface of the chassis with damper spring. In the conventional design, more screws are required to fit the motherboard to improve the rigidity. In this way the vibration resistance of the motherboard is strengthened. A two-layer framework combined with new design ideas is proposed in this paper shown in Fig. 2. A within framework is designed in the interior of the housing which is fitted inside of the chassis shell by rope spring shock absorber. In this design, the rope spring shock absorber is called GG series which is made of multiple strands of stainless steel wire ropes. The main advantage of this type damper is simple structure, good environmental adaptability, able to adapt to corrosion, high temperature and so on. Vibrations can be reduced or absorbed by reasonable arrangement of shock absorber. Within framework is molded by vacuum brazing in aluminum integrally. All of the positioning mounting holes are designed with reference to the original commercial motherboard. In this way, the motherboard can be installed as well as usually do. Within framework and the motherboard are connected rigidly by screws and then they become a complete unit. Within framework avoid the motherboard from uneven stress which can cause component failure, thereby improve the reliability of components on the motherboard. Relative to others, CD drive components inside of the vehicle-borne server are more sensitive to vibration. A shock absorber called plate series is fitted under the CD drive components. This type of shock absorber has a compact shape, which can improve the anti-vibration, impact resistance of electronic modules effectively.

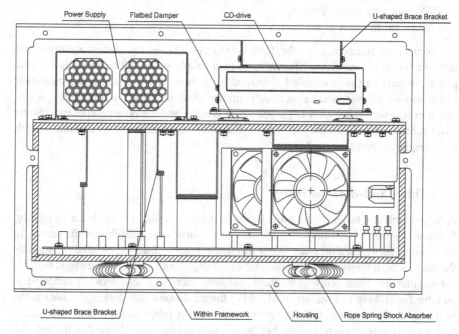

Fig. 2. Internal structure of server (front panel removed)

3.2   The Design of U-Shaped Brace Bracket

As can be seen from Fig. 2, get rid of the motherboard, the internal structure of the server to the board is also equipped with the system core components such as fans, graphics cards, network cards, serial cards. These core components are installed in the form of cantilever structure. Among all the boundary conditions, cantilever structure has the worst mechanical stability. The mechanics of materials tell us, the end of the cantilever structure generate maximum deflection as follows:

$$w_B = -\frac{Fl^3}{3EI} \tag{1}$$

A simply supported beam which pressure point is in the central the maximum deflection generated as follows:

$$w_B = -\frac{Fl^3}{48EI} \tag{2}$$

Wherein: F–force (N);
L–rod length (m);
E–Young's modulus (Pa);
I–sectional moment of inertia (m^4)

Comparing apparent from the formula (1) and (2), in the same conditions, the deformation of the cantilever beam is more than simply supported beam 16 times. This paper presents an easily installed U-shaped brace bracket which can make cantilever beam into simply supported structure. Thinking about the actual assimilability, a certain gap is reserved between U-shaped brace bracket and the core components. Some foam rubber is filled into the gap. The U-shaped brace brackets made of stainless steel, lightweight construction, and practical.

3.3   Other Anti-vibration Design

A large number of fasteners are fitted inside of the server. The correct choice of locking fasteners measures has a major significance to the structural reliability of the server. In this design many measures are taken to ensure reliable fastener installation such as thread locking adhesive, double nuts, and locknuts. Thread locking adhesive is suitable for countersink head screws. Medium and low strength thread locking adhesive is suitable for locking and sealing of M2–M12 thread. Double nuts locking manner is the best way in large space. On the assembly process requires using a pair of standard locking nuts to increase reliability, but the relevant studies have shown that the use of a thin and a thick nut locking way to has got the better performance. Installation is that a thin nut is fitted in the inside and a thick nut is on the outside. First with a predetermined tightening torque of 80% to install thin nut, and then change tightening torque to 100%, using this installation measures can get a better anti-loosening effect. Locknut is widely used in the narrow space. Locknut is different from normal nut what using a special process embeds a block of plastic permanently in the end. A greater reaction has generated when the plastic is extruded in tightening process. It has greatly enhanced friction between the internal and external threads and provided greater resistance, and thus play a role in anti-loose in the vibration.

4 Thermal Design

Rational structure is the most important element to guarantee cooling performance for the electronics. In order to determine the best method for cooling electronics, the structure of electronic products should be considered in the total power consumption of the chassis, heat distribution, thermal sensitivity, thermal environment and other factors. It should be designed the best way for heat consumption, especially for high-density assembly equipment. Research shows that the components on PCB have very strict requirements for temperature, such as the IC pin element requires less than 125 °C and CASE temperature requirements is less than 85 °C. The quickly way to export heat outside of the chassis is the key to this thermal design. Both the whole structure design and material selection will be elaborated in this paper.

4.1 Machine Design

The chassis is made of outside and within framework. Both of them are molded by vacuum brazing in aluminum integrally. On the one hand this way can improve the overall chassis anti-vibration characteristics, on the other hand is can reduce the thermal resistance to improve the thermal efficiency. The fundamental task for thermal design is to transfer heat quickly to the outside world when the components are in normal work. Radiation and convection are widely used cooling methods. The heat inside of the chassis can transmit to the plate of the outside framework by radiation and convection, the chassis's heat transmit in the same way to the surrounding air. The server designed in this paper is not fully sealed structure [4]. A fan is equipped inside of the chassis to transmit heat. The thermal design from the following two aspects: on the one hand to improve the internal heat transfer capability of components, such as the installation of the fan to improve the heat exchange capacity; on the other hand increase the heat transfer capacity of the outwardly housing, such as an external heat exchange fins processing, as shown in Fig. 1. The forms of fins are shown in Fig. 3. Fin structure may

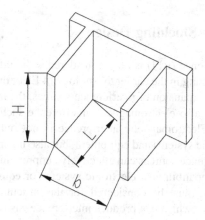

Fig. 3. Spacing between the fins

increase the structural strength, reduce weight, and increase the heat exchange area to the around air. For example, the total heat of chassis is 30 W when the ambient temperature is 50 °C if it has fins on the surface of the outside framework, high as 5 mm, thickness as 2 mm, the gap of 6 mm fins, its surface temperature can be reduced 1.6 °C.

The height and the spacing of the fins according to the following equation:

$$b = 1.5 \left(\frac{Hv^2}{\beta \Delta t Pr} \right)^{\frac{1}{4}}$$

(3)

Wherein: b–fin pitch (m);
H–Fin height (m);
v–Kinematic viscosity (m^2/s);
β–fluid expansion coefficient (1/°C);
Δt–Difference between fin temperature and ambient temperature (°C);
Pr–Prandtl number (dimensionless).

4.2 Material Selection

The server machine is made of rust-proof aluminum which Chinese Standard number is 3A21. It has such characteristics:

(1) Light weight, a density is 2900 kg/m^3;
(2) Good thermal conductivity, thermal conductivity is 204 W/(m·k), its thermal conductivity is only less than silver, copper, gold;
(3) Conductive properties, beneficial electromagnetic shielding;
(4) It has strong corrosion resistance because its surface can generate a protective film made of Al_2O_3 or $Al_2O_3 \cdot H_2O$ in air;
(5) It has high-precision milling properties so it is easy to solve the problem of electromagnetic compatibility in the gap.

5 Electromagnetic Shielding Design

Radio frequency interference (RFI) is only considered to be influenced by radio communication and broadcasting in the earlier technology of Electromagnetic Compatibility [5]. With the increasing expansion of interference sources, the interference is no longer limited to radiation, but also electromagnetic interference such as the inductive, coupling and conduction. Electromagnetic interference is not only affecting the normal operation of the electronic systems and equipment, but also having the impact on human health. To shield interference sources can effectively suppress interference and improve the electromagnetic compatibility of electronic systems or equipment, it is one of the important measures that must be considered for the structural design of electronic equipment [6]. The places which can produce interference easily such as the seams, the panel cut, power switches requires special attention in the design process.

5.1   Processing of Siding and Panel Seams

The seam on the body cavity is the main channel for electromagnetic leakage. On the project, the commonly used method is to fit conductive seal in the joints between panels and walls. Conductive seal is a widely used polymer materials in the field of EMC. Conductive seal is embedded into the groove on the wall. In the design of wall and panel which is designed to ruggedness forms will help to extend the depth of the joints, which increase shielding effectiveness [7]. The form of structure is shown in Fig. 4.

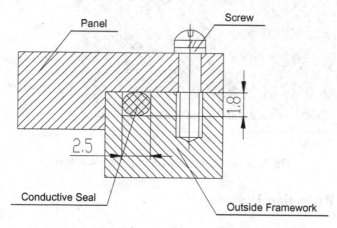

Fig. 4. A schematic diagram of joint processing

5.2   The Installation of the Connector

External data processing of the server must pass a certain number of cables and connectors. Some gap cannot be avoided because the installation of the electrical connector. In addition, the contact resistance between electrical connectors and housings is relatively large and the shield cable common mode conducted emissions increases, in order to prevent excessive radiation when the connector is installed which is equipped with conductive rubber pad [8]. Torque wrench is used to exert greater pressure on the conductive rubber pad and the connectors so that to achieve the desired results. In particular, a great galvanic corrosion will produce when the conductive rubber pad is fitted on surfaces of aluminum and magnesium. A conductive rubber pad with silver epoxy paint coating is the best choice to weaken galvanic corrosion.

5.3   Treatment for Vents of Front and Rear Panel

Effective heat dissipation and electromagnetic shielding is very important to stable operation of server system. Good thermal systems requirements the system as open as possible which is reversed to electromagnetic compatibility. There is a contradiction in the chassis design. Electromagnetic energy leakage through the ventilation holes is one important reason for the decline of shielding effectiveness. Some metal meshes are usually covered on ventilation holes in order to achieve the desired effect of shielding effectiveness while heat dissipating property is unaffected. A conductive oxide treated aluminum grid network is chosen to cover the ventilation holes. An aluminum plate is used to pin the grid network by a reasonable number of screws. A typical application is shown in Fig. 5.

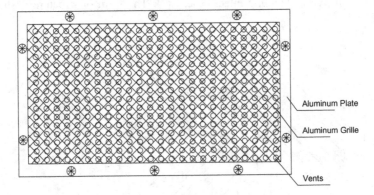

Fig. 5. A schematic diagram of grille installation

6   Noise Reduction Design

Server is installed in the vehicle-borne cabinet, taking into account the overall noise requirements, units must be designed to reduce noise. The server's main noise source is the axial fans. Studies have shown that compared to mechanical noise and air noise, the airborne noise is the major source of axial fans [9]. On view of the mechanism of noise generation point that the most effective solutions are designed muffler on the noise propagation path and selection small noise index axial fans [10]. Considering heat and noise requirements, the axial fans should provide enough air flow and produce less noise. On the side, a muffler box which is made of aluminum foam can be put on the propagation path of noise. Foam aluminum is a lightweight functional material with high porosity, generally 60% to 95%. The surface of aluminum foam is almost non-existent plane which can generate sound reflection, and therefore, when the acoustic wave propagates into the material surface the acoustic wave is diffused, and thus the noise is absorbed. Cutting the aluminum foam to appropriate size, and then arrange them uniformly at spare locations inside of the server. A foam aluminum acoustic box is set between the wall and the aluminum foam acoustic panels. The structure is shown in Fig. 6. The gap between the aluminum foam acoustic panels and the wall is about 30–60 mm. With the increase of the thickness of the gap, the absorption tank absorbs lower and lower frequency sound waves. The noise test results show that the noise can be absorbed by acoustic aluminum foam box. The better box is made of aluminum foam which porosity is 88.1%. The box's maximum sound absorption coefficient is about 0.42 in the sound wave frequency of 1000–2000 Hz caused by the axial fan.

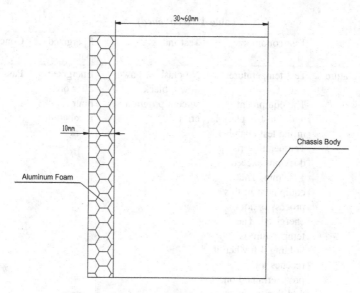

30~60mm

10mm

Chassis Body

Aluminum Foam

Fig. 6. Aluminum foam sound absorbing box

7   Environmental Test

To verify whether the design is satisfied to the standards, many tests are executed such as vibration test, low temperature test, high temperature test, electromagnetic compatibility tests and noise test. All the tests are executed in environment test center. The test conditions are in accordance with the requirements which are required by the user (Table 1).

Table 1.   Test record sheet

Projects	Test conditions	Test index	Energized state	Conclusion
Vibration Test	Vibration exposure middleweight meets People's Republic of China national military standards: GJB150.16-86 "military equipment environmental test methods - vibration test" road transport environmental requirements [5]. Vibration time: 1 h.	1. No structural damage 2. No loose fasteners or missing	Without	Pass

(continued)

Table 1. (*continued*)

Projects	Test conditions	Test index	Energized state	Conclusion
Low temperature test	Test temperature: −10 °C The equipment under test is placed in the test chamber. Temperature rising does not exceed 1 °C/min. The equipment in this process is not energized. The temperature is holding 4 h when it reaches a predetermined one and then gives the equipment power to run 1 h [5].	No crashes, power down, black screen, program error	Energized after one hour incubation work	Pass
High temperature test	Test temperature: +45 °C The equipment under test is placed in the test chamber. Temperature rising does not exceed 1 °C/min. The equipment in this process is not energized. The temperature is holding 4 h when it reaches a predetermined one and then give the equipment power to run 1 h [5].	No crashes, power down, black screen, program error	Energized after one hour incubation work	Pass

(*continued*)

Table 1. (*continued*)

Projects	Test conditions	Test index	Energized state	Conclusion
Electromagnetic compatibility tests	1. In the boot of the state to test CE102, RE102 2. In the boot of the state to test CS101, CS114–116, PS103	Meet the requirement in "People's Republic of China national military standards NO: GJB151A-97 military equipment and subsystems electromagnetic emission and susceptibility requirements"	Energized	Pass
Noise detection	In the boot of the state to test the equipment under test. The test point 1 m away before, after, left, right, above the equipment. The average noise is mean of the five test point [10]	The average noise is less than 53 dB	Energized	Pass

The tests results show that this type vehicle-borne sever is satisfied with the requirements of the user. It can work stably and reliably in the user's application environment.

8   Conclusion

This article describes a comprehensive protection design method of vehicle-borne servers. Using this idea to design vehicle-borne server can meet the requirement which has good performance on vibration, thermal, electromagnetic compatibility and noise. But the structural design in this problem involves many aspects. Each of the above directions is worth to study individually, so as to promote the continuous improvement of our design level. With the improvement of people's data exchange capabilities required in vehicle-borne environments, these vehicle-borne server products will be applied more widely. In the design phase to effectively design comprehensive protection is an important means to improve the reliability of the products.

References

1. Qiu, C., Zhao, S., Jiang, Q.: Electronic Device Structure Design Principles. Southeast University Press, Nanjing (2007)
2. Hu, T.: Vibration analysis and design for servers. Master degree thesis, University of Electronic Science and Technology (2011)
3. Hu, L.: Thermal design for reinforced computer. Mod. Electron. Techn. **16**(2), 85–90 (2009)
4. Xiang, F.: Thermal analysis and design for military electronics chassis. Master Thesis of Xi'an Technological University (2008)
5. People's Republic of China National Military Standards, GJB/Z299B-99, Handbook of reliability design for electronic equipment, Beijing, the General Armament Department Military Standard Publishing Unit (1999)
6. Jin, M., Ma, W.: Power converters EMI analysis including IGBT nonlinear switching transient model. IEEE Trans. Ind. Electron. **53**(5), 1577–1583 (2006)
7. Yuan, L.: The structure and defense design of a portable reinforcement machine. Mod. Manuf. Eng. **36**(7), 123–125 (2012)
8. Sun, C.: Design of warship control system environment protection and EMC. Marine Electric Electron. Eng. **30**(5), 53–56 (2010)
9. Hu, R.: Discussion on noise reduction method of axial flow fan. Fluid Mach. **25**(12), 31–33 (1997)
10. Huan, D.: Basic Theory of Acoustics. Nanjing University Press (2001)

Monaural Speech Separation on Many Integrated Core Architecture

Wang He[1]([✉]), Xu Weixia[1], Guan Naiyang[2], and Yang Canqun[2]

[1] Institute of Computers, College of Computer,
National University of Defence Technology, Changsha 410073, Hunan, China
kuubun@163.com
[2] Institute of Software, College of Computer,
National University of Defence Technology, Changsha 410073, Hunan, China

Abstract. Monaural speech separation is a challenging problem in practical audio analysis applications. Non-negative matrix factorization (NMF) is one of the most effective methods to solve this problem because it can learn meaningful features from a speech dataset in a supervised manner. Recently, a semi-supervised method, i.e., transductive NMF (TNMF), has shown great power to separate speeches from different individuals by incorporating both training and testing data in learning the dictionary. However, both NMF-based and TNMF-based monaural speech separation approaches have high computational complexity, and prohibit them from real-time processing. In this paper, we implement TNMF-based monaural speech separation on many integrated core (MIC) architecture to meet the requirement of real-time speech separation. This approach conducts parallelism based on the OpenMP technology, and performs the computing intensitive matrix manipulations on a MIC coprocessor. The experimental results confirm the efficiency of our implementation of monaural speech separation on MIC architecture.

Keywords: Monaural speech separation · Intel many integrated core architecture · Non-negative matrix factorization

1 Introduction

Speech separation plays an important role in many practical applications, e.g., noise reduction and speech recognition [1,2], singing voice separation [3,4], etc. Monaural speech separation aims to recover the source speeches from a single channel signal, which makes this problem even more challengeable. Traditional methods include non-negative matrix factorization (NMF) [5–7] and deep neural network (DNN) [8,9].

NMF is a linear model with non-negativity constraint incorporated. Before applying NMF to speech separation problem, the signals should be transformed to frequency-domain. The operation is based on the matrix constructed with modulus of the frequency-domain speech signals. In the training stage, NMF based speech separation first learns phonemic features on the training speech

© Springer Nature Singapore Pte Ltd. 2016
W. Xu et al. (Eds.): NCCET 2016, CCIS 666, pp. 149–156, 2016.
DOI: 10.1007/978-981-10-3159-5_14

signals, and these phonemic features take the form of spectral bases. Then in the testing stage, after learning the test mixture speech signals, the speeches of each speaker can be recovered according to the spectral bases. Another widely used technique to speech separation is DNN, which is a nonlinear model. DNN constructs deep neural networks to learn features of speech signals and has shown its efficiency in many practical tasks [10–12].

In particular, both NMF-based methods and DNN-based methods improve the separation accuracy significantly, but the computational complexities increases quickly with the increase of data. So it is difficult to apply these methods to real-time speech separation, as real-time speech separation requires the feedback time as short as possible. One useful method to solve this problem is to make use of accelerators to implement these algorithms. Nowadays, various accelerators developed quickly, including Intel MIC coprocessor [13,14] and general purpose computation on graphics processing units (GPGPU) [15,16], etc. With the help of accelerators, high parallel computations can be accelerated easily. Previous work on accelerating NMF include using graphics processing units (GPUs) to accelerate NMF [17,18], and parallel version of NMF on multicore architecture [19]. In order to meet the requirement of real-time speech separation applications, this paper proposes to implement the most effective monaural speech separation method called transductive NMF (TNMF) on Intel Many Integrated Core (MIC) architecture to reduce the execution time. As traditional NMF methods cannot utilize the training data when learning features, Guan et al. [20] proposed a semi-supervised variation of NMF, i.e., TNMF, to perform monaural speech separation. The MIC-based algorithm greatly accelerates the TNMF-based monaural speech separation with the help of Intel MIC coprocessor. Experiments on TIMIT dataset confirm its efficiency.

The remainder of the paper is organized as follows. Section 2 introduces related work, including speech separation with NMF and the Intel Many Integrated Core architecture. Section 3 introduces how to use MIC to accelerate NMF based monaural speech separation and Sect. 4 shows the experimental results. In Sect. 5, we conclude the paper.

2   Background

2.1   Monaural Speech Separation with NMF

Assuming $V \in R_+^{m \times n}$ is a non-negative matrix, NMF aims to find non-negative approximation of V, i.e.,

$$V \approx W \times H. \tag{1}$$

where $W \in R_+^{m \times r}$ and $H \in R_+^{r \times n}$, and r is usually smaller than m and n.

In particular, W and H can be optimized by solving the following problem:

$$\min_{W \geq 0, H \geq 0} ||V - WH||_F^2, \tag{2}$$

where $||\cdot||_F$ denotes the Frobenius norm. The objective function of this optimization problem measures the divergence between V and WH. As NMF incorporates non-negativity constraints over factor matrices, when applied to speech separation tasks, the original speech signals should be transformed from time-domain to frequency-domain, as time-domain signals has negative entries. The transformation can be implemented by using short-time Fourier transform (STFT).

Assuming we have p speakers and their corresponding speeches, let $V_k \in R_+^{m \times n_k}$ denote the matrix constructed with modulus of frequency-domain signal of k-th speaker. In order to conduct speech separation, we use NMF to factorize each V_k independently in the training stage, i.e.,

$$V_k \approx W_k H_k, \tag{3}$$

where $W_k \in R_+^{m \times r}$ denotes the learned phonemic features of k-th speaker, namely spectral bases, and $H_k \in R_+^{r \times n}$ denotes the activations corresponding to W_k. Let $V^m \in R_+^{m \times n}$ denotes the matrix constructed with modulus of frequency-domain mixture signals.. In testing stage, we should decompose V^m with NMF as follows:

$$V^m \approx W^m H^m, \tag{4}$$

where $W^m = [W_1, \cdots, W_p]$ is constructed by the spectral bases of corresponding speakers, $H^m \in R_+^{rp \times n}$ denotes the obtained activations. To separate the mixture speech signal, we should decompose H^m into $H^m = [H_1^{mT}, \cdots, H_p^{mT}]^T$ according to W^m. So the separated speech is

$$V_k^m \approx W_k H_k^m. \tag{5}$$

However, the NMF algorithms based on objective function (2) cannot utilize mixture signals in the training stage. To solve this problem and to improve the accuracy, a semi-supervised algorithm called transductive non-negative matrix factorization (TNMF) was presented [20]. The objective function of TNMF is

$$\min_{\forall 1 \leq k \leq p, W_k \geq 0, H_k \geq 0, H^m \geq 0} \{ \sum_{k=1}^{p} ||V_k - W_k H_k||_F^2 + \lambda ||V^m - W^m H^m||_F^2 \}. \tag{6}$$

where λ is the trade-off parameter to balance the influence of two parts of the objective function.

The TNMF model can be solved by using the multiplicative update rule (MUR) [20, 21] as follows:

$$W_k \leftarrow W_k \cdot \frac{V_k H_k^T + \lambda V^m H_k^{mT}}{W_k H_k H_k^T + \lambda W^m H^m H_k^{mT}}, \tag{7}$$

$$H_k \leftarrow H_k \cdot \frac{W_k^T V_k}{W_k^T W_k H_k}, \tag{8}$$

$$H^m \leftarrow H^m \cdot \frac{W^{mT} V^m}{W^{mT} W^m H^m}. \tag{9}$$

Based on the obtained solution, i.e., W_k, H_k and H^m, we can easily separate the mixture speech according to [20].

2.2   Intel Many Integrated Core Architecture

The Intel many integrated core (MIC) architecture aims to accelerate highly parallel and computationally intensive programs. The Intel Xeon Phi coprocessor based on the Intel MIC architecture consists of 61 cores. Each core has two level caches, includes a 32 KB L1 data cache and L1 instruction cache, and a 512 KB private L2 cache. And the Intel Xeon phi coprocessor also has a 512 bits vector processor unit (VPU) with Single Instruction Multiple Data (SIMD) architecture [22]. An important advantage of Intel MIC architecture is its compatibility with original programs, which makes it easy for developers to accelerate their programs. The Intel coprocessor is supported by a variety of numerous libraries, compilers and tuning tools, etc.

To utilize the Intel Xeon Phi coprocessor, we have both the offload mode and the native mode. The machine executes main program on the processor and offloads the selected sections to coprocessor in offload mode. The program is executed in both processor and coprocessor locally in native mode. The offload mode can further be divided into two modes, namely pragma offload mode and shared virtual memory model mode.

3   Parallel TNMF Algorithm for MIC Architecture

This paper pays attention to the TNMF-based monaural speech separation algorithm. To accelerate the TNMF-based algorithm, the main work is to parallel the matrix manipulation in Eqs. (7) to (9). In practical, we use Intel math kernel library (MKL) [24] to perform the matrix manipulation. MKL has rich functions and can compute the operations with high-efficiency.

We use OpenMP technology to perform the parallel operations on multicores. The data needed in the algorithm are constructed as matrix, so we can utilize the computational ability of coprocessor's VPU. **Algorithm 1** summarizes the MIC-based monaural speech separation algorithm.

Algorithm 1. MIC-based monaural speech separation algorithm

Input   : Training speech signals S_1 and S_2,
             Testing mixture speech signal S^m
Output: Recovered speech signals S_1^m and S_2^m
1 Transform the original speech signals from time-domain to frequency-domain, and get the signals' modulus:V_1,V_2,V^m
2 Offload V_1, V_2, V^m from CPU to coprocessor
3 Update W_k, H_k and H^m until converge with TNMF algorithm's update rules
4 Offload W_k, H_k and H^m from coprocessor to CPU
5 Compute the recovered signals: $V_k^m \approx W_k H_k^m$
6 Recover the signals to time-domain speech signals, obtain S_1^m and S_2^m.

The input of this algorithm is speech signals of training speeches and testing mixture speech. The first step of the algorithm is to transform the signals from time-domain to frequency-domain by STFT. Then we can get the modulus of transformed signals, as V_1, V_2 and V^m. To accelerate the computation, we offload the matrices to coprocessor, and update them in coprocessor. MKL has two offload modes, including automatic and compiler assisted. We use compiler assisted mode here to offload the data to coprocessor automatically. When the update stage finished, the obtained matrice W_k, H_k and H^m will be offloaded to CPU. The magnitude spectrogram of each recovered speech can be obtained by $V_k^m \approx W_k H_k^m$. Then we can easily get the time-domain signals of the recovered signals.

4 Experiments

To verify the performance of the accelerated algorithm, we compare the execution time between MIC-based monaural speech separation algorithm and original non-accelerated one. The dataset utilized in this experiment is the TIMIT dataset [23]. We randomly choose some speech segments from two speakers. The testing speech signal is generated by summing two segments from different speakers. Another two segments from the corresponding two speakers are chosen as the training data. The training speech segments is about 23 s long and the testing speech segments is about 3 s long. These speech segments are all sampled at a rate of 16 kHz. In experiments, the FFT size in all examples is set to 1024, the trade-off parameter λ is set to 0.1. All the experiment results are averages of 10 replications.

Figure 1 gives the original speech signals, which generate the testing speech segments, and the recovered speech signals by MIC-based monaural speech separation. The first row shows the time-domain signals, while the second row shows the frequency-domain signals. In particular, column (a) and column (c) represent the same speech signal while column (b) and column (c) represent the same speech signal. The original speech signals are listed in column (a) and (b) while the recovered speech signals are listed in column (c) and (d).

To verify the computational efficiency of MIC-based algorithm and the original non-accelerated one, we compare the execution time between the two algorithms in different parameters. In experiments, two parameters have significant influence on execution time, which are spectral bases number and iteration number. When spectral bases number increases, we can learn the features of speech signals more accurately, and when the iteration number increases, the decomposition result will be more accurate. Meanwhile, the computational complexity increases along with the increase of the two parameters. We set the spectral bases numbers and iteration number to different values respectively, and record the execution time of MIC-based algorithm and original algorithm. In MIC-based algorithm, the thread number is set to 8. In experiments, when the spectral bases number was set to different values, the iteration number is set to 1000. When the iteration number was set to different values, the spectral bases number is set to 120. Figure 2 presents the results.

It is obvious that MIC-based algorithm costs much less execution time. And more importantly, when the computational complexity increases, the execution

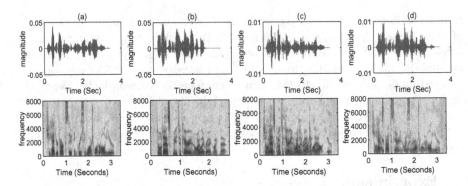

Fig. 1. The top and bottom rows represent time-domain and frequency-domain signals. Column (a) and (b) represent original signals, column (c) and (d) represent recovered signals. Columns (a) and (c) represent the same speech signals while column (b) and (d) represent the same speech signals.

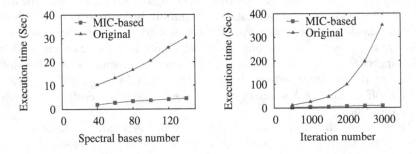

Fig. 2. Execution time with different parameter values.

time of MIC-based algorithm increases more slowly compared with the original non-accelerated algorithm.

Then, we set the thread number from 2 to 16 to test the influence of multi-thread parallelization on MIC-based algorithm. The spectral bases number is set to 120 while the iteration number is set to 1000. Table 1 shows the results.

Table 1. Execution time with different thread number

Thread number	2	4	8	16
MIC-based (Sec)	6.337	3.477	2.857	3.044

With the increase of thread number, the execution time of MIC-based algorithm has a trend of decrease. However, as the thread number is set to 16, it has a longer execution time than the thread number is set to 8. In practical, it is important to choose the correct thread number to get the best performance according to different situations.

In experiments, the MIC architecture shows its great effectiveness in NMF-based monaural speech separation. The intensitive matrix manipulations are offloaded to coprocessor and performed parallel, which makes the MIC-based monaural speech separation has a much shorter execution time than original non-accelerated algorithm. The thread number should also be chosen correctly to get a better performance. In summary, MIC-based monaural speech separation is more suitable for real-time speech separation applications.

5   Conclusion

This paper presented a MIC-based monaural speech separation. This algorithm is a parallel version of TNMF-based monaural speech separation algorithm. In practical, MIC architecture shows its power on accelerating highly parallel workloads. To verify the effectiveness of the MIC-based algorithm, we conduct experiments on TIMIT dataset to separate mixture speech signals. We compare the execution time of MIC-based algorithm and original non-accelerated algorithm under different conditions. The experiment results confirm that MIC-based monaural speech separation has much less execution time than original non-accelerated algorithm, so it is more suitable for real-time speech separation applications.

Acknowledgments. This work was supported by National High Technology Research and Development Program "863" Program) of China (under grant No. 2015AA01A301) and National Natural Science Foundation of China (under grant No. 61502515).

References

1. Vinyals, O., Ravuri, S.V., Povey, D.: Revisiting recurrent neural networks for robust ASR. In: 2012 IEEE International Conference on Acoustics, Speech and Signal Processing (ICASSP). IEEE, pp. 4085–4088 (2012)
2. Maas, A., Le, Q.V., Oneil, T.M., Vinyals, O., Nguyen, P., Ng, A.Y.: Recurrent neural networks for noise reduction in robust ASR (2012)
3. Huang, P.S., Chen, S.D., Smaragdis, P., Hasegawa-Johnson, M.: Singing-voice separation from monaural recordings using robust principal component analysis. In: 2012 IEEE International Conference on Acoustics, Speech and Signal Processing (ICASSP), pp. 57–60. IEEE (2012)
4. Huang, P.S., Kim, M., Hasegawa-Johnson, M., Smaragdis, P.: Singing-voice separation from monaural recordings using deep recurrent neural networks. In: ISMIR, pp. 477–482 (2014)
5. Lee, D.D., Seung, H.S.: Learning the parts of objects by non-negative matrix factorization. Nature **401**(6755), 788–791 (1999)
6. Wang, Z., Sha, F.: Discriminative non-negative matrix factorization for single-channel speech separation. In: 2014 IEEE International Conference on Acoustics, Speech and Signal Processing (ICASSP), pp. 3749–3753. IEEE (2014)
7. Weninger, F., Le Roux, J., Hershey, J.R., Watanabe, S.: Discriminative nmf and its application to single-channel source separation. In: INTERSPEECH, pp. 865–869 (2014)

8. Huang, P.-S., Kim, M., Hasegawa-Johnson, M., Smaragdis, P.: Deep learning for monaural speech separation. In: 2014 IEEE International Conference on Acoustics, Speech and Signal Processing (ICASSP), pp. 1562–1566. IEEE (2014)
9. Weninger, F., Hershey, J.R., Le Roux, J., Schuller, B.: Discriminatively trained recurrent neural networks for single-channel speech separation. In: 2014 IEEE Global Conference on Signal and Information Processing (GlobalSIP), pp. 577–581. IEEE (2014)
10. Erdogan, H., Hershey, J.R., Watanabe, S., Le Roux, J.: Phase-sensitive and recognition-boosted speech separation using deep recurrent neural networks. In: 2015 IEEE International Conference on Acoustics, Speech and Signal Processing (ICASSP), pp. 708–712. IEEE (2015)
11. Weninger, F., Eyben, F., Schuller, B.: Single-channel speech separation with memory-enhanced recurrent neural networks. In: 2014 IEEE International Conference on Acoustics, Speech and Signal Processing (ICASSP), pp. 3709–3713. IEEE (2014)
12. Zhang, X.-L., Wang, D.: A deep ensemble learning method for monaural speech separation. IEEE/ACM Trans. Audio Speech Lang. Process. **24**(5), 967–977 (2016)
13. Duran, A., Klemm, M.: The intel many integrated core architecture. In: 2012 International Conference on High Performance Computing and Simulation (HPCS), pp. 365–366. IEEE (2012)
14. Jeffers, J., Reinders, J.: Intel Xeon Phi coprocessor high-performance programming. Newnes (2013)
15. Tarditi, D., Puri, S., Oglesby, J.: Accelerator: using data parallelism to program gpus for general-purpose uses. In: ACM SIGARCH Computer Architecture News, vol. 34, no. 5, pp. 325–335. ACM (2006)
16. Lee, S., Min, S.-J., Eigenmann, R.: OpenMP to GPGPU: a compiler framework for automatic translation and optimization. ACM Sigplan Not. **44**(4), 101–110 (2009)
17. Platoš, J., Gajdoš, P., Krömer, P., Snášel, V.: Non-negative matrix factorization on GPU. In: Zavoral, F., Yaghob, J., Pichappan, P., El-Qawasmeh, E. (eds.) Networked Digital Technologies. Communications in Computer and Information Science, vol. 87, pp. 21–30. Springer, Heidelberg (2010)
18. Mejía-Roa, E., Tabas-Madrid, D., Setoain, J., García, C., Tirado, F., Pascual-Montano, A.: NMF-mGPU: non-negative matrix factorization on multi-GPU systems. BMC Bioinf. **16**(1), 1 (2015)
19. Alonso, P., García, V., Martínez-Zaldívar, F.J., Salazar, A., Vergara, L., Vidal, A.M.: Parallel approach to NNMF on multicore architecture. J. Supercomput. **70**(2), 564–576 (2014)
20. Guan, N., Lan, L., Tao, D., Luo, Z., Yang, X.: Transductive nonnegative matrix factorization for semi-supervised high-performance speech separation. In: 2014 IEEE International Conference on Acoustics, Speech and Signal Processing (ICASSP), pp. 2534–2538. IEEE (2014)
21. Lee, D.D., Seung, H.S.: Algorithms for non-negative matrix factorization. In: Advances in Neural Information Processing Systems, pp. 556–562 (2001)
22. Chrysos, G.: Intel xeon phi coprocessor-the architecture, Intel Whitepaper (2014)
23. Garofolo, J.S., Lamel, L.F., Fisher, W.M., Fiscus, J.G., Pallett, D.S.: DARPA TIMIT acoustic-phonetic continous speech corpus CD-ROM. NIST speech disc 1-1.1. NASA STI/Recon technical report n, vol. 93 (1993)
24. Intel, M.: Intel math kernel library (2007)

An AWGR-Based High Performance Optical Interconnect Architecture for Exascale Systems

Shi Xu[1], Lei Zhang[2(✉)], and Zhiling Li[3]

[1] College of Computer Science and Electronic Engineering,
Hunan University, Changsha, China
[2] School of Computer, National University of Defense Technology,
Changsha, China
leizhang@nudt.edu.cn
[3] Cadre Institute for Nationnalities of Urumqi, Urumqi, China

Abstract. The next milestone objective of HPC is exascale computing, which includes millions of nodes in the system. One of the key critical barrier toward realizing exascale computing is the fundamental challenge of communication networks. We propose a high performance optical interconnect architecture based on Arrayed waveguide grating router (AWGR) with WDM wavelength routing, the inherent parallelism in AWGRs and multi-hop switching provide high scalability of the network. Theoretical analysis and simulation show its better performance compared with fat-tree architecture.

Keywords: Exascale computing · Optical interconnect · AWGR · Wavelength routing · Performance evaluation

1 Introduction

The most recent world leading supercomputer, the Tianhe-2, realized 50 PetaFlops/s (PF) peak performance in June 2013. The next milestone objective of supercomputer is exascale computing, while just an scale expanding of current architecture cannot reach exascale computing, because it encounters several complex problems that range from the management of hardware failures at runtime, memory wall constraint, power consumption, identifying the adequate massively parallel programming approaches, and etc. One of the key critical barrier toward realizing exascale computing is the fundamental challenge of communication networks. It's very difficult to meet the high bandwidth, high scalability and low-latency communication requirements using conventional interconnects techniques. Furthermore, as the interconnections between supercomputer racks are usually optical fibers, it is very difficult to deploy the network with the extraordinary growth of fiber interconnections in exascale computing.

Regarding network topologies of current high performance computer systems, Fat Tree is one of the most common architecture to build large-scale computing systems and it is usually built with some level of oversubscription to reduce the number of inter-rack switches and cables. For a 3-tier Fat Tree network with 64 port electrical

© Springer Nature Singapore Pte Ltd. 2016
W. Xu et al. (Eds.): NCCET 2016, CCIS 666, pp. 157–167, 2016.
DOI: 10.1007/978-981-10-3159-5_15

switches, the scalability of Fat-Tree is well below 100,000 nodes. A recent trend in large-scale interconnection architectures is use high radix switches with a large number of ports to create directly connected networks such as dragonfly from Cray.

Optical switches attract much attention due to its low power and high radix features. The Arrayed waveguide grating router (AWGR) based optical switches and optical routers with packet switching capability have been investigated for a number of years [1, 2]. The AWGR allows the signal from one input to reach one output only on a particular wavelength, it is unique in that all-to-all communication can be realized if every node is equipped with multiple receivers and multiple transmitters working on different wavelengths so that signals on different wavelengths can be transmitted and received concurrently.

The AWGR is a passive device and low-loss at all data rates, but it encounters scalability problem when using AWGR to construct large scale interconnection network for supercomputers. One is the transceiver scalability, a $N \times N$ ports AWGR need N2 transceivers, when the number of nodes are very large, we cannot equip so many transceivers for each node. The other is interconnection scalability, because of the interior characteristics of AWGR, they cannot be directly connected as traditional routers to extend the network scale, although the number of ports for a single AWGR has reached 1024 now, the port number cannot increase unlimitedly due to the crosstalk problem, it's far more to meet the exascale computing scalability requirements.

To solve these problems, we propose a nested 2D-Tree topology for exascale computer network, which exploit the unique wavelength routing capability of AWGR to implement all-to-all interconnection in the 2D dimension, and utilize nested structure for hierarchical all-to-all interconnections, the inherent parallelism in AWGRs and multi-hop switching provide high scalability of the network.

2 Related Work

Optical links in most recent supercomputers are primarily in the form of active optical cables [4]. The main drawback is that power hungry electrical-to-optical (E/O) and optical-to-electrical (O/E) transceivers are required since the switching is performed using electronic packet switches. Recent breakthroughs in silicon photonics offer the possibility of integrating optical devices with traditional electronic logic devices in a single chip. In the past decades, passive and active silicon photonics devices capable of all of the operations required for transmission and switching have been demonstrated, such as wave guide, micro-ring resonator and modulator, arrayed waveguide grating router (AWGR), filters, detectors, and etc.

The AWGR based optical switches and optical routers with packet switching capability have been investigated for a number of years [8–10]. The AWGR allows the signal from one input to reach one output only on a particular wavelength, it can realize all-to-all communication when each node is equipped with multiple receivers and multiple transmitters. Signals from different transceivers can be transmitted and received concurrently. For example, if we have a set of wavelengths λ_i, $0 \leq i < k$, we can use $\lambda_{\text{mod}}(1 - i - j, k)$ to deliver signals from input i to output j. Figure 1 shows a

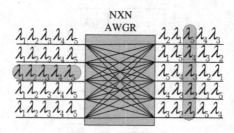

Fig. 1. Arrayed waveguide grating router example

wavelength routing map of a 5×5 AWGR with 5 input ports, 5 output ports, and 5 wavelengths per port.

References [2, 11, 12] demonstrate the some silicon photonics WDM solutions. Recently a silicon photonic LIONS Switch with 32 transmitters and 32 receivers utilizing 8×8 AWGR with kt = kr = 4 demonstrated [2] on a compact 1.2 mm $\times$ 2.4 mm silicon-on-insulator (SOI) platform.

Z. Cao [13] proposes a scalable AWGR topology for High Performance HPC Architecture, it utilizes three level interconnection to improve the network scalability. On the first level all the nodes in a chassis are connected by a single AWGR, on the second level all chassis in a cabinet are directed connected by all-to-all interconnection between AWGRs, on the third level, all cabinets are connected by two orthogonal AWGR arrays. To reduce the number transceivers, each node only has two inter-cabinet TRXs, they are multiplexed/de-multiplexed to connect to the orthogonal AWGR arrays, which need each node has a different wavelength in the same cabinet, this is very complicated for implementation and maintenance.

3 System Architecture

The whole interconnection architecture composes of five levels: CPU, node, frame, cabinet group and system.

A computing node consists of m CPUs and a switch, a switch has m electrical or optical ports that connected to the CPUs, there are also n pair of DWDM optical ports for the switch, denoted as 0, 1, 2, ..., $n-1$, each pair DWDM optical port include a horizontal interconnection port h a vertical interconnection port v, we denote the number of wavelength in each pair DWDM optical ports is $h_0, v_0, h_1, v_1, ..., h_{n-1}, v_{n-1}$, as depicted in Fig. 2. The switch DWDM ports are designed based on micro ring optical photonics technology, so that the power consumption are much lower than traditional serdes based electric switches.

A frame includes $h_0 * v_0$ computing nodes, as depicted in Fig. 3. In the horizontal direction h_0 nodes in each row is physically connected by a h_0 port AWGR, meanwhile in the vertical direction v_0 nodes in each column is physically connected by a v_0 port AWGR to form a 2D-tree connection, logically all the nodes in each row and each column are connected in an all-to-all connection.

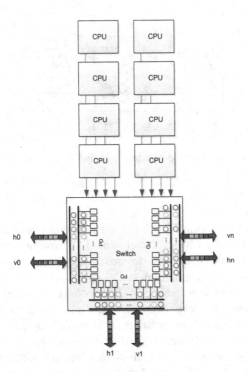

Fig. 2. Node interconnection

The number of h_1 port in the horizontal direction for each frame is $h_0 * v_0$, so does the number of v_1 port, all these ports are multiplexed/de-multiplexed into ports which include x_1 and y_1 wavelengths, so the number of x_1 port and y_1 port are $h_0 * v_0 * h_1/x_1$ and $h_0 * v_0 * v_1/y_1$ respectively, we can arrange the frames as x_1 columns and y_1 rows, so that x_1 frames in each row and y_1 frames in each column can be connected by $h_0 * v_0 * h_1/x_1$ and $h_0 * v_0 * v_1/y_1$ AWGR arrays, which construct the second level 2D-tree structure, as depicted in Fig. 4.

We can see the $x_1 * y_1$ frames in second level interconnection as a frame group, then there are $h_0 * v_0 * x_1 h_2$ type ports in horizontal direction and $h_0 * v_0 * y_1 v_2$ type ports in vertical direction, we can further multiplexed/de-multiplexed these ports to x_2 and y_2 type ports, which include x_2 and y_2 wavelengths in each port, then the number of x_2 and y_2 type ports are $h_0 * v_0 * x_1 * h_2/x_2$ and $h_0 * v_0 * y_1 * v_2/y_2$. Arrange the frame group in a 2D dimension with x_2 columns and y_2 rows, the frame groups in each row and each column are connected by $h_0 * v_0 * x_1 * h_2/x_2$ and $h_0 * v_0 * y_1 * v_2/y_2$ AWGR arrays, which is the third level 2D-tree connection, as depicted in Fig. 5.

The higher level connections can be deduced by analogy to complete the whole system interconnections. The AWGR physical connection on each level is like a two dimension tree, so we named the topology as nested 2D-tree.

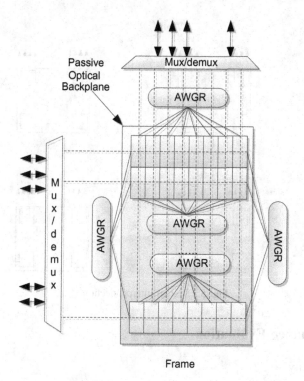

Fig. 3. Frame interconnection

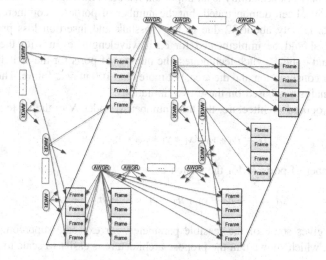

Fig. 4. Cabinet group interconnection

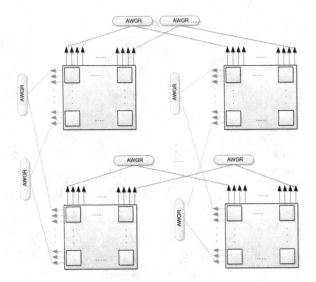

Fig. 5. System interconnection

4 Performance Evaluation

4.1 Scalability

There will be millions of nodes to be connected in future exascale supercomputers, therefore the network scalability is an important feature. Although in laboratory a 1024 port AWGR has been demonstrated, but the number of ports for commercially available AWGRs is only about 32 due to the crosstalk and insertion loss problem; the switch logic should be implemented for each wavelength, even with the emerging micro-ring and optical switch techniques, the number of ports for the switch is limited by the power consumption and die area, not more than 100 in near future. Therefore our scalability analysis is based on these two limitations.

In our proposed architecture, the total number to nodes N in the system is:

$$N = h_0 * v_0 * x_1 * y_1 * \ldots * x_{n-1} * y_{n-1}$$

The number of ports M for the switch is:

$$M = m + h_0 + v_0 + h_2 + v_1 + \ldots + h_{n-1} + v_{n-1}$$

Table 1 gives some of the feasible parameters for exascale supercomputer interconnections, which shows that the propose architecture is easily to scale to millions of nodes.

The number of wavelength is also a key factor affecting system scalability. In our proposed architecture, the wavelength can be reused on each level connection. So, the number of wavelength of the system is W:

Table 1. System scalability

Level	m	h0	v0	h1/x1	v1/y1	h2/x2	v2/y2	M	N
2	8	8	8	8/32	8/32	0/0	0/0	88	65536
2	8	16	16	16/32	16/32	0/0	0/0	72	262144
2	8	16	16	32/64	32/64	0/0	0/0	104	1048576
3	8	8	8	4/8	4/8	4/8	4/8	40	262144
3	8	8	8	16/16	16/16	8/8	8/8	72	1048576
3	8	8	8	16/16	16/16	16/16	16/16	88	4194304

$$W = max(max(h_0, v_0), max(x_1, y_1), max(x_2, y_2), \ldots, max(x_{n-1}, y_{n-1}))$$

For example, to build a system with 262144 nodes, if we use two level 2D-tree $(h_0 = v_0 = 16, x_1 = y_1 = 32)$, 32 wavelengths are needed; if we use three level 2D-tree $(h_0 = v_0 = 8, x_1 = y_1 = 8, x_2 = y_2 = 8)$, only 8 wavelengths are needed. The more levels of the 2D-tree, the fewer wavelengths are needed, which means we can use fewer ports AWGRs to build the same size system.

4.2 Inter Frame Links and Switches

Inter frame links is usually connected by optical fibers, which has important impact on system deployment and cost. In our proposed architecture, the total number of inter cabinet links are:

$$L = h_0 * v_0 * h_1 * y_1 + h_0 * v_0 * v_1 * x_1 + h_0 * v_0 * x_1 * y_1 * h_2 * y_2 + h_0 * v_0 * x_1 * y_1 * v_2 * x_2 + \ldots$$
$$+ h_0 * v_0 * x_1 * y_1 * \ldots * x_{n-2} * y_{n-2} * h_{n-1} * y_{n-1} + h_0 * v_0 * x_1 * y_1 * \ldots * x_{n-2} * y_{n-2} * v_{n-1} * x_{n-1}$$

The number of inter frame switches is:

$$S = h_0 * v_0 * h_1/x_1 * y_1 + h_0 * v_0 * v_1/y_1 * x_1 + h_0 * v_0 * x_1 * y_1 * y_2 * h_2/x_2$$
$$+ h_0 * v_0 * x_1 * y_1 * x_2 * v_2/y_2 + \ldots + h_0 * v_0 * x_1 * y_1 * \ldots * x_{n-2} * y_{n-2} * y_{n-1} * h_{n-1}/x_{n-1}$$
$$+ h_0 * v_0 * x_1 * y_1 * \ldots * x_{n-2} * y_{n-2} * x_{n-1} * v_{n-1}/y_{n-1}$$

Figures 6 and 7 compare the inter frame links and switches of our proposed architecture and fat-tree, which show that our proposed architecture needs only about 50% cables and 35% switches of fat-tree in a 100000 nodes system. Even compared to the far-tree network with 3:1 oversubscription ratio, our architecture can save up to 25% cables and 50% switches.

4.3 Maximum Hop Counts and Average Hop Counts

We can treat switching among the switch ports as one hop, so the maximum hop count to be 5 for 2 level 2D-tree and 7 for 3 level 2D-tree in our proposed architecture. Two hops to destination cabinet group(for 3 level 2D-tree), two hops to the destination

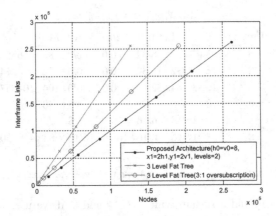

Fig. 6. The number of inter frame links

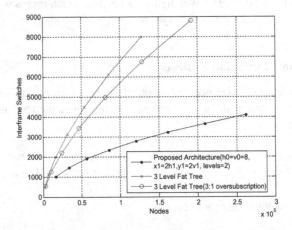

Fig. 7. The number of inter frame switches

frame and three hops to the destination CPU in the frame. For 3 tree fat tree, the maximum hop count is 5, so their maximum hop counts are same.

We simulate the average hop counts under uniform random traffic, the average hop count is of our proposed architecture and 3 tree fat tree is depicted in Fig. 8, which shows that the average hop counts are lower than fat tree architecture.

4.4   Power Consumption

Fat tree is an indirect network, the total power consumption includes network interface in each node and switch power consumption in the network. Our proposed architecture is a direct network, the AWGR power consumption is zero, the network power mainly consumed by the optical switch in each node. To compare the total network power consumption, we can use the number of network ports to estimate the total network

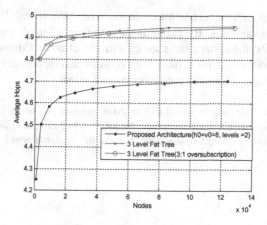

Fig. 8. The average hop counts

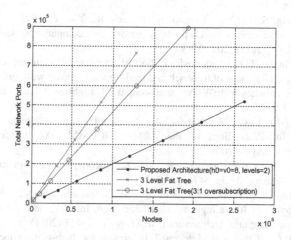

Fig. 9. The average hop counts

power consumption, as depicted in Fig. 9. We can see the power consumption of our proposed architecture is much lower than fat tree. For example, for a 100000 nodes system, the power consumption of our proposed architecture is about 60% and 40% lower than a fat tree and 3:1 oversubscription fat tree architecture.

5   Conclusion

Scalability and power consumption are the main challenges for future exascale computing network design. Among all the proposed and existing optical interconnect architectures for HPC and datacenters, the arrayed waveguide grating router (AWGR) based solutions have attracted much attention due to WDM parallelism, dense interconnectivity and unique wavelength routing capability. We propose a high performance optical interconnect architecture based on AWGR with WDM wavelength routing for exascale systems. By exploiting the unique all-to-all wavelength routing property of AWGRs, the system can scale to millions of node. Compared with fat-tree network with 3:1 oversubscription ratio, 60% power consumption can be reserved with less switches and cables for inter-cabinet communication.

Acknowledgements. The authors would like to thank the anonymous reviewers for the feedback and revision suggestions. Then, we would thank China 863 Program (2015AA015302) and NSFC (61572509) for providing the assistance to make this research possible.

References

1. Kamei, S., Ishii, M., Itoh, M., Shibata, T., Inoue, Y., Kitagawa, T.: 64 × 64-channel uniform-loss and cyclic-frequency arrayed-waveguide grating router module. Electron. Lett. **39**, 83–84 (2003)
2. Yu, R., Cheung, S., Li, Y., Okamoto, K., Proietti, R., Yin, Y., et al.: A scalable silicon photonic chip-scale optical switch for high performance computing systems. Opt. Express **21**, 32655–32667 (2013). 2013/12/30
3. Chia, M.C., Hunter, D.K., Andonovic, I., Ball, P., Wright, I., Ferguson, S.P., et al.: Packet loss and delay performance of feedback and feed-forward arrayed-waveguide gratings-based optical packet switches with WDM inputs-outputs. J. Lightwave Technol. **19**, 1241–1254 (2001). 2013/12/30
4. Al-Fares, M., Loukissas, A., Vahdat, A.: A scalable, commodity data center network architecture. In: Proceedings of the ACM SIGCOMM 2008 Conference on Data Communication, August 2008
5. Rumley, S., Nikolova, D., Hendry, R., Li, Q.: Silicon photonics for exascale systems. J. Lightwave Technol. **33**(3), 547–562 (2015)
6. Binkert, N., Davis, A., Jouppi, N.P., McLaren, M., Muralimanohar, N., Schreiber, R., et al.: The role of optics in future high radix switch design. In: 2011 38th Annual International Symposium on Computer Architecture (ISCA), pp. 437–447 (2011)
7. Beausoleil, R.G.: Large-scale integrated photonics for high-performance interconnects. ACM J. Emerg. Technol. Comput. Syst. (JETC) **7**, 6 (2011)
8. Yoo, S.J.B.: Optical packet and burst switching technologies for the future photonic Internet. J. Lightwave Technol. **24**, 4468–4492 (2006)
9. O'Mahony, M.J., Simeonidou, D., Hunter, D.K., Tzanakaki, A.: The application of optical packet switching in future communication networks. IEEE Commun. Mag. **39**, 1280135 (2001)
10. Guillemot, C., Renaud, M., Gambini, P., Janz, C., Andonovic, I., Bauknecht, R., et al.: Transparent optical packet switching: the European ACTS KEOPS project approach. J. Lightwave Technol. **16**, 2117–2134 (1998)
11. Absil, P.P., De Heyn, P., Dumon, P., Van Thourhout, D., Verheyen, P., Selvaraja, S., et al.: Advances in silicon photonics WDM devices, pp. 90100J-1–90100J-7 (2014)
12. Fang, Q., Liow, T.-Y., Song, J.F., Ang, K.W., Yu, M.B., Lo, G.Q., et al.: WDM multi-channel silicon photonic receiver with 320 Gbps data transmission capability. Opt. Express **18**, 5106–5113 (2010). 2010/03/01

13. Cao, Z., Proietti, R., Yoo, S.J.B.: Photonics Conference (IPC), pp 180–181, October 2014
14. Feng, Q.Y., Sang, X.Z., Dou, W.H.: Demonstration of a 5 Gb/s 24 interchip optical interconnect system. Microw. Opt. Technol. Lett. (2012)
15. Xie, M., Lu, Y.T., Wang, K.F., Liu, L., Cao, H.J., Yang, X.J.: TIANHE-1A interconnect and essage-passing services. IEEE Micro Mag. (2012)

Accelerating Nyström Kernel Independent Component Analysis with Many Integrated Core Architecture

Lei Shan$^{(\boxtimes)}$, He Wang, Weixia Xu, Canqun Yang, and Minxuan Zhang

Institute of Microelectronics, Institute of Software, College of Computer,
National University of Defence Technology, Changsha 410073, Hunan, China
ssll2999@163.com

Abstract. Kernel independent component analysis (KICA) penalizes the correlations among components in a reproducing kernel Hilbert space (RKHS) and performs well in many practical tasks such as speech separation due to its robustness on varying source distributions. Recently, Nyström-KICA (NKICA) incorporates a low-rank approximation and low-complexity sampling method to reduce the computational complexity of KICA. In this paper, we show that the computational complexity of NKICA can be further decreased by implementing the algorithm on the many integrated core (MIC) architecture to meet the requirement of large data processing. Particularly, we parallelize the critical segments with the OpenMP technology and perform the intensive matrix manipulations on a MIC coprocessor. This MIC-based approach has been evaluated on both simulated dataset and the TIMIT dataset. The experimental results confirm the efficiency of our implementation of NKICA on the MIC architecture, and show that it achieves a consistent speedup rate of around 10 on average, and of 12.3 at best, comparing with that performed on single CPU.

Keywords: Kernel ICA · Nyström method · MIC · OpenMP · MKL

1 Introduction

Independent component analysis (ICA) [1] is a signal processing technique of recovering sources from observation data. The observations are linear combinations of statistic independent sources. ICA aims to find out the latent independent components with a set of observations of random variables, which has been widely used in practice, e.g., blind source separation, speech separation and feature extraction [2,3], etc. The traditional ICA algorithms were based on objective functions defined in terms of expectations of a single fixed nonlinear function, which makes them suitable for some specific problems. Kennel ICA (KICA, [4]) define the objective function in a reproducing kernel Hilbert space (RKHS), and make use of the "kernel trick" to search over this space efficiently. The use of a function space makes it possible to adapt to a variety of sources and thus makes KICA algorithm more robust to varying source distributions.

© Springer Nature Singapore Pte Ltd. 2016
W. Xu et al. (Eds.): NCCET 2016, CCIS 666, pp. 168–176, 2016.
DOI: 10.1007/978-981-10-3159-5_16

Although KICA algorithm is very effective, the high computational complexity prohibits it form practical applications [5]. The kernel matrices get larger and larger, and the computational complexity has a cubic growth when the scale of data to be processed increases. A usual solution to this problem is constructing low-rank approximations of the kernel matrices because the spectra of kernel matrices decays rapidly [6]. Recently, Wang et al. use Nyström [8] method to construct such low-rank approximation termed Nyström KICA (NKICA). NKICA is proposed to solve the computation problem of prior incomplete Cholesky decomposition KICA (IDC-KICA). With the increase of the scale of data, both time and space complexities of ICD-KICA are unacceptable. In contrast to ICD method, the Nyström method uses a low-complexity sampling technique [7]. NKICA cuts down the computational complexity of KICA effectively, from $O(m^3N^3)$ to $O(mM^2N)$.

Although NKICA reduces the computational complexity effectively, with the scale of practical data increases, the computation complexity of algorithm grows quickly. It prohibits NKICA form big data applications. To solve the problem, we consider hardware implementation to accelerate computation of NKICA. Nowadays, various accelerators developed quickly, including Intel MIC coprocessor [9,10] and general purpose computation on graphics processing units (GPGPU) [12,13], etc. With the help of the accelerators, highly parallel computations can be accelerated easily.

Intel MIC architecture provides many computational cores, and conveniently exploits parallelism with technology such as OpenMP and TBB. On the other hand, MIC is very suitable for matrix manipulations, which are the most manipulations in NKICA. In this paper, we implement the NKICA on Intel Many Integrated Core (MIC) architecture to reduce the computational complexity of KICA to meet the requirement of large data processing. Particularly, we parallelize the critical segments with the OpenMP technology and perform the intensive matrix manipulations on a MIC coprocessor. Experiments on both simulated dataset and the TIMIT dataset confirm its efficiency.

The remainder of the paper is organized as follows. Section 2 introduces related work including Nystrom Fast KICA and nd the Intel Many Integrated Core architecture. Section 3 discusses how to use MIC to accelerate Nystrom KICA algorithm and Sect. 4 presents the experimental results. Section 5 concludes the paper.

2 Background

2.1 Kernel Independent Component Analysis

Independent component analysis (ICA) [3] aims to recover a latent random vector $s = (s1; \ldots; sm)$ from observations of m unknown linear functions of that vector. The components of s are assumed to be mutually independent, and their distributions are usually assumed unknown. x is modeled as

$$x = As, \tag{1}$$

where s is the independent components, and A is A is an $m \times m$ mixing matrix of parameters. ICA finds the optimal demixing matrix $W = A^{-1}$ by solving a objective function, and recovers $s = Wx$. The traditional ICA algorithms were based on objective functions defined in terms of expectations of a single fixed nonlinear function, such as kurtosis, negentropy. KICA define the objective function in a reproducing kernel Hilbert space(RKHS), and make use of the "kernel trick" to search over this space efficiently. The objective function of KICA is relates to the kernelized first canonical correlation between variables. Mathematically, the kernalized first canonical correlation can be obtained by finding the minimal eigenvalue of the following matrix.

$$\widetilde{K_k} = \begin{pmatrix} I & r_k(K_1)r_k(K_2) & \cdots & r_k(K_1)r_k(K_m) \\ r_k(K_2)r_k(K_1) & I & \cdots & r_k(K_2)r_k(K_m) \\ \vdots & \vdots & & \vdots \\ r_k(K_m)r_k(K_1) & r_k(K_m)r_k(K_2) & \cdots & I \end{pmatrix} \quad (2)$$

where $K_1, \ldots, K_m$ denote the kernel matrices of the observations, where $r_k(K_i) = K_i(K_i + \frac{Nk}{2}I)^{-1}$, and $K_i + \frac{Nk}{2}I$ denotes the regularization of K_i and $\frac{Nk}{2}$ is called jitter factor [6]. The minimal generalized eigenvalue, denoted as λ_{min}, and the objective function can be defined as $C(W) = -\frac{1}{2}\log \lambda_{min}$. The value of the objective function is nonnegative, and equals zero if and only if the variables are pairwise independent [4].

An ICA objective function is actually a function of demixing matrix W. Estimating the independent components means minimizing the objective function with respect to W. It is quite challenging because the scale of the constructed kernel matrices are quite large. Recently, Wang et al. proposed Nyström KICA(NICA) to perform low-rank approximations of the kernel matrices. NKICA randomly sample M data points form the observations consist of N samples, $M \ll N$. The NKICA algorithm is shown in Algorithm 1. The total computational complexity of NKICA Algorithm 1 is $O(mM^2N)$.

2.2 Intel Many Integrated Core Architecture

Intel many integrated core (MIC) architecture is designed to accelerate highly parallel and computational intensive applications. Intel Xeon Phi coprocessor is a commercial product based on MIC architecture. One coprocessor consists of up to 61 cores. Each core has two level caches, includs a 32 KB L1 data cache and L1 instruction cache, and a 512 KB private L2 cache. A 512 bits vector processor unit (VPU) based on Single Instruction Multiple Data (SIMD) architecture is implemented on MIC.

Intel MIC architecture is easy to program for developers. Applications on other platform can also be ported to MIC with little modification. The MIC coprocessor is supported by a variety of libraries, compilers and tuning tools, etc. In practical, developers usually use the parallel programming interface, such as OpenMP and TBB, to utilize the abundant computational core resources. The

---

Algorithm 1. NKICA Algorithm[8]

Input : Data vectors $x^1, x^2, \cdots, x^N$,
       Kernel function $K(x, y)$.
Output: Estimated independent components s.
1 Whiten the data
2 perform the low-rank approximation via Nyström method, randomly choose $M \times M$, $K_i \approx P_i A_i^{-1} P_i^T$
3 Compute the orthogonal eigenvectors and eigenvalues of K_i, U_i and L_i, $K_i \approx U_i L_i U_i^T$
4 Compute the kernel matrix R_K based on U_i and L_i, find the minimal eigenvalue of R_K λ_{min}
5 Define objective function $C(W) = -\frac{1}{2} \log \lambda_{min}$
6 Minimize the objective function, obtain the demixing matrix W
7 Output the estimated independent components $s = Wx$.

MIC coprocessor is often treated as an accelerator to perform the computational intensive tasks offloaded from CPU. Lager scale matrix computations are main tasks for MIC coprocessor. With the help of Intel math kernel libraryMKL, matrix computations can be performed effectively on MIC.

3   Analysis of Parallelism

This paper aims to parallelly accelerate NKICA algorithm on MIC. So the main work is to parallelize the most time consuming parts, i.e. the critical segments, of the algorithm, and perform the computations on the MIC. By analysing the NKICA algorithm in Algorithm 1, we find the critical segment is the computation of the objective function. The objective function is computed many times in Algorithm 1 to find the minimal value. Table 1 shows the simulated execution of NKICA, the components number sets to 2, 6, 10. We can see the total time of computing objective function accounts for more than 80% of the execution time of NKICA algorithm. Therefore, the computation of objective function is the critical segment needs to be parallelized.

Table 1. Simulated excution of NKICA

Number of independent components	2	6	10
Execution time of NKICA Algorithm	8.25 s	86.06 s	316.68
Total time of computing objective function	7.33 s	73.98 s	267.51
Percentage	88.85%	85.96%	84.47%

There are two levels of parallelism inhered in NKICA algorithm. The first level is the parallelism of computing K_i of each observation, and the second level is the parallelism inhered in matrix manipulations, including matrix multiplication, singular value decomposition and eigenvalues decomposition. In practical, We use OpenMP technology to exploit the first level of parallelism, and Intel math kernel library (MKL) to realize the second level of parallelism. MKL has rich functions and can perform matrix manipulation with high-efficiency. The data needed in the algorithm are constructed as matrix, so we can utilize the computational ability of coprocessors VPU. Algorithm 2 summarizes the NKICA algorithm with MIC.

Algorithm 2. NKICA algorithm with MIC

Input : Data vectors $x^1, x^2, \cdots, x^N$,
           Kernel function $K(x, y)$.
Output: Estimated independent components s.
1 Whiten the data
2 Generate the initial demixing matrix W', compute the corresponding source
   $s' = W'y$
3 offload s' and Kernel function $K(x, y)$ from CPU to MIC
4 perform the low-rank approximation via Nyström method, randomly choose
   $M \times M$, $K_i \approx P_i A_i^{-1} P_i^T$
5 Compute the orthogonal eigenvectors and eigenvalues of K_i, U_i and L_i,
   $K_i \approx U_i L_i U_i^T$
6 Compute the kernel matrix R_K based on U_i and L_i, find the minimal eigenvalue
   of R_K λ_{min}
7 Return objective function $C(W) = -\frac{1}{2} \log \lambda_{min}$ to CPU
8 Minimize the objective function, obtain the demixing matrix W
9 Output the estimated independent components $x = Wy$.

In Algorithm 2, Step 3 to step 7 are performed on MIC, use OPENMP technology to realize parallelization, and MKL to perform the matrix manipulation. We adopt offload mode of MIC in Step 3. Step 5 and step 6 perform singular value decomposition and eigenvalues decomposition on A_i and R_K respectively. In practice, the regularization scheme in NKICA enables us to ignore the eigenvalues less than the jitter factor, which significantly reduces the computational complexity.

4   Experiments

To verify the performance of the accelerated algorithm, we compare the execution time between MIC-based NKICA algorithm and original non-accelerated one only on CPU. The CPU is Intel Xeon server CPU, 2.6 GHz, two way 8 cores. the only CPU-based algorithm also uses MKL to perform matrix manipulation. The datasets used in experiments include the simulated dataset and the TIMIT dataset. The input kernel function is Gaussian Kernel in all experiments. All the experiment results are averages of 10 replications.

There are three parameters have significant influence on execution time, which are components number m, observations data size N and sampling number M. When m and N increases, we can perform NKICA algorithm on larger datasete. When M increases, the results will be more accurate. Meanwhile, the computational complexity increases along with the increase of the three parameters. We set the three parameters to different values respectively, and record the execution time of the MIC-based algorithm and the only CPU-based algorithm on different dataset.

4.1 Simulated Dataset

The simulated dataset consists of data obtained from a variety of source distributions. In this paper, we use five basic distributions to generate a large dataset. Figure 1 shows the five basic distributions. We set different parameters to the distributions to get different data.

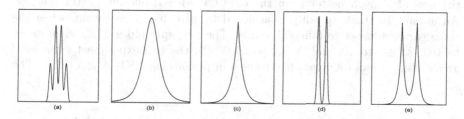

Fig. 1. Probability density functions of sources in simulated dataset with their kurtoses: (a) Mixtures of four Gaussians; (b) Student; (c) Double exponential; (d) Mixture of two Gaussians; (e) Mixtures of two double exponential.

Figure 2 shows the results of two experiment sets on simulated dataset. We compare the execution time between the MIC-based and the only CPU-based NKICA algorithm. The results show that the MIC-based algorithm runs much faster than the only CPU-based one, an around 10 times speedup is achieved by MIC-based algorithm, when the three parameters set to different values.

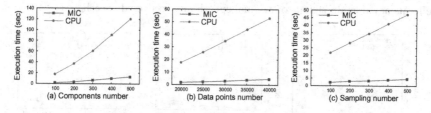

Fig. 2. Execution time with different parameter values: (a) Components; (b) Data points; (c) Sampling points.

4.2   TIMIT Dataset

TIMIT dataset [14] consists of large amount of speech segments of different speakers. We use it to test our MIC-based algorithm for practical applications, such as speech separation [15]. Speech segments are all sampled at a rate of 16 kHz.

Figure 3 compares the original speech signals, which used to generate observation data, and the recovered speech signals by MIC-based NKICA algorithm. The first row shows the time-domain signals, while the second row shows the frequency-domain signals. The estimated 1 signal is the corresponding recovery of the source 1, while the estimated 2 corresponds to source 2. The results demonstrate that MIC-based NKICA algorithm can perform speech separation effectively.

Figure 4 shows the results of the two experiment sets on TIMIT dataset. We also compare the execution time between the MIC-based and only CPU-based NKICA algorithm. The results show that the performance of MIC-based algorithm is also much better than the only CPU-based one on TIMIT dataset. An around 10 times speedup is achieved by MIC-based algorithm, when the three parameters set to different values. The best speedup is 12.3, when m set to 100, M set to 40, and N set to 50000. In the two experiments, the MIC architecture shows its great effectiveness in performing NKICA algorithm. The

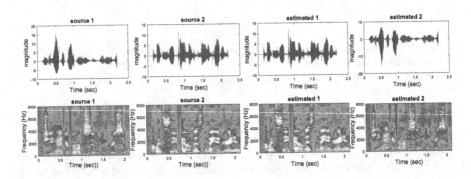

Fig. 3. Decomposition result on TIMIT dataset by NKICA. The first row shows the time-domain signals of original speech and recovered speech, and the second row shows the frequency-domain signals of original speech and recovered speech

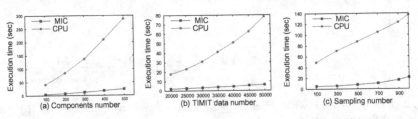

Fig. 4. Execution time with different parameter values: (a) Components; (b) Data points; (c) Sampling points.

intensive matrix manipulations are offloaded to coprocessor and performed parallel, which makes the NKICA algorithm has a much shorter execution time on MIC. In summary, MIC implementation is a very effective way to accelerate NKICA algorithm.

5 Conclusion

The NKICA algorithm reduces the computational complexity of the KICA algorithm effectively. However, with the scale of the dataset increases, the computational complexity of NKICA algorithm grows quickly. This paper presented a MIC-based implementation of the NKICA algorithm. We analyzed the parallelism of the NKICA algorithm, and parallelized the critical segments by offloaded the intensive computations to MIC. Our implementation took advantage of the OPENMP and MKL technology, and made best use of the parallelism provided by MIC. The experiment results on simulated dataset and TIMIT dataset show that MIC-based NKICA algorithm costs much less execution time, When comparing with the only CPU-based one. The speedup is around 10 on average, and 12.3 at best. The experiment results confirmed that MIC-architecture is suitable for accelerating NKICA algorithm.

References

1. Hyvärinen, A., Oja, E.: A fast fixed-point algorithm for independent component analysis. Neural Comput. **9**(7), 1483–1492 (1997)
2. Du, K.L., Swamy, M.: Independent Component Analysis: Neural Networks and Statistical Learning, pp. 419–450. Springer, London (2014)
3. Hyvärinen, A., Karhunen, J., Oja, E.: Independent Component Analysis. Wiley, New York (2004)
4. Bach, F.R., Jordan, M.I.: Kernel independent component analysis. J. Mach. Learn. Res. **3**, 1–48 (2003)
5. Shen, H., Jegelka, S., Gretton, A.: Fast kernel-based independent component analysis. IEEE Trans. Sign. Process. **57**(9), 3498–3511 (2009)
6. Williams, C., Seeger, M.: The effect of the input density distribution on kernel-based classifiers. In: Proceedings of the 17th International Conference on Machine Learning, no. EPFL-CONF-161323, pp. 1159–1166 (2000)
7. Kumar, S., Mohri, M., Talwalkar, A.: Sampling techniques for the Nyström method. In: International Conference on Artificial Intelligence and Statistics, pp. 304–311 (2009)
8. Wang, H., Xu, W., Guan, N., Yang, C.: Fast kernel independent component analysis with Nyström method. In: International Conference on Signal Processing (2016)
9. Duran, A., Klemm, M.: The intel many integrated core architecture. In: 2012 International Conference on High Performance Computing and Simulation (HPCS), pp. 365–366. IEEE (2012)
10. Jeffers, J., Reinders, J.: Intel Xeon Phi coprocessor high-performance programming. Newnes (2013)
11. Chrysos, G.: Intel xeon phi coprocessor-the architecture. Intel Whitepaper (2014)

12. Tarditi, D., Puri, S., Oglesby, J.: Accelerator: using data parallelism to program gpus for general-purpose uses. In: ACM SIGARCH Computer Architecture News, vol. 34, no. 5, pp. 325–335. ACM (2006)
13. Lee, S., Min, S.J., Eigenmann, R.: OpenMP to GPGPU: a compiler framework for automatic translation and optimization. ACM Sigplan Notices **44**(4), 101–110 (2009)
14. Garofolo, J.S., Lamel, L.F., Fisher, W.M., Fiscus, J.G., Pallett, D.S.: DARPA TIMIT acoustic-phonetic continous speech corpus CD-ROM. nist speech disc 1–1.1, NASA STI/Recon Technical report N, vol. 93 (1993)
15. Guan, N., Lan, L., Tao, D., Luo, Z., Yang, X.: Transductive nonnegative matrix factorization for semi-supervised high-performance speech separation. In: 2014 IEEE International Conference on Acoustics, Speech and Signal Processing (ICASSP), pp. 2534–2538. IEEE (2014)

Technology on the Horizon

A High-Radix Switch Architecture Based on Silicon Photonic and 3D Integration

Jian Jie[1(✉)], Xiao Liquan[1], Lai Mingche[1], and Xu Shi[2]

[1] College of Computer, National University of Defense Technology,
Changsha, Hunan, China
jianj06@mails.tsinghua.edu.cn
[2] College of Computer Science and Electronic Engineering,
Hunan University, Changsha, Hunan, China

Abstract. The design of high-radix switch chips is becoming a challenging research field in EHPC (Exascale High-Performance Computing). Recent development of silicon photonic and 3D integration technologies has inspired new methods of designing high-radix switch chips. In this paper, we propose a high-radix switch architecture called Grahpein, which improves the radix and bandwidth while lowering switch chips power consumption by 3D integration and silicon photonic technology. The simulation result also shows that the average latencies under both random and hotspot patterns are less than 10 cycles, and the throughput under random pattern is more than 95%. Compared to hi-rise architecture, the proposed architecture ensures the packets from different source ports receive fairer service, thereby yielding more concentrated latency distribution. In addition, the power consumption of the Graphein chip is about 19.2 W, which totally satisfies the power constraint on a high-radix switch chip.

1 Introduction

As the core infrastructure of HPC (High-Performance Computing), interconnection network plays a key role to the realization of large-scale parallel computing, by determining the performance and scalability of the system. ITRS predicts that by 2022, the peak performance of HPC will reach exascale (10^{18}), with over 200,000 computational nodes [1]. Such large scale and high performance raises higher requirements to the bandwidth, power consumption, and latency of the EHPC interconnection network. High-radix switch chip, as the key component of the interconnection network, determines the power and cost of the network. In 2015, Mellenox proposed a 36 port IB router for the interconnection of supercomputing and large-scale datacenter [2]. Intel proposed a 48-port switch based on Omni-Path architecture [3], yielding performance 2.3 times higher than that of IB network switches. Despite these achievements, they cannot satisfy the demands from EHPC (Exascale High-Performance Computing) for the efficacy and density of interconnection network. Therefore high-radix switch chips with more ports and higher throughput (over tens of Tbps per port) are highly expected.

© Springer Nature Singapore Pte Ltd. 2016
W. Xu et al. (Eds.): NCCET 2016, CCIS 666, pp. 179–190, 2016.
DOI: 10.1007/978-981-10-3159-5_17

However, the design of high-radix switch chips raises following challenges to the conventional technologies: (1) **Power and area bottleneck of LR-Serdes.** Most existing high-radix switch chips connect with other chips through LR-Serdes, which have relatively high BTE (Bit Transport Energy), resulting in high port power. The high power of LR-Serdes makes it difficult to physically realize high-radix switch chips. (2) **Buffer layout bottleneck.** Typical YARC architectures usually contain multiple large buffers, in order to compensate for the negative effects of round-trip credit delay on persistent switch throughput. With the increase of IO bandwidth and number of ports, the numerous buffers can cover over 60% of the chip's overall area. Besides, the large amount of row/column buses within the YARC architecture causes high density of lines on the chip, resulting in heavy RC and cross talk, which hinders effective chip layout.

In order to develop a realistic high-radix switch chip, we must first overcome the aforementioned two bottlenecks, which require innovative high-radix switch chip technologies. In 2015, OIF (Optical Connection Forum) defined SR-Serdes and USR (Ultra-Short Reach)-Serdes standards [4], which respectively support 20 cm and 5 cm signal transmission. The power of USR Serdes is only 4pj/bit, only 1/5–1/10 of LR Serdes, and the area is only 1/5 of LR Serdes. This means, with the development of silicon photonic, it is possible to solve the power bottleneck caused by LR Serdes, by directly applying the SR-Seders and USR-Serdes in switch chips with the help of on-board E/O transmission and 2.5D/3D photonic integration.

In this paper, we deal with the intra-chip data switching problem by applying on-chip photonic interconnection technology. As this technology advances, it is already possible to apply a complete on-chip photonic transmission component in an interconnection network of multi-core processors [5,6]. Compared to the conventional electric transmission network, silicon photonic networks have the advantage of high bandwidth density, low latency, low dynamic power and repeater-less communication, which makes it a viable choice for designing next-generation high-radix switch chips with up to 128–256 ports. In this work, we stack multiple layers of the 3D chip using silicon photonic on-chip network and TSV (Through Silicon Via)-based 3D integration technology [7], (1) to realize high-speed communication among multiple layers using inter-layer connections, and (2) to separate the optical data plane and the electric control plane. We can thus distribute the switch network and buffer of a high-radix switch chip into multiple layers, and realize 3D implementation of a high-radix switch network. Our approach is able to (1) decrease the length of waveguides on each layer, and (2) relieve the pressure of power, layout and bandwidth of the high-radix switch chip, thereby facilitating the design of high-radix switch chip.

In this paper, we propose Graphein – a novel Optical High-radix Switch Architecture for 3D Integration, which combines the advantages of silicon photonic and 3D integration. Graphein stacks 5 optical layers and 1 bottom port layer. Each optical layer is equipped with an optical switch network, which realizes intra- and inter- layer high-speed switching by using an intra-layer crossbar network and an inter-level TSV, The multi-layer network is able to lower the intra-layer crossbar radix, thereby (1) reducing the length of each optical waveguide, (2) reducing the count of micro-rings attached to each optical waveguide, and (3) lowering the overall power of the interconnection network. Using a PhoenixSim simulator, we have empirically evaluated our architecture in terms of latency, throughput, power and fairness.

2   Related Work

With the recent progress in silicon nanophotonics, many recent researches have turned their attention to optical on-chip interconnection network [8,9]. Silicon photonic components are CMOS-compatible and have lower production cost than electric components. 3D integrated circuits (3D-ICs) with wafer-to-wafer bonding technology show promising capability in improving the scalability of chips. In wafer-to-wafer bonded 3D-ICs, active devices (processors, memories, peripherals) are placed on multiple active layers, while vertical Through Silicon Vias (TSVs) are used to connect modules across the stacked layers. The appearance of 3D-ICs provides new opportunities for enabling higher performance and design efficiency of ICs [10]. Multiple active layers in 3D ICs can enable increased integration of chip within the same area footprint as traditional single layer 2D ICs. In addition, long global interconnects between ports can be replaced by shorter inter-layer TSVs, improving performance and reducing on-chip power dissipation. Recent 3D IC test chips from Intel, IBM, and Tezzaron [11–13] have confirmed the benefits of 3D IC technology.

Supreet Jeloka [14] proposes a high-radix switch for 3D integration called Hi-Rise. The Hi-Rise architecture puts the 64 ports in 4 layers of the 3D architecture to improve the scalability of the chip, and the arbitration of the switch is also divided into intra switch layer and inter switch layers. This architecture guarantees the fairness and efficiency of the arbitration by CLRG scheme, however, the bandwidth of the TSV channels between layers is the bottleneck of the network, which also limits the throughput cannot reach 100%.

The flattened butterfly [15] and dragonfly [16] are also architectures used to build high-radix switches. When compared to the traditional architectures such as mesh, these architectures improve the IO bandwidth and scalability of the switch chip. However, these architectures cannot satisfy the demand of EHPC. S. Scott [17] proposes the YARC architecture with 64 port. The bandwidth of YARC achieves 2.4 Tb/s. In order to solve the HOL problem, the YARC divides the switch process into 2 steps by placing a large amount of buffers and row/column buses. The demand of these resource makes it hard to scale to a higher radix. Nathan Binkert [18] rebuilds the YARC architecture by silicon photonic technology. The novel architecture replaces the buses by waveguides, and also decrease the buffer size. But it changes the arbitration process to only one step, and cannot guarantee the efficiency of the arbitration.

The channel allocation strategies of photonic network can be divided into 3 models, SWMR (single-write-multiple-read), MWSR (multiple-write-single-read), MWMR (multiple-write-multiple-read). The MWSR model is the most

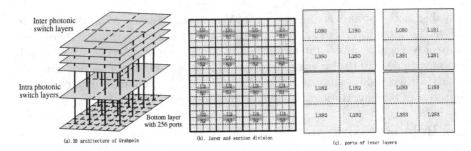

Fig. 1. Graphein architecture and its layers

popular one due to its high utilization of channels and low complexity of arbitration. MWSR crossbars provide each router with a dedicated receiving channel, and all the routers transmit data on the receivers' channels, forming a crossbar at the senders' end. Many MWSR arbitration schemes [19–21] have proposed in the last few years, most of them uses tokens to improve the efficiency of arbitration, and they also use broadcast waveguides or longer arbitration waveguides to improve the fairness. The existing literatures demonstrate that the MWSR arbitration schemes in optical network work well on fairness, power consumption and arbitration efficiency.

3   The Graphein Architecture

Graphein is an optical high-radix switch architecture for 3D integration, containing 256 ports. Using optical interconnection and stacked 3D packaging, Graphein architecture is able to (1) divide the switch network into many layers and (2) provide efficient intra-chip routing according to the relative positions of source and destination ports.

3.1   Graphein Architecture and Optical Switch Layers

In the Graphein architecture, all the 256 switch ports are distributed on the bottom port layer of the 3D multi-layer chip, and the high-radix switch network is realized on the optical switch layers upon the port layer. In order to decrease the radix of switch network, we propose two kinds of switch layers, the intra-switch layer and the inter-switch layer. Different layers connect with each other by TSVs (see Fig. 1(a)). When the packets enter Graphein from the bottom port layer, they will be transmitted through the TSVs to the corresponding inter-/intra- switch optical switch layer according to the respective positions of source and destination ports. After completing the switching process in the optical switch network, they will return to the bottom port layer and leave the Graphein chip.

In order to allocate the flow rate of packets into the switch network, the Graphein divides its 256 ports into 4 layers with 64 ports per layer. Each layer is further divided into 4 sections. Figure 1(b) shows the overall layout of the ports and the way they are divided into layers and section. We use coordinate (L, S, P) to denote the position of ports, where (1) L represents the layer number of the port, (2) S represents the port's section number in its layer, and (3) P represents the port's position in its section. For example, given port coordinate (L, S, P), we can get its number N by using the following formula:

$$N = L \cdot 64 + S \cdot 16 + P$$

and

$$0 \leq L \leq 3, 0 \leq S \leq 3, 0 \leq P \leq 15$$

Similarly, if we know a port's number is K, we can deduce its coordinate (L_k, S_k, P_k) by

$$L_k = K/64$$
$$S_k = (K/16)/4$$
$$P_k = K\%16$$

The switch network of the intra switch layer contains 4 crossbars – each of which consists of 64 ports from the corresponding layer (see Fig. 1(b)). Each inter-layer switch network chooses the crossbars which belong to 4 different layers but have the same intra-layer section number, and connects them into a fully connected switch network (see Fig. 1(c)). The entire Graphein architecture is thus composed of 4 inter-layer switch layers. For example, port 19 (with coordinate $(0, 1, 3)$), in the intra-switch layer, is connected with all the other ports in layer 0 into a crossbar network; while in the inter-switch layer, since its section number is 1, all the ports from Sect. 1 (i.e. 16–31, 80–96, 144–160, 208–224) form a 64-port crossbar network.

3.2   Switch

Packets that are injected into Graphein through input ports will leave from destination output port after going through the high-radix switching. The processes of switching can be classified as below according to the relative positions of the source and target ports. For the convenience of description, we abstract all 16 ports of the same section into one switch node, i.e., all the ports with layer number $L = i$ and section number $S = j$, are abstracted into one switch node $R(i, j)$, of which the port numbers (N) are within the following range:

$$i \cdot 64 + j \cdot 16 \quad \sim \quad i \cdot 64 + (j + 1) \cdot 16$$

Therefore, the optical switch network formed by multiple optical switch layers can be abstracted into the network shown in Fig. 2, where (1) the green lines denote the intra-switch network and the blue lines denote the inter-switch network, which are both realized by optical waveguides; and (2) the yellow lines denote the TSVs used to connect different switch layers.

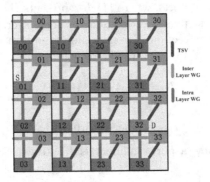

Fig. 2. Switch network of Graphein (Color figure online)

The network is a two dimension unidirectional torus network. Here, we use the classic XY-dimension routing algorithm for transmitting packets in this network. The inter-switch network forms the X-dimension paths and intra-switch network forms the Y-dimension paths. The inter-layer TSVs (the yellow oblique lines) are used for data transmission during the shifting between local and global switching.

The flows can be classified into 4 types according to the relative positions of source and target ports: (1) If both the source port and the target port of the packet are in the same layer, but with different section numbers (i.e., $L_s = L_d; P_s \neq P_d$), then it only needs to be switched within the intra-switch layer, i.e., the Y-dimension switching in Fig. 2. In this case, the packet first enters the intra-switch network through TSV and then leaves the Graphein from the bottom port switch after being switched. (2) If the source port and the target port of the packet are in different layers, but with the same section numbers (i.e., $L_s \neq L_d; P_s = P_d$), then it only needs to be switched within the inter-switch layer. In this case, the packet first enters the inter-switch network through TSV, reaches the target port through inter-layer switching network, and then returns to the port layer through TSV. (3) If the source and target ports of the packet are in different layers, with different section numbers (i.e., $L_s \neq L_d; P_s \neq P_d$), then it requires following two steps of optical switching: (i) inter-layer switching on X-dimension, i.e., transmits the packet to the intermediate node in the inter-layer; (ii) intra-layer switching on Y-dimension, i.e., transmit the packet through the inter-switch network to the target port. (4) If the source and target ports of the packet share the same layer number and section number, apply the same switching process as case 1, i.e., the packet is only transmitted in the intra-switch layer. The pseudo code of the switch process is as follows:

```
       The switch process of Graphein architecture
1. When a packet pk inject to the switch:
2.          Ls ← Ps/64; Ss ← (Ps/64)/4;
3.          Ld ← Pd/64; Sd ← (Pd/64)/4;
4. if ( Ls == Ld)
5.      Transmit pk to intra-layer by TSV;
6.      Switch pk to Dest port;
7.      Transmit pk to port-layer by TSV;
8. endif
9. else if ( Ss == Sd)
10.      Transmit pk to inter-layer by TSV;
11.      Switch pk to dest port;
12.      Transmit pk to port-layer by TSV;
14. else
15.      Transmit pk to inter-layer by TSV;
16.      Switch pk to intermediate (Ld,Ss);
17.      Transmit pk to intra-layer by TSV;
18.      Switch pk to dest port;
19.      Transmit pk to port-layer by TSV;
20. endif
```

4 Evaluation

The simulation is based on a cycle accurate simulator, the PhoenixSim simulator. This simulator can analyze and evaluate the key metrics such as delay, throughput and power consumption of the multi-processor systems connected by optical interconnection network. We use this simulator to model our high radix router architecture Graphein and the compared architectures Hi-Rise. We define the port number of switch architecture as P, the channel multiplicity between layers of hi-rise architecture as c.

The optical path length $T = 8$ cycles, and the frequency of the system is set to 8 GHz. The size of crossbar (N) is 256 with a packet size of 64 bytes. The depth of the queues is 8. We use synthetic traffic models to test these proposed architectures. For destination node selection, two distributions are used: (1) Normal Random (NR) and (2) Hotspot. When under the hotspot traffic, the hotspot is port 1.

4.1 Latency

We use the parameter P denotes the port count of the switch architecture, and the parameter c denotes the channel multiplicity of the hi-rise architecture. We build the simulation modes of hi-rise architecture [16] when $P = 64, c = 4; P = 256, c = 4; P = 256, c = 8$ and the simulation models of Graphein when $P = 64$ and $P = 256$, then statistics the average latency when the injection rate changes under the uniform random and hotspot traffic patterns. The results are in Figs. 3a and b.

When the injection rate is low, the Hi-Rise architectures with different parameters all have higher latencies than the Graphein architecture, this is because the arbitration latency of the optical network is lower than the electric network in the Hi-Rise. The more nodes in the network, the more write nodes to compete the write channel, which makes the arbitration latency is higher. This situation also occurs under the hotspot traffic patterns.

Meanwhile, under the random traffic pattern, the latency lines of the hi-rise architecture reach saturation faster than the Graphein, and the larger the ratio of P/c, the faster the line reaches saturation. As in the Hi-Rise architecture, the TSV channels between layers is the bottleneck of the network, and the larger of the value of P/c, the heavier of the congestion in the TSVs, which results in the average latency of packets increases rapidly. While in the Graphein architecture, there is no bottleneck in the network, and the latency line reaches saturation until the injection rate is almost 100%. When under the hotspot traffic pattern, all the nodes only send packets to the hotspot, the traffic in the TSVs is not so heavy that the TSV channels are not hotspot in the Hi-Rise architecture. Thus the saturation points of all the models are almost the same.

4.2 Throughput

We examine the performance with random and hotspot traffics and set the parameter $P = 256, c = 8$. Figure 4 shows the throughput of 16 ports choosing from all the 256 ports. The graphein architecture achieves almost ideal throughput under both traffic patterns, the simulation result agrees well with the analysis in Sect. 4. As the TSV channel is the bottleneck of the Hi-Rise architecture under the random traffic pattern, the throughput of nodes in Hi-Rise architecture is low. Generally, when the injection rate is r, the unidirectional flow between any layers is:

$$f = r \cdot P/L \cdot 1/L$$

L is the layer count of Hi-Rise, in this paper, is 4. When the utilization ratios of all the c TSV channels reach 100%, and the network is saturate, then, the flow between any layers is

$$f = r \cdot 256/(4 \cdot 4) = 8$$

That means only half of the flows can transmit through the TSVs timely. The throughput of the Hi-Rise architecture can only be 50%. The result is the same as Fig. 4 shows. While under the hotspot traffic pattern, there is no bottleneck in the Hi-Rise network and the throughput can approach to the ideal value.

4.3 Fairness

In order to evaluate the fairness of the Hi-Rise and the Graphein architecture, we draw the quartile diagram of the packets' latencies, the value of parameter P is 256 and c is 8. The result is shown in Fig. 5.

Under the random traffic, the 25%, 50% and 75% lines of the Graphein architecture all concentrate on about 15 cycles. This shows that most of the packets in Graphein have similar latencies. The fairness of the Graphein is good. The 25% line and 50% line of the Hi-Rise architecture is concentrate on about 20 cycles,

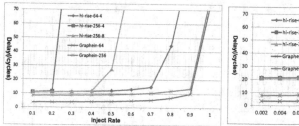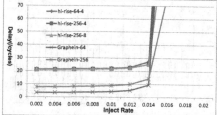

Fig. 3. Latency of hi-rise and Graphein under (a) random (b) hotspot patterns

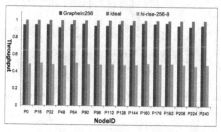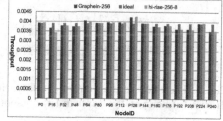

Fig. 4. Throughput of hi-rise and Graphein under (a) random (b) hotspot patterns

while the 75% line is scattered, most of the values are above 40 cycles, which demonstrates that under the saturate injection rate, the congestion between layers occurs. Though most of the packets can be transmitted timely, almost half of the packets cannot be serviced promptly and suffer a large latency. Under the hotspot traffic, the unfairness of the Hi-Rise is more significant. As shown in Fig. 5c, the distribution of the 25%, 50%, 75% lines of the Graphein is concentrated in a small range. Most of the packets have an similar latency in the architecture and they have a fair chance to gain the service. Meanwhile, we also notice that there is difference between nodes in the same layer: the nodes at the beginning of each layer have higher latencies and the nodes at the end of each layer have lower latencies. This is due to the unfairness of the 2-pass arbitration scheme in optical crossbar. The opportunity of nodes near to the downstream of the destination node is higher than that of the upstream ones, and the latencies of the nodes from the downstream are also lower.

However, when turn to Hi-Rise architecture, as can be seen in Fig. 5d, the latencies become various. Latencies of the packets from those nodes in the same layer with the hotspot node are small and their distribution is concentrate, while the latencies of packets from other layers are larger and their distribution is separate. This result shows that the TSV channels are the bottleneck of the Hi-Rise architecture, which make the architecture cannot be fair.

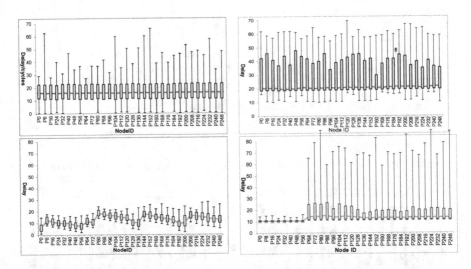

Fig. 5. The quartile diagram of the latencies (a) random & Graphein (b) random & Hi-Rise (c) hotspot & Graphein (d) hotspot & Hi-Rise

4.4 Power Consumption

Power consumption of an optical network consists of both static and dynamic components. The static component includes external laser power and ring heating power. The laser power includes distribution loss (laser coupling loss, beam splitter loss, laser E/O efficiency et al.) and ring resonance power. The ring heating power is generated by trimming the rings to the corresponding wavelengths. The dynamic power is expended by ring modulation and electrical back-end components including amplifier and detector. When to model the overall power consumption, we set the frequency of optical network as 8 GHZ, The data channels are each a waveguide with 16 wavelengths. It is also important to choose the parameters of optical devices. From some sets of technology parameters, we adopt the optical model in [22]. We also list the parameters of photonic devices and the optical resource inventory in Table 1.

According to the parameters, we can work out the bidirectional bandwidth of each port in the Graphein architecture:

$$B = 2 \cdot 16 \cdot 8G = 256\,\text{Gbps}$$

The assumption and parameters setting in this paper all satisfy the performance demand of EHPC. The ITRS predicts that, the demand of a single port in EHPC will not exceed 200 Gbps. The overall power consumption of the Graphein architecture is worked out to be no more than 19.2 W when following the parameters above, and this is within acceptable limits under the current industry process.

Table 1. Parameters and resource inventory

Parameters of photonic devices			
Photonic device	Loss	Photonic device	Loss
Waveguide loss	1 dB/cm	Coupling	1 dB
Insertion	0.017 dB	Ge RCEPD	3 dB
Scattering	0.001 dB	Trim	22 uW
Laser efficiency	5 dB	Biasing	91 uW
Detector sensitivity	0.15 fJ/b	Modulation	474 uW
Optical resource inventory			
Photonic network	Waveguides		Micro ring
Data network	Intra	256	256 K
	Inter	256	256 K
2-pass arbitration	Intra	4	8 K
	Inter	4	8 K

5 Conclusion

We propose a high-radix switch architecture based on silicon photonic and 3D integration in this paper. The proposed high-radix switch chip combines low cost photonic crossbars on multiple photonic layers with ports and switch logic modules in bottom electric port layers to reduce power dissipation and extend the scalability of the switch. Experimental comparisons with the previously proposed Hi-Rise architecture indicate a strong motivation for considering Graphein for future high-radix switch ICs as it can provide high throughput for every port and fairness for all packets. Our future work will explore the adaptive switch in the interconnection network on chip.

Acknowledgment. This work was partially supported by 863 Program of China (2015AA015302), NSFC (61572509).

References

1. International Technology Roadmap for Semiconductors, ITRS
2. SB7700: 36-port Non-blocking Managed EDR 100 Gb/s InfiniBand Switch, Mellanox Technologies (2015)
3. OIF Next Generation Interconnect Framework, April 2013
4. Birrittella, M.S., Debbage, M.: Intel@ Omni-Path Architecture: Enabling Scalable, High Performance Fabrics. IEEE (2015)
5. Biberman, A., Bergman, K.: Optical interconnection networks for high-performance computing systems. IOP sci. Rep. Prog. Phys. **75**, 046402 (2012). 15 pp
6. Ophir, N., Mineo, C., Mountain, D., Bergman, K.: Silicon photonic microring links for high-bandwidth-density, low-power-chip I/O. In: IEEE MICRO, January 2013

7. Koonath, P., Jalali, B.: Multilayer 3-d photonics in silicon. Opt. Express **15**(20), 12686C12691 (2007)
8. Morris Jr., R.W.: The three-dimensional stacked nanophotonic network-on-chip architecture with minimal reconfiguration. IEEE Trans. Comput. **63**(1), 243–255 (2014)
9. Dang, D., Patra, B., Mahapatra, R., A 2-layer laser multiplexed photonic network-on-chip. In: 16th International Symposium on Quality Electronic Design (2015)
10. Pavlidis, V., Friedman, E.: Three-dimensional Integrated Circuit Design. Morgan Kaufmann Pub, San Francisco (2009)
11. Vangal, S., et al.: An 80-Tile 1.28 TFLOPS network-on-chip in 65 nm CMOS. In: IEEE International Solid State Circuits Conference, February 2007
12. Bernstein, K., et al.: Interconnects in the third dimension: design challenges for 3D ICs. In: DAC (2007)
13. Patti, R.S.: Three-dimensional integrated circuits and the future of system-on-chip design. In: Proceedings of IEEE, vol. 94, no. 6, June 2006
14. Jeloka, S., Das, R.: Hi-Rise: a high-radix switch for 3D integration with single-cycle arbitration. In: MICRO (2014)
15. Kim, J., Balfour, J., Dally, W.: Flattened butterfly topology for on-chip networks. In: MICRO (2007)
16. Kim, J., Dally, W.J.: Technology-driven, highly-scalable dragonfly topology. In: ISCA (2008)
17. Scott, S., Abts, D., Kim, J.: The black widow high-radix clos network. In: ISCA (2006)
18. Binkert, N., Davis, Al.: The role of optics in future high radix switch design. In: ISCA (2011)
19. Vantrease Corona, D., et al.: System implications of emerging nanophotonic technology. In: ISCA (2008)
20. Pan Flexishare, Y., et al.: Channel sharing for an energy-efficient nanophotonic crossbar. In: HPCA (2010)
21. Vantrease, D., et al.: Light speed arbitration and flow control for nanophotonic interconnects. In: MICRO (2009)
22. Joshi, A., Batten, C., Kwon, Y.: Silicon-photonic clos networks for global on-chip communication. In: IEEE International Symposium on Network-on-Chip (NOCS), San Diego, CA (2009)

A Radiation Hardening Algorithm on 2nd Order CDR

Hu Chunmei[1](✉), Chen Shuming[1,2], Liu Yao[1], Chen Jianjun[1], and Xu Jingyan[1]

[1] School of Computer, National University of Defense Technology,
Deya Street 109, Changsha 410073, People's Republic of China
chmhu001@163.com
[2] National Laboratory for Parallel and Distributed Processing,
National University of Defense Technology,
Deya Street 109, Changsha 410073, People's Republic of China

Abstract. A radiation hardening algorithm named as state-conservation on 2nd order clock and data recovery (CDR) system is presented in this paper. This proposed algorithm is used to resist the single event transient (SET) of CDR tracking loop. A MATLAB model is established to fast evaluate the sensitive position of the system. A circuit model of 5 Gbps half rate CDR together with the hardening algorithm is set up to verify the effect of the proposed algorithm in Cadence design environment. The simulation result shows that SET does not lead to any error data and no loop delay is added. Compared to the RHBD standard-cell technique, the hardening algorithm saves area about 15.3% and reduces power consumption about 47.8%.

Keywords: Clock and data recovery · Pulse injection · State-conservation algorithm · Accumulator

1 Introduction

CDR using digital tracking loop has become increasingly popular for high-speed serial transceivers on both ground and space applications such as Backplane, Copper Cables, Optical Converters [1–3]. It has the advantage of low jitter, low power, small area requirements and no-affection by PVT variations [4, 5]. As the technology scales down, SET becomes more reliability-concerned in those devices and soft errors caused by SET increases [6, 7].

The previous SET hardening techniques on CDR are power and area consuming. For example, HXSRD01 Trivor of Honeywell Corporation is hardened by redundant method with cost of double area and power on 150 nm silicon-on-insulator CMOS technology [8]. Some research is carried on about single characterization and mitigation in the analog part of CDR [9, 10]. However, radiation hardening technique on entire CDR system has not been found according to the best knowledge of the authors. This paper focuses on aspect of hardening method which is about algorithm level.

This paper is organized as follow: Sect. 2 presents 2nd order CDR architecture. Section 3 analyses sensitive position in the CDR loop due to SET. Sections 4 and 5

© Springer Nature Singapore Pte Ltd. 2016
W. Xu et al. (Eds.): NCCET 2016, CCIS 666, pp. 191–199, 2016.
DOI: 10.1007/978-981-10-3159-5_18

propose state-conservation algorithm and show the simulation result on circuit level. Conclusions are presented in Sect 6.

2   CDR Structure and 2nd order Tracking Algorithm

According to the orders of digital low pass filter, the CDRs are divided into three types: 1st order [11], 2nd order and 3rd order [4, 12, 13]. Compared to 1nd order algorithm, 2nd order has the advantage of larger jitter tolerance. Third order loops are complicated because of the trade-offs by the frequency-dependent 3rd order loop behavior [13]. Second order loop is moderate and is adopted in this paper.

The architecture of 2nd CDR based on interpolator is shown in Fig. 1. The CDR consists of two samplers, one digital module and one phase interpolator (PI). In the frontend of the CDR, the samplers which work with the half of data rate sample the data to obtain the edge and data information. Due to the request of high bit rate which is 5 Gbps, the sampler is designed with high speed dynamic comparator with CML logic [10]. PI is the core analog circuit of CDR which receives the coefficients from digital module and interpolates four orthogonal clocks to accommodate the variety of input serial data in. The clock after PI is ensured to align with the center of input data eye.

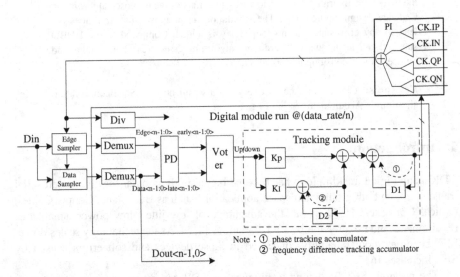

Fig. 1. 2nd order CDR block diagram

In this paper, we mainly focus on the digital module. In the Fig. 1, Demux is introduced after two samplers to slow down the frequency of CDR digital module. The n value in "<n − 1:0>" is decided by the format of deserializing data, the algorithm of digital module. Phase detector (PD) analyzes the two edges and one data information which are neighborhood and judges early or late. To suppress the effect of input jitter, Voter is introduced in the CDR. Voter sums early <n − 1:0> and late <n − 1:0> and up/down is come into being. The following tracking module suppresses input jitter using 2nd order algorithm and generate PI coefficient to restore the phase and frequency difference between input serial data and orthogonal clock. Tracking module is illustrated in Fig. 2.

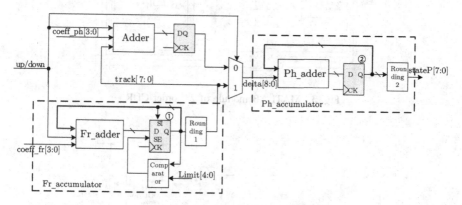

Fig. 2. Tracking module block digram

Tracking module is a 2nd order algorithm. It consists of Ph_accumulator and Fr_accumulator module which accumulate phase and frequency difference respectively. The accumulator of frequency difference has saturated characteristic which will be stabilized when serial data and orthogonal clock matchs. The accumulator of phase tracking has cycle characteristic which will clean to zero when overflow. To improve the flexibility of controlling, coeff_fr[3:0], coeff_ph[3:0] and limit[4:0] are set. These parameters can be adjusted to adapt KP and KI in Fig. 1. The Cadence Spectre simulation result shows that deterministic jitter of the recovered data is less than 0.3 UI and 1000 ppm frequency difference can be tracked in this system.

3   Analyzing Sensitive Position of SET

In this paper, MATLAB module of 2nd order CDR is established as shown in Fig. 3. In the prophase of designing, MATLAB module is usually used to evaluate performance of whole system such as jitter, loop delay and bandwidth because parameters such as KP and KI can be adjusted easily and quickly. Compared with circuit level simulation, using MATLAB is much faster and the running time can be reduceded two orders of magnitude.

The sensitive position of SET can also be located quickly in this period with the method of pulse injection. As illustrated in Fig. 4, pulse injection is realized by subtraction of two step-function signals with different delay. The amplitude of signal determines the bit precedence of bus <n − 1:0> . The delay of two signals is defined as one clock period. As a result, pulse injection can simulate SET in MATLAB.

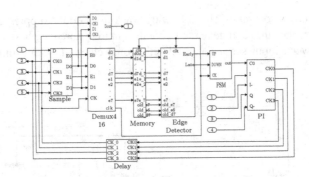

Fig. 3. MATLAB module of 2nd order CDR

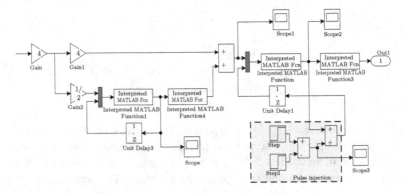

Fig. 4. MATLAB module of tracking module

The pulse injections are carried on DEMUX, Detector, VOTER, frequency accumulator, and phase accumulator in the module. Due to the characteristic of low pass filtering, the pulse injection on DEMUX, Detector and VOTER has very little impact on the coefficient of PI. But the action of two accumulators are much more worsen.

Figure 5 indicates the stabilization process and the eye diagrams of clock after PI on three situations. In (a), no pulse injection, the coefficient of PI is stable after 1 us. In (b) and (c), there is a pulse injection at 2 us and the amplitude of pulse is 512 which is equivalent to sum<9> = 1 in sum<10:0>. When SET happens, the coefficient of PI changes unexpectedly and the CDR enters restoration moment. In (c), it takes 1.56 us for restoration and the time in (b) is 0.08 us. The eye diagram becomes worsened. The eye diagram closes partly in (b), and the eye diagram closes entirely in (c). It also shows that the data of sampler in (b) and (c) is not correct during the restoring moment. Pulse injection can be executed at any combination cell in accumulator. As long as the glitch which is induced by SET can be latched by the accumulator's register, it is hazardous to the system. So in the 2nd order CDR the two accumulators are sensitive to SET.

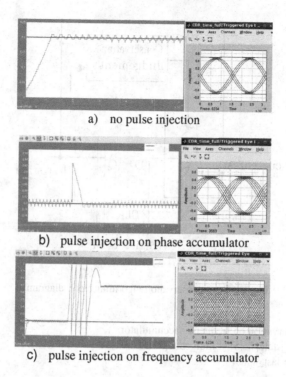

a) no pulse injection

b) pulse injection on phase accumulator

c) pulse injection on frequency accumulator

Fig. 5. The stabilization process of PI and the eye diagrams of clock

4 State-Conservation Algorithm on 2nd order CDR

State-conservation algorithm is presented in this paper to reject SET on accumulators in 2nd order CDR. Figure 6 shows the structure of the proposed algorithm. The new algorithm detects the input signal of accumulator's register every clock period. If the subtraction between input signal of register (means the state of current clock) and output signal of register (means the state of last clock) exceeds utmost tolerance, the output of accumulator's register will be forced back to the value of last clock shown in Fig. 6. As a result, the abnormal glitch cannot be transferred to PI coefficient. The implementation of the proposed algorithm uses an extra judgement module and a MUX. Another implementation method is using register with scan input (SI) and scan enable (SE) to unite MUX and register. The proposed algorithm does not add new register and the last state just maintains another one cycle, so loop delay and clock jitter will be invariable. The disadvantage of this algorithm is that it needs to add judgement logic which may has influence on critical path.

In this paper, state-conservation algorithm is implemented on a 5 Gbps 2nd order CDR based on Fig. 2 at circuit level. The registers at the end of accumulators are enhanced and conversation judgement is added. The state-conservation logic pseudocode is illustrated in Fig. 7.

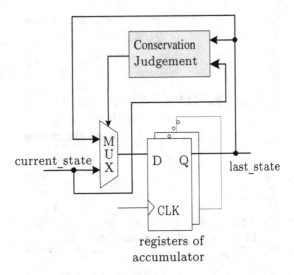

registers of
accumulator

Fig. 6. State-conservation algorithm block diagram

```
// state-conservation on frequency accumulator
if ( |current_state[11:5]— last_state[11:5] | > 1)
then state* = last_state;
else
state* = current_state;
endif

// state-conservation on phase accumulator
if ( |current_state[8:0] — last_state[8:0] | > 2coeff_ph [3:0] + |track[7:0]| +2)
then state* = last_state;
else
state* = current_state;
endif
```

Fig. 7. State-conservation logic pseudo codes

On frequency accumulator, rounding1 in Fig. 2 is 5 bit. The criterion of judgement is not relevant to state[4:0] and the coeff_pr[3:0] is shielded. The criterion is that the absolute value between current_state[11:5] and last_state[11:5] is larger than 1. For phase accumulator, when the result of voter changes from down to up, the difference is at least 2 * coeff_fr[3:0]. At the same time, owing to rouding2 is 1 bit, constant "2" is added to the criterion. On both pseudocodes, if Δ exceeds the criterion, the last_state will be reloaded by register once again instead of current_state.

5 Simulation Result

Cadence Spectre simulator is used for simulation at circuit level and SET is injected by the means of double exponential current source. The double exponential current source is expressed as

$$I(t) = I_0[\exp(-\alpha t) - \exp(-\beta t)] \tag{1}$$

Where I_0 is approximately the maximum current, $1/\alpha$ is the collection time constant of the junction, and $1/\beta$ is the time constant for initially establishing the ion track. Those parameters of current source are extracted from 3D device simulation under the same technology with Synopsys Sentaurus DeviceVersion H-2013.03. The I_0 is 200 uA, $1/\alpha$ is 10 ps and $1/\beta$200 ps. The testbench is PRBS7 with 10 feet channel model.

As showed in Fig. 8, the injection is happened at 100 ns, and the coefficient of PI drops from 219 to 153 suddenly. After that, the coefficient restores step by step and reaches at balance again. The opening degree of PI clock descends to 0.8 UI in Fig. 9. And worse yet, there are about 75 error-bits in the output of CDR during restoration which cannot be tolerated under the request of BER 10^{-12}.

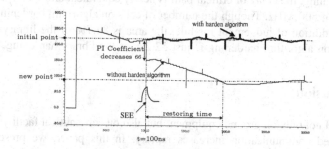

Fig. 8. The coefficient of PI in circuit simulation

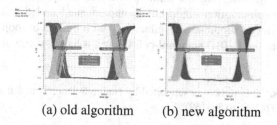

(a) old algorithm   (b) new algorithm

Fig. 9. Eye diagrams in circuit simulation

After using state-conservation algorithm, the coefficient of PI is well-balanced and there has no restoring time because the coefficient under SET cannot be transferred through the register of accumulator. In addition, the eye-opening is 0.86 UI which is almost the same compared to simulation result without SET. As a result, there is no error-bit in output.

To evaluate the cost of state-conservation algorithm, logic synthesis is performed on both the algorithm hardening and the RHBD standard-cell library which is proved to be effective in our research group [14–16]. The RHBD standard-cell library refers to all cells in library are radiation hardened by design. The result is shown in Table 1.

Table 1. The result of logic synthesis

	Library hardening	Algorithm hardening	Comparison
Stages of critical path	8	13	Meet the request of 500 MHz
Delay of critical path	1.21 ns	1.19 ns	
Area	5555.4 um^2	4703.5 um^2	84.7%
Power	2.9548 mW	1.5411 mW	52.2%

Though the stages of critical path on algorithm hardening is more than that of library hardening, the delay of critical path is nearly equivalent and both methods meet the request of 500 MHz. Though the number of cells on algorithm hardening increases due to the addition of judgement module, the area is 84.7% of the library hardening. The power on algorithm hardening is just 52.2% of the library hardening.

6 Conclusion

CDR is used not only on ground equipment but also on aeronautical facility as the need of high-speed communication increases rapidly. In this paper, we present a novel state-conservation algorithm to resist the SET on tracking logic of 2nd order CDR. Matlab modeling is used to fast locate the sensitive position of the CDR loop with the method of pulse injection, thus the running time can be spared. The 2nd order CDR circuit with state-conservation algorithm is implemented and the simulation results show the algorithm can suppress SET effectively with no loss of loop delay and clock jitter. Compared to the RHBD standard-cell library, it has less area and almost half of power.

Acknowledgments. This work was supported by Nature Science Foundation of China (Grant No: 61434007, 61376109, 61504169).

References

1. He, M.Y., Poulton, J.: A CMOS mixed-signal clock and data recovery circuit for OIF CEI-6G+ backplane transceiver. IEEE J. Solid-State Circ. **41**(3), 597–606 (2006)
2. Kromer, C., Sialm, G., Menolfi, C., Schmatz, M.: A 25-Gb/s CDR in 90-nm CMOS for high-density interconnects. In: IEEE International Solid-state Circuits Conference, vol. 41, pp. 1266–1275 (2006)
3. Savoj, J., Hsieh, K., Upadhyaya, P., An, F.T., Im, J., Jiang, X., et al.: Design of high-speed wireline transceivers for backplane communications in 28 nm CMOS. In: Proceedings of the Custom Integrated Circuits Conference, pp. 1–4 (2012)
4. Zhang, Y., Gai, W.: SSC tracking analysis and a deeper-SSC estimator. In: IEEE International Symposium on Circuits & Systems, pp. 1408–1411 (2013)
5. Chang, H.H., Yang, R.J., Liu, S.I.: Low jitter and multirate clock and data recovery circuit using a MSADLL for chip-to-chip interconnection. IEEE Trans. Circ. Syst. I **51**(12), 2356–2364 (2004)
6. Premkishore, S., Michael, K., Stephen, W.K., Burger, D., Lorenzo, A.: Modeling the effect of technology trends on the soft error rate of combinational logic. In: Proceedings International Conference on Dependable Systems and Networks, DSN 2002, pp. 389–398 (2010)
7. Mahatme, N.N., Jagannathan, S., Loveless, T.D., Massengill, L.W., Bhuva, B.L., Wen, S.J., et al.: Comparison of combinational and sequential error rates for a deep submicron process. IEEE Trans. Nucl. Sci. **58**(6), 2719–2725 (2011)
8. datasheet of HXSRD01 Trivor. www.honeywell.com
9. Armstrong, S.E., Olson, B.D., Holman, W.T., Warner, J., Mcmorrow, D., Massengill, L.W.: Demonstration of a differential layout solution for improved ASET tolerance in CMOS A/MS circuits. IEEE Trans. Nucl. Sci. **57**, 3615–3619 (2010)
10. Hu, C., Chen, S., Huang, P., Liu, Y., Chen, J.: Evaluating the single event sensitivity of dynamic comparator in 5Gbps SerDes. IEICE Electron. Express **12**(23), 1–6 (2015)
11. Liu, Y., Yum, T.Y., Xue, Q., Chan, C.H.: A 50-mW/ch 2.5-Gb/s/ch data recovery circuit for the SFI-5 interface with digital eye-tracking. IEEE J. Solid-State Circ. **39**(4), 613–621 (2004)
12. Chen, W.C., Tsai, C.C., Chang, C.H., Peng, Y.C.: A 2.5-8 Gb/s transceiver with 5-tap DFE and second order CDR against 28-inch channel and 5000 ppm SSC in 40 nm CMOS technology. In: IEEE Custom Integrated Circuits Conference, pp. 1–4 (2010)
13. Wang, S., Mei, H., Baig, M., Bereza, W.: Design considerations for 2nd-order and 3rd-order bang-bang CDR loops. In: Custom Integrated Circuits Conference, pp. 317–320 (2005)
14. Du, Y., Chen, S., Liu, B.: Impact of pulse quenching effect on soft error vulnerabilities in combinational circuits based on standard cells. Microelectron. J. **44**(2), 65–71 (2013)
15. Bin, L., Yankang, D., Hui, X.: Mitigating the SERs of large combinational circuits by using half guard band technique in CMOS bulk technology. IEICE Electron. Express **11**(19), 1–6 (2014)
16. Bing, L., Ruiqiang, S.: Analyzing and mitigation the internal single-event transient in radiation hardened flip-flop at circuit-level. Sci. China Tech. Sci. **57**, 1834–1839 (2014)

Sub-threshold Performance Driven Choice in Tunneling CNFETs

Hailiang Zhou[1(✉)], Xiantuo Tang[2], Minxuan Zhang[1,2], and Yue Hao[1,2]

[1] The School of Computering, National University of Defense Technology,
Changsha 410073, China
hlzhou@nudt.edu.cn
[2] China National Digital Switching System Engineering and Technological
Research and Design Center, Zhengzhou, China

Abstract. The working mechanism of Tunneling Carbon Nanotube Feild Effect transistors (TCNFETs) has been analyzed firstly by defining the sub-threshold plunging voltage and subdividing sub-threshold region into Band-To-Band Tunneling (BTBT) burst region, BTBT sharp region and BTBT smooth region. And then, the effects of device parameters, such as source/drain doping level, oxide thickness, working voltage, on the transfer characteristics are studied with an eye kept on the effect of BTBT burst region. As a conclusion, a reference device parameters choice flow and corresponding criterion are brought out. Research results show that: (1) BTBT burst region make a non-ignorable contribution to the sub-threshold slope. (2) Proper device parameters would contribute to ultra-low sub-threshold slope. (3) BTB tunneling at channel-drain interface would have a negative effect on device performance, which is even could not be suppressed for TCNFETs with small enough energy gap.

Keywords: Sub-threshold slope · Band-to-band tunneling · Ambipolar conductance · Carbon nanotube field effect transistor · Non-equilibrium green's function

1 Introduction

In recent years, much attention has been directed to Carbon Nanotube Field Effect Transistors (CNFETs) due to better device performance [1] and scaling ability [2] as to conventional silicon based Metal-Oxide-Semiconductor Field Effect Transistors (MOSFETs). And CNFETs are considered as building blocks of future nano-electronic systems. Although a CNFETs-based prototype circuit has been fabricated, the optimization of device performance would never stop. According to the device structure, CNFETs could be categorized into conventional MOS-like CNFETs (C-CNFETs), Schottky barrier CNFETs

The work is supported by National Natural Science Foundation of China (No. 61204130).

W. Xu et al. (Eds.): NCCET 2016, CCIS 666, pp. 200–211, 2016.
DOI: 10.1007/978-981-10-3159-5_19

(SB-CNFETs) and Tunneling CNFETs (TCNFETs). TCNFETs receive much research due to the possibility of ultra-low sub-threshold slope SS.

Both high dynamic performance and low OFF-state leakage current could be obtained with the assumption of steep enough SS. As a consequence lots of subthreshold performance optimization researches have been carried out. The ambipolar conductance of TCNFETs, resulting from the symmetrical device structure, would weaken not only the device OFF-state but also sub-threshold performance [3,4]. [5] analyzed the effect of oxide thickness on the band structure and thus on the device sub-threshold performance, as well as the effect of gate structure on the transfer characteristics. [6] made a deep insight into the depending factors of SS and the effect of source/drain doping level on sub-threshold performance in TCNFETs. And a conclusion was concluded that high driving current and steep SS cannot be obtained at the same time in TCN-FETs with planar bulk structure. Further comparing research results show that TCNFETs with 1-D device layout behaved more affirmatively in performance optimization.

A fact would be revealed later is sub-threshold performance optimization is a complicated project. Many factors such as CNT energy gap, source/drain doping level (N_{SD}), working voltage (V_{DD}), device structure, affect the transfer characteristics and sub-threshold performance in different manner. These factors even interact with each other sometimes. Therefore we try to present a reference device parameters choice flow and corresponding criterion to optimize the sub-threshold performance.

2   Numerical Modeling

NEGF [7,8] method is adopted to develop the CNFETs model in order to take the quantum phenomena such as carrier tunneling, phonon assisted tunneling [9,10] and quantum capacitance into account. The NEGF formalism, which solves Schrodinger equation and Poisson equation iteratively, provides a sound basis for quantum device simulation.

Much work has been done on CNFET modeling based on NEGF method, and several CNFETs simulators have been set up. There are some very famous and authentic ones such as "moscnt" (set up by Guo Jing research group of Purdue University) [9], "NANOTCAD" (set up by Gianluca Fiori research group of Purdue University) [11,12], and "NEMO" (set up by research group of Pisa University) [13]. Large quantities of comparing studies show that these models, which are open source, can describe the carriers transporting in CNFETs exactly.

For the authenticity of the research results, the research are carried out based on "moscnt" in this work, but with some important modifications. Schottky contact between CNT and metal electrode is taken into account. As a result, the simulation of SB-CNFETs and C-CNFETs or TCNFETs with metal contacting electrode can be carried out based on this model. At the same time, in order to deal with effect of phonon assisted tunneling in CNFETs, the modeling of phonon assisted tunneling is added into the model. And the corresponding detailed method and modeling flow could be found in [14].

3   Subthreshold Performance Is the Key

Scaling is the most important method to improve the density and performance of integrate circuit. But a interesting phenomenon is that V_{DD} of high performance MOSFETs would just scale to 0.64 V by 2018 according to ITRS (International Technology Roadmap for Semiconductors) 2013 [15], while V_{DD} is about 1.2 V on 2000. The scaling speed of V_{DD} is seriously slower than that of device size. [16] considered that the following two facts contribute mainly to this phenomenon. Firstly, the OFF-state current I_{OFF} increases exponentially with the decrease of threshold voltage V_T [16]. Secondly, the device dynamic performance depends on V_{DD}/V_T. It's easy to find, by seeing through the appearance to perceive the essence, the essential limitation of V_{DD} scaling ability is the mild SS. It's well-known that there is a theoretic limitation to the SS of 60 mv/dec for silicon based MOSFETs. Due to the existence of such theoretic limitation, certain inversion region length should be preserved for large enough driving current.

As a result, the V_T value could not be too small [17] to decrease the OFF-state leakage power on one hand, and not be too large to ensure demand-meeting dynamic performance on the other hand in application. Both high dynamic performance and low OFF-state leakage current could be obtained with the assumption of steep enough SS. Therefore, considerable amounts of research has already be carried out for smaller SS [18,19], and certain progress has been made. [20] presented a novel device structure to obtain SS with value even smaller than kT/q by making use of schottky barrier tunneling and the amplifying effect of the device structure. America scientist organization web reported on Feb. 2012 that scientists from University of NotreDame and the Pennsylvanias State University have manufactured tunneling FETs working on quantum tunneling [21]. Toshiba declared, considering the outstanding characteristics of tunneling FETs on low-power, on Sep. 2014 to develop ultra-low power MCU (Memory Control Unit) based on tunneling FETs [22]. About the application of tunneling FETs in ultra-low power area, Swiss scientist Lonescu forecasted that the device power would be decreased to about one percent by scaling V_{DD} from 1 V to 0.2 V.

It's necessary to take a deep insight into the sub-threshold characteristics of TCNFETS. For convenience of analysis, a parameter of sub-threshold plunging voltage V_{STP} should be defined as the gate voltage value when the conductance band bottom of channel E_{CH}^C has just be pushed down lower than the valence band top of source region E_V^S.

When Vg $< V_{STP}$, there is almost no conductance channel, excepting the thermal diffusion which is small enough to be neglected, between source and drain. Further increase of Vg decreases the band gap between E_C^{CH} and E_V^S. When Vg $> V_{STP}$, E_C^{CH} was pushed down under E_V^S just as the solid curve in Fig. 1 shows. The carriers in source could transfer into channel via BTBT and form the source drain current I. The barrier, that conducting carriers should tunneling through, is shown as the dark region in Fig. 1. The width of the barrier is noted with Λ. It's obvious that the barrier shape is not a strict triangle, but with Λ changing sharply at the bottom.

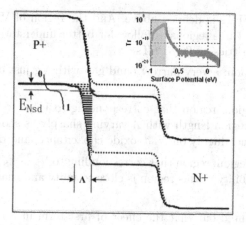

Fig. 1. Sketches of the band profiles of TCNFET.

The numerical computing expression and detailed corresponding deduction flow for SS were described in [6, 23, 24]. According to the conclusion in [6], SS can be expressed as:

$$SS = \ln(10)(\frac{\partial I_d}{\partial V_g}\frac{1}{I})^{-1} \tag{1}$$

$$\frac{\partial I}{\partial V_g} = \frac{2e^2}{h}\left(\frac{\partial T_{WKB}}{\partial E_C^{CH}}F(E_C^{CH}, N_{SD}) + T_{WKB}\frac{\partial F(E_C^{CH}, N_{SD})}{\partial E_C^{CH}}\right) \tag{2}$$

where $F(E_C^{CH}, N_{SD})$ is the transfer carriers integral between E_C^{CH} and E_V^S. $F(E_C^{CH}, N_{SD})$, with the value equaling to energy state number multiplied by the corresponding carrier occupancy probability, depends not only on the value of E_C^{CH} and also N_{SD}. T_{WKB} is the approximated BTB tunneling probability. By treating the barrier gap as strict triangle, it can be be expressed as $T_{WKB} \approx \exp(-\frac{4\Lambda\sqrt{2m^*Eg^{3/2}}}{3|e|\hbar(\Delta\Phi+Eg)})$ with $\Delta\Phi = E_C^{CH} - E_V^S$ and Eg being the energy gap. However, as mentioned above the shape of the barrier is not a strict triangle. Λ near E_V^S varies sharply with the change of Vg. But what we can sure is that T_{WKB} is function of Eg, $\Delta\Phi$, Λ, and the carrier effective mass m^*.

It's obvious that ultra low SS can be obtained by increasing either the first term or second term or even both of them in Eq. 2. [6] pointed out that the first term in Eq. 2 dominated when T_{WKB} is small but rapidly changes with Vg. E_C^{CH} is pushed down under E_V^S for just a narrow gap right now. And the author emphasized further that a ultra-low SS may be obtained due to first term of Eq. 2, but a small SS at certain limited Vg region is not sufficient. Therefore, what affects the average sub-threshold performance mainly is the second term, while the first term is insignificant.

The conclusions in [6] that listed above is reasonable at some point of view and for some cases. But is it suitable for all cases?

V_{STP} in TCNFETs is defined above. And the region of Vg > V_{STP} would be subdivided into three regions as follow for better understatement of the sub-threshold characteristics of TCNFETs.

– BTBT burst region: a very narrow band gap with Vg just exceeding or even equaling to V_{STP}.

– BTBT sharp region: region that corresponding to V_{STP} < Vg < $V_{STP} + \Gamma$, where Γ is the region length with Λ varying sharply as shown in Fig. 1. The value of Γ depends highly on Nsd, oxide capacitance, and device structure.

– BTBT smooth region: region that corresponding to Vg > $V_{STP} + \Gamma$. The BTB tunneling probability in this region is close to unity and changes only slightly with Vg.

Authors in [6] pointed out that the effect of first term in Eq. 2 is insignificant due to the narrowness of BTBT burst region. A series of simulation has been carried out for verification in this paper. And the simulation results are shown in Fig. 2. The gray solid line in Fig. 2(a) is the transfer characteristics with $N_{SD} = 10 \times 10^{-8}\,\mathrm{m}^{-1}$. It's obvious that I increases sharply during 0.55 V < Vg < 0.6 V. A fine-granularity simulation for this region is carried out with the results displayed as Fig. 2(c). It's obvious the current increases in a non-linear manner. I increases by 4 magnitudes during 0.55 V < Vg < 0.555 V, and increases by 4 magnitudes during a much wider region of 0.555 V < Vg < 0.6 V. That's to say, the burst of I during 0.55 V < Vg < 0.555 V results from $\frac{\partial T_{WKB}}{\partial E_V^{CH}}$ and thus the first term in Eq. 2. What should be pointed out further is that, the leap of the $\frac{\partial T_{WKB}}{\partial E_V^{CH}}$ value is due to not only the varying of Λ as mentioned in [6], but also the emergence of BTB tunneling within BTBT burst region. And the later even dominates.

For convenience of introduction, two sub-threshold performance correlative parameters are introduced:

– S_{min}: the minimum SS value during the whole Vg region with certain varying step.

– S_{ave}: the average SS value of the whole Vg region. There is not any specific definition for average SS of FETs. The value of S_{ave} affects mainly the choice of V_{DD}, OFF-state current, driving current etc. And these effects are all considered in the effect of sub-threshold performance on ON/OFF-state current ratio I_{ON}/I_{OFF}. Therefore, S_{ave} is defined as the average SS during the Vg region that started from V_{STP} and corresponds to I increased by six magnitudes.

The gray and black columns of Fig. 2(a) inset show the dependence of S_{min} and S_{ave} on Nsd respectively. It's obvious the ultra-low SS during 0.55 V < Vg < 0.555 V leads to S_{min} and S_{ave} of just 6 mV/dec when Nsd is $8 \times 10^{-8}\,\mathrm{m}^{-1}$ or $10 \times 10^{-8}\,\mathrm{m}^{-1}$. With the increase of Nsd, the sub-threshold performance corresponding to BTBT burst region decline, and S_{min} and S_{ave} increase accordingly. Now, we would come to the conclusion that any sub-threshold region with ultra-low SS could not be neglected.

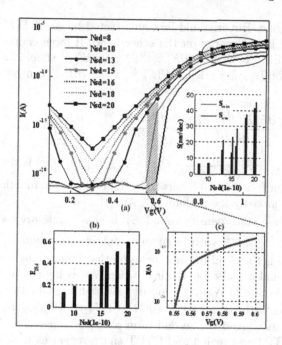

Fig. 2. Sketches of the effect of source/drain doping level on the transfer characteristics of TCNFET with CNT chirality of (7, 0), source/drain/channel length Lg = 28 nm, oxide thickness Tox = 2 nm, oxide dielectric constant $\varepsilon_{ox} = 16$, drain-source voltage Vds = 0.6 V, N_{SD} varying from $8 \times 10^{-8} \mathrm{m}^{-1}$ to $20 \times 10^{-8} \mathrm{m}^{-1}$, the work function of gate material equal to that of CNT

4   The Art of Choice

Just as described in Sect. 3, TCNFETs take the potential of ultra-low SS, which is crucial for high working frequency and low power. But we must note that the sub-threshold performance depends highly in the choice of device parameters. The choice of device parameters is very important. The correlative parameters that should be taken into account are listed as follow in priority order.

4.1   Doping Level Nsd

Nsd affects Eq. 2 in multiple mode. Nsd would affect, due to the P-N diode theory, the depletion region length and thus BTB tunneling probability T_{WKB} and even $\frac{\partial T_{WKB}}{\partial E_C^{CH}}$ on one hand. And the Fermi energy and thus the carriers distribution in source/drain region depends highly on the value of Nsd on the other hand. This means that both $F(E_C^{CH}, N_{SD})$ and $\frac{\partial F(E_C^{CH}, N_{SD})}{\partial E_C^{CH}}$ depend on Nsd. When Nsd is relatively high, the first term in Eq. 2 could is not so important due to two facts. $\partial T_{WKB}/\partial E_C^{CH}$ in BTBT smooth region is small on one hand. High enough value could be obtained for $\partial T_{WKB}/\partial E_C^{CH}$ in BTBT burst and

BTBT sharp region. But it would be counteracted by small $F(E_V^{CH}, N_{SD})$ due to large enough Fermi energy on the other hand. If large enough value of the second term in Eq. 2 is wanted, $\partial F(E_C^{CH}, N_{SD})/\partial E_C^{CH}$ should be large enough with the value of T_{WKB} settled. $\partial F(E_C^{CH}, N_{SD})/\partial E_C^{CH}$ can be subdivided as follow.

$$\frac{\partial F(E_C^{CH}, N_{SD})}{\partial E_C^{CH}} = \frac{\partial D(E)}{\partial E_C^{CH}} f(E) + \frac{\partial f(E)}{\partial E_C^{CH}} D(E) \qquad (3)$$

where $D(E) = \frac{8}{3\pi a_{cc}|t|} \frac{|E|}{\sqrt{E^2 - (E_G/2)^2}} \Theta(|t| - E_G/2)$ [25]. $\Theta(x)$ is the step function which equals 1 for $0 > x$ and 0 otherwise. $f(E)$ is the Fermi function. When Nsd is high, E_f^S is markedly lower than E_V^S. And the energy states located mainly close to E_V^S, while state density round E_f^S is small and varies slowly. On the other hand, $\partial f(E)/\partial E_C^{CH}$ with large value only exists round E_f^S but not E_V^S. This two facts together lead to the conclusion that large enough value of second term in Eq. 2 could not also be obtained when Nsd is high enough.

With the decrease of Nsd, E_f^S moves toward E_V^S gradually. The first term of Eq. 2 increases with the increase of $F(E_C^{CH}, N_{SD})$ in BTBT burst region and BTBT sharp region. And the second term of Eq. 2 increases with the increase of $f(E)$ in BTBT burst region and BTBT sharp region as well as the increase of $D(E)$ in BTBT smooth region. With the further decrease of Nsd to certain degree, small enough SS would be obtained due to the outstanding transfer characteristics in BTBT burst region and BTBT sharp region.

What should be pointed out is that both terms in Eq. 2 would increase with the decrease of Nsd. Then here comes the question which part or both contribute mainly to the ultra-low SS? The parameter $E_{Nsd} = E_V^S - E_f^S$ is introduced here for further analysis. The dependence of E_{Nsd} on Nsd is shown as Fig. 2(b). The value of E_{Nsd} is about 0.12 V when $Nsd = 10 \times 10^{-8} m^{-1}$. And the length of gate bias region corresponding to such ultra-low SS is even smaller than 0.05 V as Fig. 2(c) shows. So according to the analysis in Sect. 3, it's proper to make a conclusion that the ultra-low SS is mainly due to the first term in Eq. 2 and especially to the ultra-large $\partial T_{WKB}/\partial E_C^{CH}$ in BTBT burst region.

The decrease of Nsd would increase the sub-threshold performance, but widen the BTB Tunneling barrier width and thus decrease the ON-state current markedly just as the ellipse in Fig. 2(a) shows. When just one CNT is integrated in CNFETs, this would decrease the device driving ability and thus increase the gate delay $C_g V_{DD}/I$ greatly. However, multiply CNTs are integrated in technique application [26,27]. So I_{ON}/I_{OFF} denotes the device driving ability more reasonably than I_{ON}. And the former increases, but not decreases, by about 3.5 magnitude with Nsd decreased from $20 \times 10^{-8} \, m^{-1}$ to $8 \times 10^{-8} \, m^{-1}$ as Fig. 2(a) shows.

Therefore the choice criterion of Nsd is: $0 < E_{Nsd} < \Delta$ should be maintained with Δ is quite small positive number if steep SS is wanted. Such conclusion has been concluded before such as in [6]. But the conclusion in this paper is drew based on a subdivision of the sub-threshold region and detailed analysis of SS expression.

4.2 Oxide Capacitance

The source-channel interface could not be dealt as a common P-N junction due to the existence of oxide capacitance. For instance, depletion locates mainly on the lightly doped side according to P-N junction theory. But this is not the fact in CNFETs according to all corresponding researches. The cause is just the existence of oxide capacitance. The oxide capacitance affect the BTB Tunneling barrier and thus the transfer characteristics on certain degree. Figure 3 show the effect of oxide thickness Tox on the transfer characteristics of TCNFET with Tox varying from 0.5 nm to 4 nm.

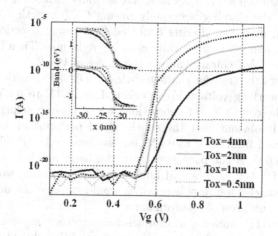

Fig. 3. Sketches of the effect of oxide thickness on the transfer characteristics of TCN-FET with CNT chirality of (7, 0), Lg = 28 nm, $Nsd = 10 \times 10^{-8}$ m^{-1}, $\varepsilon_{ox} = 16$, Vds = 0.6V, the work function of gate material equal to that of CNT

Just as the inset of Fig. 3 shows that the barrier width Λ decreases, due to the increase of the gate control ability, with the decrease of Tox. With an insight into the effect of Tox on the device band profile, it's easy to conclude that not only T_{WKB} but also $\frac{\partial T_{WKB}}{\partial E_V^{CH}}$ increases with the decrease of Tox. And this would lead to the increase of first term of Eq. 2. Therefore, just as the main of Fig. 3 shows, the sub-threshold performance increases with the decrease of Tox. At the same time, a larger I_{ON} could be obtained due to the decrease of Λ. This would further enhance the device driving ability.

Therefore the choice criterion for Tox is: If the gate leakage current is neglectable and no dielectric breakdown happens, the value of Tox should be as small as possible. And the similar effects would be obtained by increasing the dielectric constant ε_{ox} in application.

4.3 Working Voltage

The transfer characteristics of TCNFETs with Vds (with value being the same with that of working voltage V_{DD}) value of 0.3 V, 0.6 V and 0.9 V are simulated as the black solid, gray solid, black dotted curves in Fig. 4 show respectively. And the corresponding band profiles are shown as the inset of Fig. 4. Just as the curves in the inset of Fig. 4 show that the change of Vds value just affect the band profile of drain and source-channel interface. Further insight into inset of Fig. 4 will found that no BTB tunneling channel come into existence even when Vg = 0.9 V. The maximum working voltage value is smaller than 1.0 V in technique at present. Therefore, the choice of Vg value within technique bias region would not affect the sub-threshold performance just as the curves in main of Fig. 4 show.

However, what should be pointed out is that the CNT chirality in all above simulations is assumed as (7, 0). A fact that we must be faced is that it's impossible to control the chirality accurately during CNT growth. Techniques like electric burning, diameter filtering could perform rough selection of chirality, but could not obtain CNTs with unity chirality right now. Then here comes the question whether CNT chirality affects the choice of V_{DD}?

Figure 5 shows the transfer characteristics of TCNFETs with CNT chirality of (19, 0) and working voltage V_{DD} varying from 0.3 V to 0.6 V respectively. According to the conclusion of subsection A, the corresponding Nsd value is $2 \times 10^{-8}\,\text{m}^{-1}$. It obvious that the subthreshold performance keeps the same with Vds increased from 0.3 V to 0.5 V, but weakens suddenly when Vds varies from 0.5 V to 0.6 V. A comparing study of the band profiles corresponding to Vds = 0.5 V and Vds = 0.6 V would find that BTB tunneling would come into existence at channel-drain interface, which would increase the off-state current and weaken the subthreshold performance.

Therefore, if BTB tunneling at channel-drain interface is not wanted to affect the device subthreshold performance, the must condition should be maintained:

$$\frac{E_g}{2} + \frac{Vds}{2} + \Delta_{sub} > Vds + E_{Nsd} \tag{4}$$

where Δ_{sub} denotes the steep subthreshold region just as inset of Fig. 5 shows.

Equation 4 could be transferred into:

$$Vds < Eg + 2\Delta_{sub} - 2E_{Nsd} \tag{5}$$

That's to say, the suppression of the effect of BTB tunneling at channel-drain interface on the subthreshold performance sets a upper limitation to V_{DD}. And it's denoted with V_{MAX} in this paper. The value of V_{MAX} depends on Eg and thus on CNT chirality.

Large V_{DD} is favorable for I_{ON}/I_{OFF}, OFF-state leakage power, V_T tuning, driving ability of the device and so on. But the dynamic power and gate leakage power would increases exponentially with the increase of V_{DD}. At the same time dielectric breakdown would even take place with the device size scaling. Therefore, V_{DD} should not be set too large while larger enough I_{ON}/I_{OFF} and

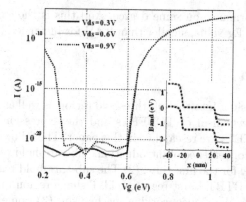

Fig. 4. Sketches of the effect of Vds value on the transfer polarity of TCNFET with CNT chirality of (7, 0), Lg = 28 nm, $Nsd = 8 \times 10^{-8}\,\mathrm{m}^{-1}$, $Tox = 2\,\mathrm{nm}$, $\varepsilon_{ox} = 16$, the work function of gate material equal to that of CNT. And the corresponding band profile with Vg = 0.65 V(inset).

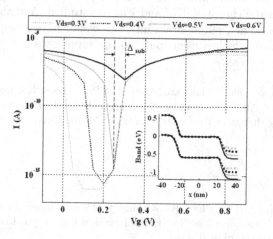

Fig. 5. Sketches of the effect of Vds value on the transfer polarity of TCNFET with CNT chirality of (19, 0), Lg = 28 nm, $Nsd = 2 \times 10^{-8}\,\mathrm{m}^{-1}$, $Tox = 2\,\mathrm{nm}$, $\varepsilon_{ox} = 16$, the work function of gate material equal to that of CNT. And the corresponding band profile with Vg = 0.3 V(inset).

V_T tuning region are ensured. As someone pointed out that V_{DD} would be triple of the sub-threshold region. Such value is defined as V_{MIN}, and set a lower limit to V_{DD}.

When $V_{MAX} > V_{MIN}$, outstanding sub-threshold performance could be obtained with Vds value within $[V_{MIN}, V_{MAX}]$. This is the case for TCN-FETs with with Eg value not too small. When $V_{MAX} < V_{MIN}$, the BTB tunneling at channel-drain interface would have a negative effect on the device subthreshold performance on some degree. And this is the case for TCNFETs with small enough Eg value, smaller than 0.2 V for instance.

5 Conclusion

Based on a deep insight into the sub-threshold region as well as a system analysis of the working mechanism of TCNFETs and the expression for SS, the sub-threshold of TCNFETs are researched in this paper. The following work has been done: (1) For the convenience of introduction, sub-threshold plunging voltage of TCNFETs is define for the first time. (2) The sub-threshold region in TCNFETs is subdivided into BTBT burst region, BTBT sharp region and BTBT smooth region according to the device working mechanism. (3) Some modification has been done to conclusions in [6] by confirming the non-ignorable contribution of BTBT burst region to the sub-threshold performance. (4) A reference device parameters choice flow and corresponding criterions for Nsd, Tox, V_{DD}, ε_{ox} are presented to obtain outstanding sub-threshold performance. (5) The effect of CNT chirality on the choice of Nsd and Vds are studied. And the results show that BTB tunneling at channel-drain interface would have a negative effect on device performance, which is even could not be suppressed for TCNFETs with small enough energy gap.

Acknowledgement. The authors are indebted to Prof. Zoheir Kordrostami from Shiraz University, Prof. Ali Naderi from Semnan University for their helpfull discussion and kindly help. Many thanks to Prof. Guo Jing from Purdue University for the CNFETs model.

References

1. Martel, R., Wong, H.P., Chan, K., Avouris, P.: Carbon nanotube field effect transistors for logica applications. In: IEDM Technical Digest, pp. 159–162 (2001)
2. ITRS 2008. http://public.itrs.net
3. Zhou, H.L.: Numerical study of carbon nanotube Field effect transistors based on Non-Equilibruim Green's Function. National University of Defense technology, Cshangsha, China (2010)
4. Koswatta, S.O., Nikonov, D.E., Lundstrom, M.S.: Computational study of carbon nanotube p-i-n tunnel FETs. Institute of Electrical and Electronics Engineers Inc., Washington, DC, MD, United states, pp. 518–521 (2005)
5. John, D.L., Pulfrey, D.L.: Issues in the modeling of carbon nanotube FETs: structure, gate thickness, and azimuthal asymmetry. J. Comput. Electron. **6**(1–3), 175–178 (2007)
6. Knoch, J., Mantl, S., Appenzeller, J.: Impact of the dimensionality on the performance of tunneling FETs: bulk versus one-dimensional devices. Solid-State Electron. **4**(51), 572–578 (2007)
7. Guo, J., Datta, S., Lundstrom, M., Anantram, M.: Towards multiscale modeling of carbon nanotube transistors. Int. J. Multiscale Comput. Eng. **2**, 257–276 (2004). Special Issue on Multiscale Methods for Emerging Technologies

8. Paulsson, M.: Non Equilibrium Green's Functions for Dummies: Introduction to the One Particle NEGF Equations. http://arxiv.org/abs/cond-mat/0210519v2
9. Koswatta, S.O., Lundstrom, M.S., Nikonov, D.E.: Band-to-band tunneling in a carbon nanotube metal-oxide-semiconductor field-effect transistor is dominated by phonon-assisted tunneling. Nano Lett. **5**(7), 1160–1164 (2007)
10. Koswatta, S.O., Lundstrom, M.S., Anantram, M.P., Nikonov, D.E.: Simulation of phonon-assisted band-to-band tunneling in carbon nanotube field-effect transistors. Appl. Phys. Lett. **25**(87), 3107 (2005)
11. Fiori, G., Iannaccone, G., Klimeck, G.: A three-dimensional simulation study of the performance of carbon nanotube field-effect transistors with doped reservoirs and realistic geometry. IEEE Trans. Electron Devices **53**(8), 1782–1788 (2006)
12. Fiori, G., Iannaccone, G., Klimeck, G.: Coupled Mode space approach for the simulation of realistic carbon nanotube field-effect transistors. IEEE Trans. Nanotechnol. **6**(4), 475–480 (2007)
13. Neophytou, N., Ahmed, S., Klimeck, G.: Non-equilibrium Green's function (NEGF) simulation of metallic carbon nanotubes including vacancy defects. J. Comput. Electron. **6**, 317–320 (2007)
14. Koswatta, S.O., Hasan, S., Lundstrom, M.S., Anantram, M.P., Nikonov, D.E.: Nonequilibrium green function treatment of phonon scattering in carbon-nanotube transistors. IEEE Trans. Electron Devices **54**(9), 2339–2351 (2007)
15. The International Technology Roadmap for Semiconductors (2013). http://www.itrs.net/ITRS
16. Chen, L.Y.: Low-Power CMOS Circuits: Technology, Logic Design and CAD Tools (Christian Piguet). CRC Press, Beijing (2011)
17. Knoch, J., Appenzeller, J.: Tunneling phenomena in carbon nanotube field-effect transistors. Physica Status Solidi a-Applications Mater. Sci. **205**(4), 679–694 (2008)
18. Zhou, H.L., Hao, Y., Zhang, M.X.: Numerical study of the sub-threshold slope in T-CNFETs. J. Semicond. **31**(9), 4005 (2010)
19. Appenzeller, J., Lin, Y.M., Knoch, J., Avouris, P.: Band-to-band tunneling in carbon nanotube field-effect transistors. Phys. Rev. Lett. **93**(19), 6805 (2004)
20. Gopalakrishnan, K., et al.: I-MOS: a novel semiconductor device with a subthreshold slope lower than kT/q. In: IEDM Technical Digest, pp. 289–292 (2002)
21. http://news.sciencenet.cn/htalnews/2012/3/261886.shtm
22. http://www.businesswire.com/news/home/20140916005387/zh-CN/VSNNv71gdNA
23. Zhang, Q., Zhao, W., Seabaugh, A.: Low-subthreshold-swing tunnel transistors. IEEE Electron Dev. Lett. **27**, 297–300 (2006)
24. Knoch, J., Appenzeller, J.: A novel concept for field-effect transistors -the tunneling carbon nanotube FET. In: Device Research Conference Digest, Santa Clara, CA, United states, pp. 153–156 (2005)
25. Guo, J.: Carbon nanotube electronics: modeling, physics, and applications. Purdue University (2004)
26. Chen, C.X., Xu, D., Kong, E.S.W., Zhang, Y.F.: Multichannel carbon-nanotube FETs and complementary logic gates with nanowelded contacts. IEEE Electron Device Lett. **27**(10), 852–855 (2006)
27. Chen, C.X., Zhang, W.: Multichannel carbon nanotube field-effect transistors with compound channel layer. Appl. Phys. Lett. **95**(19), 3 (2009)

A Novel Separated Pre-discharging Sense Amplifier for STT-MRAM

Huan Li[✉], Zhenyu Zhao, Quan Deng, Peng Li, Haoyue Tang,
and Lianhua Qu

College of Computer, National University of Defense Technology,
Changsha 410073, Hunan Province, People's Republic of China
{lihuan15,zyzhao,qulianhua14}@nudt.edu.cn

Abstract. This paper presents a novel sense amplifier for Spin Transfer Torque Magnetic Random Access Memory (STT-MRAM), named Separated Pre-discharging Sense Amplifier (SPDSA). By inverting the pre-charging path of Separated Pre-charging Sense Amplifier (SPCSA) to a pre-discharging path, a couple of inverters that used to transfer the voltage can be eliminated, and thus the area overhead of SPCSA is reduced. We develop a compact magnetoresistance model for MTJ to perform hybrid CMOS/magnetic HSPICE simulations. Based on 45 nm CMOS technology, simulation results exhibit that compared with SPCSA, SPDSA can reduce the power consumption by 35.6% and improve the read reliability by 29%.

Keywords: Read reliability · Sense amplifier · SPCSA · STT-MRAM

1 Introduction

In the past few decades, SRAM was a dominating memory technology for on-chip cache thanks to its high speed and easy integration with CMOS logic process [1,2]. However, as CMOS technology node scaling down, many obstacles like increased leakage power and limited scalability make SRAM design more difficult to meet the demand of sufficient stability. To overcome those issues, many memory technologies have been proposed. Among them, Spin Transfer Torque Magnetic Random Access Memory (STT-MRAM) is considered one of the most promising next-generation emerging memory technology to replace SRAM [3].

STT-MRAM can achieve long endurance (>10 years), nonvolatility, low write energy with fast writing speed. Magnetic tunnel junction (MTJ) as the cornerstone of STT-MRAM, is composed of two ferromagnetic layers (FM, e.g., CoFeB) separated by one tunneling oxide layer (e.g., MgO). The magnetization of one ferromagnetic layer is fixed while the other can change freely, as shown in Fig. 1. When the magnetization direction of the two FM layers are parallel (P),

This work is supported by the Research and Development of Supercomputer Processors (2015ZX01028-101).

© Springer Nature Singapore Pte Ltd. 2016
W. Xu et al. (Eds.): NCCET 2016, CCIS 666, pp. 212–217, 2016.
DOI: 10.1007/978-981-10-3159-5_20

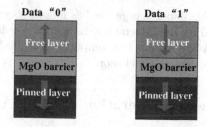

Fig. 1. The compositions of MTJ in two opposite configurations.

MTJ performs low-resistance, whereas, when the magnetization direction of the two FM layers are antiparallel (AP), MTJ performs high-resistance. Based on the different resistances of MTJ in different status, sense amplifiers can read out two different digital information through current or voltage [4].

To read the digital information stored in MTJs with high reliability, various sense amplifiers have been proposed. Zhao et al. proposed Pre-Charged Sense Amplifier (PCSA) in 2009 [5] and proposed Separated Pre-charge Sense Amplifier (SPCSA) later in 2014 [6], both of them exhibit high speed and low power consumption in deeply scaled CMOS technology nodes. The structure of PCSA and SPCSA are shown in Fig. 2(a) and (b), respectively. Both of them read a pair of MTJs (MTJ0 and MTJ1) in opposite magnetization configuration and exhibit very low power consumption and high sensing speed. Compared with PCSA, the readability of SPCSA has been greatly improved, while its area overhead is not a patch on PCSA. In order to reduce the area overhead of SPCSA, and improve its functionalities, we propose SPDSA.

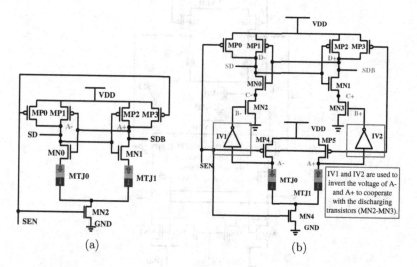

Fig. 2. (a) The schematic of PCSA. (b) The schematic of SPCSA.

The remainder of this paper is organized as follows. Section 2 introduces the proposed structure and its read operation. In Sect. 3, we demonstrate the high performance of SPDSA and exhibit the comparison results between SPCSA and SPDSA. Finally, Sect. 4 gives a conclusion.

2   The Structure and Operation of SPDSA

As can be observed, the structure of PCSA is more compact than that of SPCSA. However, due to the PVT variations and voltage headroom problem [6], the high sensing reliability of PCSA cannot maintain in deeply scaled submicrometer technology nodes. Base on PCSA, Zhao et al. proposed SPCSA. By separating the discharging and evaluation stages with two different paths, its immunities to the voltage headroom and PVT variations are greatly improved, and then, the sensing reliabilities ameliorated. However, the area overhead of SPCSA is too large.

In order to take advantage of the good merit of SPCSA while reduce the area overhead, meanwhile, improve the whole performance, we propose SPDSA as represented in Fig. 3. By inverting the pre-charging path of SPCSA to pre-discharging path, IV1 and IV2 that used to transfer the voltage can be eliminated, thus, the area overhead are reduced by four transistors. Unlike the SPCSA, which pre-charging the D− and D+ nodes to VDD and then discharging them during read operations, SPDSA pre-discharging the B− and B+ nodes to GND first and charging them during read operations. One thing to be noticed

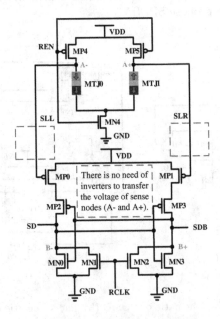

Fig. 3. The schematic of SPDSA.

is that, we also separate the discharging and evaluation paths, and simulation results show that SPDSA can achieve higher readability than SPCSA.

As shown in Fig. 3, SPDSA consists of a couple of inverters (MP2-3, MN0 and MN3), three NMOS (MN4 and MN1-2) that control discharging paths, and four PMOS (MP4-5 and MP0-1) that control charging paths. The basic sensing operation of SPDSA is similar to SPCSA, including three phases: charging, discharging and evaluation.

When set the REN = 0 and RCLK = 1, MP2-5 and MN1-2 are opened, while MP0-1, MN0 and MN3-4 are closed. A− and A+ nodes are charged to VDD, while B− and B+ nodes are discharged to GND. Then REN and RCLK are set to 1 and 0, respectively. MP4 and MP5 are closed and MN4 is opened. As the resistances of MTJ0 and MTJ1 are separately configured to be low and high, the discharging speed of A− and A+ nodes are different, and thus, the MP0 and MP1 are in different conduction conditions. Once the voltage of B− node reaches to the threshold voltage of the MN3, B+ node starts discharging to GND, while B− node continues charging to VDD.

One thing to be noted is that there hardly exit any stationary currents in the whole sensing operation. Just like SPCSA. Therefore, low power consumption can be expected in SPDSA.

3 Simulation and Comparison Results

In order to evaluate the performance and read reliability of the proposed SPDSA, we employed a compact MTJ model that integrates process variations, and a CMOS 40-nm design kit with 3 worse case parameters (for the Vth, channel length and width) [5,7], to perform 1,000 Monte-Carlo simulations. Some other default parameters used in HSPICE are listed as follows: (1) supply voltage VDD = 0.9 V; (2) the resistance of the parallel state is 3.8 k and (3) TMR = 120%. We designed the layout of SPDSA, as shown in Fig. 4, and extracted the parasitic resistance and capacity to perform transient simulations.

Figure 5 presents the timing of the sense process of SPDSA in transient simulations. Before T1, we set the REN = 0 and RCLK = 1, A− and A+ nodes are charged to VDD, and B− and B+ nodes are discharged to GND; when the REN and RCLK separately changed to 1 and 0, B− node reaches first to the threshold voltage of the MN3 and continues charging to VDD, and B+ node starts discharging. The sensing latency of SPDSA that taken from point T1 to point T3 is about 122 ps, while the latency of SPCSA is about 132 ps. Moreover, we calculate that the power consumption of SPDSA is about 1.855 fJ, far less than the power consumption of SPCSA, which is about 2.883 fJ. All these improvements are owing to the elimination of the couple of inverters in SPCSA.

Both sensing margin and read disturbance are related with the bias voltage. High bias voltage will generate read disturbance, whereas low bias voltage will lead to the sensing margin decreased. Both cases cause readability issues. Therefore, our proposed sense amplifier should maximize the sensing margin and meanwhile, minimize the read disturbance. As shown in Fig. 6, compared with

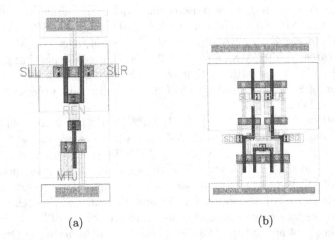

(a)   (b)

Fig. 4. (a) The layout of memory cell and the pre-charging circuit. (b) The layout of SPDSA.

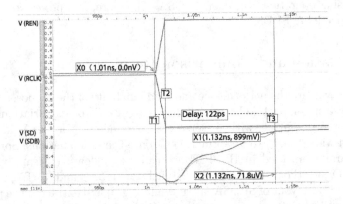

Fig. 5. The timing of the read process.

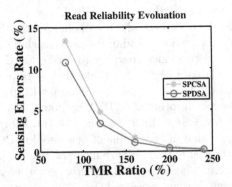

Fig. 6. Sensing error rate versus TMR ratio using Monte Carlo statistical simulations in 45 nm technology node.

Table 1. Comparison results of SPCSA and SPDSA at TT corner (TMR = 120%)

Circuit	Latency	Power	Reliability error rate
SPCSA	132 ps	2.883 fJ	4.8%
SPDSA	122 ps	1.855 fJ	3.4%

SPCSA, SPDSA presents a better read reliability. The reason of this improvement is that the sensing nodes (A− and A+) of SPDSA drive the charging transistors directly rather than via inverters, and which reduces parametric variations. All the comparison results of SPDSA and SPCSA are listed in Table 1.

4   Conclusion

In this paper, a novel sense amplifier has been proposed and verified through HSPICE simulations. Like SPCSA, SPDSA separates discharging and evaluation paths but achieves a higher sensing readability. Meanwhile, SPDSA presents higher sensing speed and lower power consumption than SPCSA. Furthermore, compared with SPCSA, the area overhead of SPDSA is reduced by 4 transistors. It should be noted that SPDSA can also be operated with all known writing modes developed for MRAM and be used to realize nonvolatile logic.

References

1. Ryu, J.W., Kwon, K.W.: A reliable 2T2MTJ nonvolatile static gain cell STT-MRAM with self-referencing sensing circuits for embedded memory application. IEEE Trans. Magn. **52**, 1–10 (2016)
2. Kang, W., Zhang, L., Zhao, W., Klein, J.-O., Zhang, Y., Ravelosona, D., Chappert, C.: Yield and reliability improvement techniques for emerging nonvolatile STT-MRAM. IEEE J. Emerg. Sel. Top. Circ. Syst. **5**, 28–39 (2015)
3. Lee, H., Alzate, J.G., Dorrance, R., Cai, X.Q., Markovic, D., Amiri, P.K., Wang, K.L.: Design of a fast and low-power sense amplifier and writing circuit for high-speed MRAM. IEEE Trans. Magn. **51**, 1–7 (2015)
4. Kang, W., Zhang, L., Klein, J.-O., Zhang, Y., Ravelosona, D., Zhao, W.: Reconfigurable codesign of STT-MRAM under process variations in deeply scaled technology. IEEE Trans. Electron. Devices. **62**, 1769–1777 (2015)
5. Zhao, W., Chappert, C., Javerliac, V., Noziere, J.-P.: High speed, high stability and low power sensing amplifier for MTJ/CMOS hybrid logic circuits. IEEE Trans. Magn. **45**, 3784–3787 (2009)
6. Kang, W., Deng, E., Klein, J.-O., Zhang, Y., Zhang, Y., Chappert, C., Ravelosona, D., Zhao, W.: Separated precharge sensing amplifier for deep submicrometer MTJ/CMOS hybrid logic circuits. IEEE Trans. Magn. **50**, 1–5 (2014)
7. Umeki, Y., Yanagida, K., Yoshimoto, S., Izumi, S., Yoshimoto, M., Kawaguchi, H., Tsunoda, K., Sugii, T.: A 0.38-V operating STT-MRAM with process variation tolerant sense amplifier. In: 9th IEEE Asian Solid-State Circuits Conference (A-SSCC), Singapore, pp. 249–252. IEEE (2013)

Dynamic Response Characteristics of the PCB Under Thermo-Acoustic Load

Cunxian Cao[✉], Jiangfeng Huang, Daoqing Qu, and Miao Zhang

The Computer Department, Jiangsu Automation Research Institute,
Lianyungang, China
ccx1237@126.com, huangjiangfeng@jari.cn,
wfwfcu@163.com, zm86325@126.com

Abstract. The temperature of thermal buckling of the PCB is very low. The dynamic response characteristics of the PCB are very different from pre-buckling and post-buckling. The snap-through motion between multiple post buckled equilibrium positions introduces high level of alternating stress which reduces the fatigue life of the structures. The vibration equation for the PCB under thermo-acoustic load is derived in this paper. Thermal post buckling equilibrium Path is solved using the finite element method. The affection of the thermo-acoustic load on the dynamic response is analyzed with the study of the difference of dynamic response characteristics of the PCB from pre-buckling and post-buckling. The conclusions provide a reference for the calculation of stochastic dynamics with the consideration of the thermal buckling and the prediction of the PCB fatigue life under thermo-acoustic load. Furthermore, it lays a foundation for the structural optimization, which aims to increase the fatigue life of the PCB.

Keywords: PCB · Thermal buckling · Buckling equilibrium path · Stochastic dynamics · Snap-through

1 Introduction

The PCB is common seen in the electronic devices, usually as a support platform installation components. The electronic components are packaged on the PCB using the ball grid array (BGA) method. The PCB is widely used in many areas, especially the PCB in the control platform of ship engine and strengthening computer of aerospace faced a certain degree of thermo-acoustic load. Studies have shown that the damage of solder joint caused by the thermo-acoustic load is the main reason for the failure of electrical components [1]. Salvatore Liguore et al. [2] have shown that reliability analysis and the prediction of fatigue life of electronic equipment must consider the thermal and vibration environment. Many research about the reliability analysis of the PCB under the thermal and vibration load have been carried out [3–7]. Thermal and vibration load generates mutual coupling effect rather than a simple additive effect. Barker et al. [8, 9] proposed a linear superposition to consider the coupling effect of thermal and vibration load to reliability of PCB, which calculated the damage caused by the coupling load and the two effects are linear superposition.

© Springer Nature Singapore Pte Ltd. 2016
W. Xu et al. (Eds.): NCCET 2016, CCIS 666, pp. 218–229, 2016.
DOI: 10.1007/978-981-10-3159-5_21

However, the reliability analysis of the PCB under thermo-acoustic load didn't consider the impact of thermal buckling in most recent investigation. And the temperature of thermal buckling of the PCB is very low. The warpage of the PCB can increase the damage and failure of solder joint. The PCB in the post-buckling state would generate snap-through phenomenon under stochastic acoustic, which greatly improves the stress level of the PCB and reduces the fatigue life of the PCB.

The relevant affection of the thermal and acoustic load on the PCB is analyzed in the paper with the theory of thermal buckling and stochastic dynamics.

The thermal buckling equilibrium path and dynamic response of the simply-supported PCB is investigated under a combination of temperature and random acoustic load using the finite element method. The time curve of displacement, probability distribution function of displacement (PDF), root mean square (RMS) of displacement and stress, power spectral density of displacement (PSD) calculated by the Fourier transform method are analyzed. Based on the parameters above, the relationship between random response of the PCB and thermo-acoustic load is investigated. And the snap-through phenomenon of the random response is analyzed as a focal point.

2 Theory of Thermal Buckling and Stochastic Dynamics

2.1 Theory of Thermal Buckling

In the stable equilibrium state, the balance equation is derived as Eq. (1) based on the principle of stationary potential energy.

$$(K_E + K_G)U = P \tag{1}$$

where K_E is the initial elastic stiffness matrix, K_G is the geometric stiffness matrix, U is the displacement vector of the node, P is the load vector of the node cause by the thermal load, Eq. (1) also been called geometric nonlinear balance equation.

The second order variation of the potential energy of the system is derived and make it zero, then the balance equation is obtained as Eq. (2)

$$(K_E + K_G)\delta U = 0 \tag{2}$$

So we can get

$$|K_E + K_G| = 0 \tag{3}$$

In Eq. (3), the structural stiffness matrix is known, the load make Eq. (3) zero is buckling load. It is assumed that there is a set of external load P^0(the corresponding geometric stiffness matrix K_G^0), if the buckling load is λ time of P^0, therefore $K_G = \lambda K_G^0$, the above equation can be derived as Eq. (4)

$$\left| K_E + \lambda K_G^0 \right| = 0 \tag{4}$$

The corresponding eigenvalue equation is:

$$(K_E + \lambda_i K_G^0)\{\phi_i\} = 0 \tag{5}$$

where λ_i is the ith-order eigenvalue; $\{\phi_i\}$ is the ith-order eigenvector, also called buckling modes.

The Newton-Raphson method is always used to solve the Eq. (1), which use the piecewise linear method to solve nonlinear equations. The nonlinear equations of equilibrium is written as iterative formula using NR methods:

$$\left. \begin{array}{l} [K_T(\{u\}_i)]\{\Delta u\}_{i+1} = \{P\} - \{P\}_i \\ \{u\}_{i+1} = \{u\}_i + \{\Delta u\}_{i+1} \end{array} \right\} \tag{6}$$

where $\{P\}_i = [K_T(\{u\}_i)]\{\Delta u\}_i$.

2.2   Theory of Stochastic Dynamics

The displacement field is assumed with the consideration of transverse shear strain based on the Mindlin-Reissner theory. Then the strain-displacement relation is derived with the nonlinear Von Karman. The vibration equation under thermo-acoustic load is obtained based on energy principle and Hamiltonprinciple.

$$\begin{bmatrix} m_b & 0 \\ 0 & 0 \end{bmatrix} \begin{Bmatrix} \ddot{w}_b \\ \ddot{w}_m \end{Bmatrix} + \begin{bmatrix} c_b & 0 \\ 0 & 0 \end{bmatrix} \begin{Bmatrix} \dot{w}_b \\ \dot{w}_m \end{Bmatrix}$$
$$+ \left(\begin{bmatrix} k_b & k_{bm} \\ k_{bm}^T & k_m \end{bmatrix} + k_{ij}^2 \begin{bmatrix} k_s & 0 \\ 0 & 0 \end{bmatrix} + \begin{bmatrix} k_{Nm} - k_{\Delta T} & 0 \\ 0 & 0 \end{bmatrix} \right) \begin{Bmatrix} w_b \\ w_m \end{Bmatrix} = \begin{Bmatrix} p_{b\Delta T} \\ p_{m\Delta T} \end{Bmatrix} + \begin{Bmatrix} p_{vib} \\ 0 \end{Bmatrix} \tag{7}$$

where m_b is the mass matrix for the PCB; the first two of the stiffness matrix do not count for the influence of thermal; k_{Nm} is the additional bending stiffness caused by the displacement of inner surface; $k_{\Delta T}$ is the additional bending stiffness caused by the strain of thermal; $p_{b\Delta T}$ 、 $p_{m\Delta T}$ is the additional force and moment caused by the thermal; p_{vib} is the acoustic load.

As for the PCB structure, $k_{bm} = 0$, $p_{b\Delta T} = 0$, then Eq. (7) can be derived as Eq. (8):

$$\begin{cases} k_m w_m = p_{m\Delta T} \\ m_b \ddot{w}_b + (k_1 + k_2)w = p_{vib} \end{cases} \tag{8}$$

where $k_1 = k_b + k_{ij}^2 k_b$ is stiffness matrix without the consideration of the thermal; $k_2 = k_{Nm} - k_{\Delta T}$ is the correction term of stiffness caused by the thermal.

In the actual solving, we solve the first static equation of Eq. (8) firstly to get the displacement field w_m. Then the displacement is applied to the structure, which means that we introduce the correction item k_2 into the stiffness matrix in the dynamic analysis. Based on the solving above, we can obtain the dynamic characteristics of the PCB in a certain thermal with the consideration of thermal load.

3 Numerical Computation and Analysis

3.1 Finite Element Model of the PCB and Load

A simply supported rectangular the PCB plate with dimensions of 233.5 × 160 1.6 mm is considered here. The material properties of the PCB are listed in Table 1.

Table 1. Material properties of the PCB

	Density	Young's modulus	Poisson's ratio	Thermal expansion coefficient
PCB	1900 kg/m³	22 GPa	0.28	18e−6/K

The finite element model is constructed with shell181 as shown in Fig. 1.

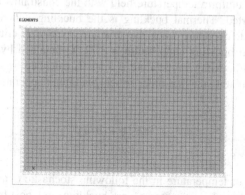

Fig. 1. Finite element model of the PCB

The actual temperature load the PCB faced with is extremely complex. The uniform temperature field is investigated in this paper, which ranges from 0 to 10 times in the buckling temperature rise.

The acoustic load investigated in this paper is simplified as white Gaussian noise, whose noise level amplitude agrees to Gaussian distribution and the power spectral density is constant. The bandwidth of the Gaussian white noise ranges 0–1500 Hz. The time curve and probability density distribution (PSD) of the Gaussian white noise which the SPL is 120 dB and cutoff frequency is 1500 Hz as shown in Figs. 2 and 3. The thermo-acoustic load are applied on the surface of the PCB in vertical.

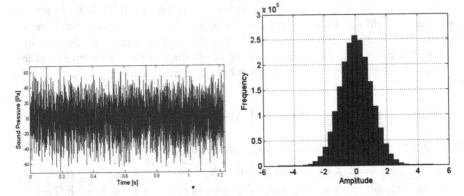

Fig. 2. The time curve of the Gaussian white noise   **Fig. 3.** The PSD of the Gaussian white noise

3.2   Thermal Buckling Analysis of the PCB

The buckling critical temperature and buckling equilibrium path are solved in this section with the eigenvalue buckling and nonlinear static analysis using the finite element method, thereby laying the foundation for analysis of thermo-acoustic stochastic dynamics.

The PCB is at a uniform temperature field with the constraints in the form of four sides simply supported. Thermal buckling is the buckling which is caused by the thermal stress. The temperature when the structure buckled is critical buckling temperature. The critical buckling temperature is 3.72 °C obtained by the finite element method. The critical buckling temperature is 3.56 °C calculate by the formula [10] as bellow used for calculating the first-order critical buckling temperature. Both results are close.

$$T_C = \frac{\pi h^2 [1 + (b/a)^2]}{12\alpha b^2 (1 + \mu)} \tag{9}$$

Since the range of temperature in the following stochastic dynamic analysis is so wider that covers the whole process of pre-buckling and post-buckling, while the stochastic dynamic analysis needs to remodel the structure after buckling, that is we must update the displacement of the nodes to the post-buckling structure, it is necessary to strike the buckling equilibrium path. The arc method is used in this paper to get the path in ANSYS.

The first-order buckling mode is extracted in the analysis of eigenvalue, which is updated to the structure in 1 percent in the analysis of large deflection. Then the buckling equilibrium path is obtained as shown in Fig. 4.

Where $S = \Delta T / T_{Cr}$, ΔT is the temperature rise.

From the buckling equilibrium path as shown in Fig. 4, it is found that the structure has almost no displacement before buckling, while the structure displacement has a sudden increase in the critical temperature. The increasing of displacement slows down

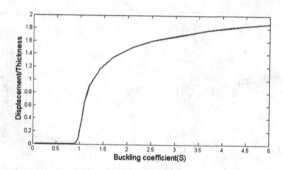

Fig. 4. Buckling equilibrium path of simply supported the PCB

as the temperature continues to increase. This indicates that the stiffness is reduced by the thermal stress induced by the binding of the deformation in the critical temperature, while the stiffness begins to increase when the temperature increases after buckling.

From the buckling equilibrium path, we can obtain the stress and displacement fields of the structure in the whole process of pre-buckling and post-buckling, which are introduced into the analysis of the stochastic dynamic as the boundary condition.

3.3   Dynamic Response of the PCB Under Thermo-Acoustic Load

In this section, the time curve of dimensionless displacement, the PDF of dimensionless displacement, the RMS of displacement and stress, and the PSD of displacement are obtained from the analysis of stochastic dynamic response of PCB under different combinations of thermal and acoustic load.

3.3.1   Dynamic Response of the PCB Before Buckling

The dynamic response characteristics are investigated when the sound pressure level changes at S = 0, and the time curve and PDF of dimensionless displacement of central node is obtained as shown in Fig. 5.

From Fig. 5, the simply supported PCB vibrates randomly around the initial equilibrium position.

The displacement of the PCB increases when the sound pressure level increases. The maximum dimensionless displacement is 0.2 when S = 0 and SPL = 160 dB, the value is 2 when SPL = 140 dB, and the value is 2 when SPL = 160 dB. Also with the sound pressure level increases, time curve becomes denser, indicating that as the sound pressure level increases, the frequency increases.

From the PDF of dimensionless displacement at four different SPL when S = 0, it is found that the PDF becomes flat when the SPL increases.

In order to study the effects of different SPL on the simply supported PCB before buckling, the displacement and stress variation of dynamic response under various conditions of SPL are investigated. The RMS of the displacement and stressare as shown in Figs. 6 and 7. In order to investigate the relationship between displacement and stress and pressure on nature, we transform the SPL to analyze the sound pressure.

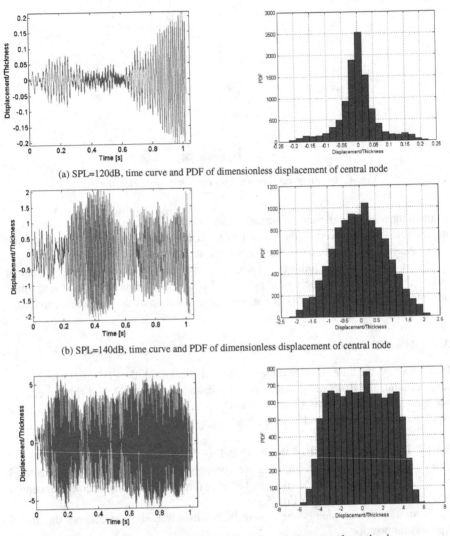

(a) SPL=120dB, time curve and PDF of dimensionless displacement of central node

(b) SPL=140dB, time curve and PDF of dimensionless displacement of central node

(c) SPL=160dB, time curve and PDF of dimensionless displacement of central node

Fig. 5. S = 0, dynamic response of central node at different SPL

As can be seen from Fig. 6, at a certain temperature before buckling, the RMS of displacement increases as the sound pressure increases. And to a lesser extent in the sound pressure, the increasing of sound pressure has a greater impact on the RMS of displacement, while the SPL is over 160 dB, the RMS of displacement changes less noticeable when the SPL increases. This is because the stiffness of the membrane increases sharply when the displacement of THE PCB increases to a certain extent, resulting that the RMS of displacement is no longer change as the SPL increases. From Fig. 7, the RMS of Von Misses stress increases as the SPL increases. And there is a

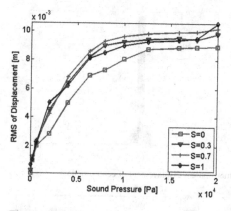
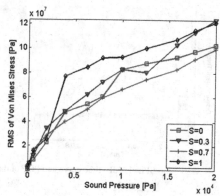

Fig. 6. Relation between RMS of displacement and pressure

Fig. 7. Relation between RMS of stress and pressure

slowdown of the rate of increasing as the RMS of displacement, but it is slighter than the degree of the RMS of displacement.

3.3.2 Dynamic Response of the PCB After Buckling

The analysis of dynamic response is carried on the model which is rebuilt after buckling.

The dynamic response characteristics are investigated when the sound pressure level changes at S = 5, and the time curve and PDF of dimensionless displacement of central node is obtained as shown in Fig. 8.

When at a low sound pressure level in the post-buckling, the PCB structure vibrates around the equilibrium position, as shown in Fig. 8(a). And the amplitude of the PCB increases when the SPL increases. When the SPL increases to a certain degree, the PCB vibrates between two equilibrium positions beyond the initial equilibrium position, appears the snap-through phenomenon, as shown in Fig. 8(b). As the sound pressure level increases further, the structure of the snap-through phenomenon of the two equilibrium positions will become more and more frequent, as shown in Fig. 8(c).

From the PDF of dimensionless displacement at four different SPL when S = 5, the evolution of snap-through phenomenon as the SPL increases is shown more clearly. Figure 8(a) shows the PDF of dimensionless displacement around the initial equilibrium position. Figure 8(b) shows the PDF of dimensionless displacement snap-through intermittently around two equilibrium positions, where the PDF appears two peaks. Figure 8(c) shows the PDF of dimensionless displacement snap-through frequently around two equilibrium positions, where the peaks of PDF becomes flat.

As before, in order to study the effects of different SPL on the simply supported PCB before buckling, the displacement and stress variation of dynamic response under various conditions of SPL is investigated. The RMS of the displacement and stress are as shown in Figs. 9 and 10.

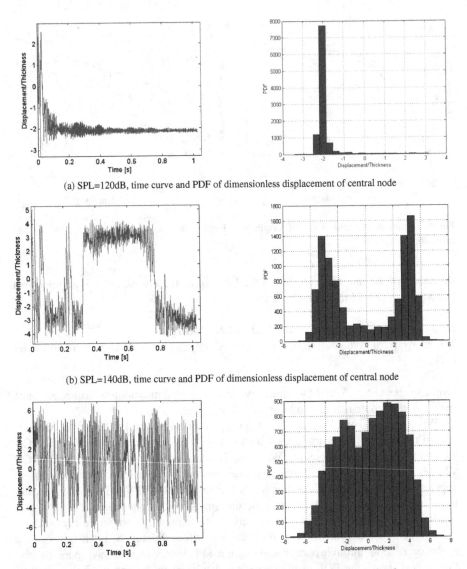

(a) SPL=120dB, time curve and PDF of dimensionless displacement of central node

(b) SPL=140dB, time curve and PDF of dimensionless displacement of central node

(c) SPL=160dB, time curve and PDF of dimensionless displacement of central node

Fig. 8. S = 5, dynamic response of central node at different SPL

As can be seen from Fig. 9, the RMS variation of displacement is basically the same as pre-buckling when the buckling factor is less than a certain range. But in a larger buckling factor, such as Fig. 5, it is found that the RMS of displacement firstly decreases, and then increases, and finally becomes stability as the SPL increases and the overall changes slightly. As for the RMS of stress, it is basically the same as pre-buckling. But the RMS of stress changes slightly in a larger buckling factor.

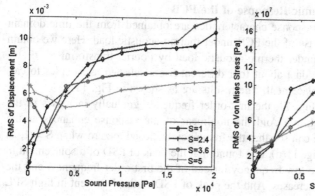

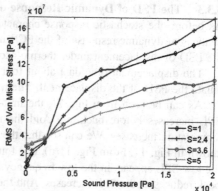

Fig. 9. Relation between RMS of displacement and pressure

Fig. 10. Relation between RMS of stress and pressure

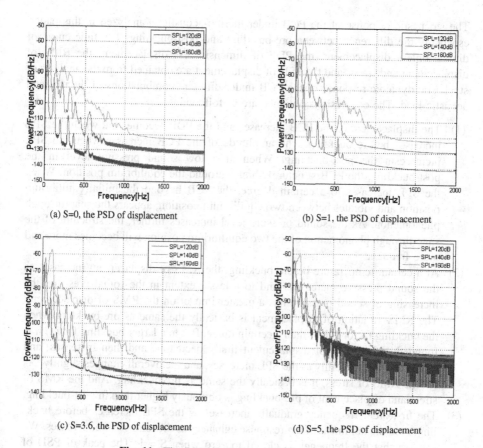

(a) S=0, the PSD of displacement

(b) S=1, the PSD of displacement

(c) S=3.6, the PSD of displacement

(d) S=5, the PSD of displacement

Fig. 11. The PSD of displacement in different SPL

3.3.3   The PSD of Dynamic Response of the PCB

As before, the stochastic response characteristics are obtained from the time-domain analysis of dynamic response of the PCB under thermo-acoustic load. Here we obtain the PSD of displacement under thermo-acoustic load by Fourier transform.

The displacement-time data about four different S are selected as samples to calculate the PSD of the displacement. The results are as shown in Fig. 11.

As can be seen from Fig. 11, the first-order frequency gradually increases as the SPL increases before buckling. And the nonlinear of the response enhances as the temperature increases. We can see that the frequency is closed to zero when S = 1, as shown in Fig. 11. From Fig. 11(d), it is found that the peak of PSD of displacement in the low SPL appears in the low frequency instead of the first-order frequency, and the peak reduces as the SPL increases. And the peak of PSD of displacement in high SPL appeared in the first-order frequency.

4   Conclusions

The stochastic response of the PCB under thermo-acoustic is analyzed in this paper, especially the difference between pre-buckling and post-buckling. The time curve of dimensionless displacement, the PDF of dimensionless displacement, the RMS of displacement and stress, and the PSD of displacement are obtained from the analysis of stochastic dynamic response of the PCB under different combinations of thermal and acoustic load. The conclusions obtained are as followings:

(1) The displacement of the PCB increases and the PDF becomes flat when the SPL increases before buckling. The amplitude of the PCB increases when the SPL increasesin the post-buckling. When at a low sound pressure level in the post-buckling, the PCB structure vibrates around the equilibrium position. When the SPL increases to a certain degree, the PCB beyond the initial equilibrium position and vibrates between two equilibrium position, appears the snap-through phenomenon. As the sound pressure level increases further, the structure of the snap-through phenomenon of the two equilibrium position will becomes more and more frequent.

(2) At a certain temperature before buckling, the RMS of displacement increases as the sound pressure increases. And to a lesser extent in the sound pressure, the increasing of sound pressure has a greater impact on the RMS of displacement. The RMS variation of displacement is basically the same as pre-buckling when the buckling factor is less than a certain range. But in a larger buckling factor, it is found that the RMS of displacement firstly decreases, and then increases, and finally becomes stability as the SPL increases, and the overall changes slightly. As for the RMS of stress, it is basically the same as pre-buckling. And the RMS of stress and displacement of pre-buckling is obviously higher than in post-buckling.

(3) The first-order frequency gradually increases as the SPL increases before buckling. And the nonlinear of the response enhances as the temperature increases. We can see that the frequency is closed to zero when S = 1. The peak of PSD of displacement in the low SPL appears in the low frequency instead of the

first-order frequency, and the peak reduces as the SPL increases, while the peak of PSD of displacement in high SPL appears in the first-order frequency. In the actual layout of the electrical components and dynamic design, the design is needed to be adjusted based on the actual service environment.

References

1. Martin, P.L.: Electronic failure analysis handbook. McGraw-Hill Press, New York (1999)
2. Salvatore, L., David, F.: Vibration fatigue of surface mount technology (SMT) solder joints. In: IEEE Proceedings Annual Reliability and Maintainability Symposium, America, pp. 18–26 (1995)
3. Luo, M.Z., Kang, R., Liu, F.W.: A review of reliability prediction methods for electronic products. J. Electron. Sci. Technol. 1(2), 246–256 (2014)
4. Li, R., Kang, R.: A review of reliability prediction modifying methods for electronic systems (2007)
5. Ding, Y., Tian, R., Wang, X., et al.: Coupling effects of mechanical vibrations and thermal cycling on reliability of CCGA solder joints. Microelectron. Reliab. 4(11), 2396–2402 (2015)
6. Yong, Z., Ma, L., Liu, S., et al.: The coupling effects of thermal cycling and high current density on Sn58Bi solder joints. J. Mater. Sci. 48(6), 2318–2325 (2013)
7. Ghaffarian R.: Thermal cycle and vibration/drop reliability of area array package assemblies. In: Structural Dynamics of Electronic and Photonic Systems, pp. 519–574 (2011)
8. Barker, D., Vodzak, J., Dasgupta, A., et al.: combined vibrational and thermal solder joint fatigue—a generalized strain versus life approach. J. Electron. Packag. 112(2), 129–134 (1990)
9. Basaran, C., Chandaroy, R.: Thermo mechanical analysis of solder joints under thermal and vibrational load. J. Electron. Packag. 124(1), 279–284 (2002)
10. Fan, X.: The Analysis and Application of Thermal Structure of Hypersonic Vehicle. National Defense Industry Press, Beijing (2009)

Author Index

Printed in the United States
By Bookmasters